## DICKENS' NEW AGE CLAS~~~~

Charles Dickens' *A Christmas Carol* is the story of ~~~~
This hero overcame family neglect, abandonment and years of rage and hurtful behavior toward himself and others. He underwent a near-death experience and alien encounter/abduction. He experienced a sudden kundalini awakening, grieved for his wounded inner child and learned compassion for the pain of others. The hero of this story is Ebenezer Scrooge.

Most of us don't think of Scrooge as a spiritual hero. Yet *Transforming Scrooge* explains how he serves as an inspiring role model for today's seekers. Dr. Joseph Cusumano examines Scrooge's transformation from curmudgeon to convert in light of contemporary psychological theories: the inner child work of John Bradshaw, John Selby's work on kundalini, Raymond Moody on near-death experiences, and Kenneth Ring on the similarities between near-death experiences and alien abductions.

*Transforming Scrooge* brings *A Christmas Carol's* great truths to life—and it reveals the specific psychological and spiritual challenges Scrooge worked through to experience a true psychospiritual awakening. With the help of this inspiring guide, you too can overcome the fears keeping you from reaching your glorious potential.

"An illuminating and penetrating psychospiritual analysis of Dickens' classic story of human redemption. Cusumano's revisioning of this classic tale is loaded with surprising insights that enable us not only to see it with new eyes, but also to appreciate its special significance for this critical time in humanity's evolution toward higher consciousness."

—Kenneth Ring, Ph.D.
author of *The Omega Project*, *Heading Toward Omega*, and *Life at Death*

"*Transforming Scrooge* takes us to the farthest reaches of our own nature. Like astronauts walking on the moon, Cusumano shows us we too are capable of giant evolutionary steps."

—Barbara Harris Whitfield
author of *Full Circle* and *Spiritual Awakenings*

## ABOUT THE AUTHOR

Joseph D. Cusumano, Ph.D., has a dual career, which includes teaching literature to high school students, and running a private practice mental health office that specializes in psychospiritual growth. In addition to teaching, counseling, and writing, Joseph leads many workshops using Scrooge as a role model for change; he has also served as a facilitator for workshops conducted by John Bradshaw in his area. Joseph lives in the Midwest with his wife and children.

## TO WRITE TO THE AUTHOR

If you wish to contact the author or would like more information about this book, please write to the author in care of Llewellyn Worldwide, and we will forward your request. Both the author and the publisher appreciate hearing from you and learning of your enjoyment of this book and how it has helped you. Llewellyn Worldwide cannot guarantee that every letter written to the author can be answered, but all will be forwarded. Please write to:

Joseph D. Cusumano, Ph.D,
℅ Llewellyn Worldwide
P.O. Box 64383 Dept. K198–8
St. Paul, MN 55164-0383, U.S.A.
Please enclose a self-addressed, stamped envelope for reply or
$1.00 to cover costs.
If outside the U.S.A., enclose international postal reply coupon.

## FREE LLEWELLYN CATALOG

For more than ninety years, Llewellyn has brought its readers knowledge in the fields of metaphysics and human potential. Learn about the newest books in spiritual guidance, natural healing, astrology, occult philosophy, and more. Enjoy book reviews, New Age articles, a calendar of events, plus current advertised products and services. To get your free copy of *Llewellyn's New Worlds*, send your name and address to:

*Llewellyn's New Worlds of Mind and Spirit*
P.O. Box 64383, Dept K198–8, St. Paul, MN 55164-0383, U.S.A.

Joseph D. Cusumano, Ph.D.

# TRANSFORMING SCROOGE

## Dickens' Blueprint for a Spiritual Awakening

1996
Llewellyn Publications
St. Paul, Minnesota 55164-0383

FIRST EDITION
First Printing, 1996

Cover illustration: Anatol Woolf
Cover design: Maria Mazzara
Book design, layout, and editing: Laura Gudbaur
Project management: Jessica Thoreson and Marilyn Matheny
Photos: T. van Renterghem © 1996

An effort has been made to acquire proper permission for the use of copyrighted material used in this book. Upon notification, we will make appropriate acknowledgements in subsequent editions.

Material from *Kundalini Awakening* by John Selby, copyright © 1992 by John Selby. Illustrations © 1992 by Zachary Jay Selig. Used by permission of Bantam Books,.a division of Bantam Doubleday Dell Publishing Group, Inc.
Material from *Awareness* by Anthony deMello, S. J. and J. Francis Stroud, S. J., editor, copyright © 1990 by the Center for Spiritual Exchange. Used by permission of Doubleday, a division of Bantam Doubleday Dell Publishing Group, Inc.
Material from *Making Sense of Suffering* by J. Konrad Stettbacher. *Wenn Leiden einen Sinn haben Soll* © copyright 1990 by Hoffmann unde Campe Verlag, Hamburg, Germany.
Material from *Heading Toward Omega* by Kenneth Ring, copyright © 1985 by Kenneth Ring. Used by permission of William Morrow and Company, Inc.
Material from *The Omega Project* by Kenneth Ring, copyright © 1992 by Kenneth Ring. Used by permission of William Morrow and Company, Inc.
Quotes from *Power Through Constructive Thinking* by Emmet Fox, copyright © 1940 by Emmet Fox. Copyright renewed 1968 by Kathleen Whelan. Reprinted by permission of HarperCollins Publishers, Inc.
Material from *The Secret Teachings of Jesus* copyright © 1984 by Marvin W. Meyer. Used by permission of Random House, Inc.

Illustrations by John Leech (some hand-colored) are from the 11th edition of Charles Dickens' *A Christmas Carol* (1846). Dickens—having quarreled with his regular publisher, Chapman & Hall—put out this edition himself through Bradbury & Evans, 90 Fleet and White Briars, London.

Library of Congress Cataloging-in-Publication Data
Cusumano, Joseph D., 1953–
   Transforming Scrooge: Dickens' blueprint for a spiritual awakening / Joseph D. Cusumano. — 1st ed.
         p.    cm.
   Includes bibliographical references.
   ISBN 1-56718-198-8 (trade pbk.)
   1. Dickens, Charles, 1812-1870. Christmas carol. 2. Dickens, Charles, 1812-1870--Characters--Ebenezer Scrooge. 3. Scrooge, Ebenezer (Fictitious character) 4. Spiritual life in literature. 5. Spiritual life. I. Title.
PR4572.C7C87  1996                                                    96-22000
823'.8--dc20                                                               CIP

Llewellyn Publications
A Division of Llewellyn Worldwide, Ltd.
P.O. Box 64383, Dept. K198–8, St. Paul, MN 55164-0383

*To my life-partner, Donna;*
*my children, Matt and Monica;*
*and to Sharon and Nancy.*
*Thanks for your love, support,*
*and belief in me.*

# TABLE OF CONTENTS

## Part One: Transforming Scrooge

## Part Two: A Christmas Carol

*According to* The Gospel of Truth, *the process of self-discovery begins as a person experiences the "anguish and terror" of the human condition, as if lost in a fog or haunted in sleep by terrifying nightmares.*

—Elaine Pagels
The Gnostic Gospels

# TRANSFORMING SCROOGE

## Dickens' Blueprint for a Spiritual Awakening

# Introduction

In Paul Davis' comprehensive book, *The Lives and Times of Ebenezer Scrooge*, he informs us that from its inception, Charles Dickens' *A Christmas Carol* has been the subject of cultural interpretation. At its beginnings in the 1840s, "The Carol" was thought of as a parable, which also served the dual purpose of saving the Christmas holiday from extinction as the world began to urbanize. During the 1870s, the story was viewed by the Victorians as a Biblical Christmas story. Around World War I, "The Carol" was thought of primarily as a children's story. During the Great Depression, its interpretation reflected the hard economic realities gripping the world. By the 1960s, the story was filtered through the ongoing cultural revolution, with its attendant questioning of all traditional values. During the narcissism and gluttony of the 1980s, "The Carol" once again took on an economic interpretation.

The intention of this book is to help bring to light the next cultural interpretation of the story as we approach the twenty-first century. It is my contention that Scrooge suffered the trauma of severe parental neglect and abandonment during his childhood. Because the pain associated with that abusive behavior was left unresolved, he manifested abusiveness in adulthood, hurting himself and many others. Ultimately, and fortunately, his defense mechanisms crashed, and he experienced a sudden psychospiritual awakening. Because of this, he was liberated to lead "an altered life."

During Scrooge's night of transformation, Dickens provided us with a completely valid blueprint for change, which included all the fundamental principles that we, too, need to realize and deal with in order to be reborn into spiritual awareness. Those steps are brought to light as this book progresses, and it is clear that they include a combination of psychological and spiritual elements. From this nineteenth century work, we are given a glorious gift that can help make our twenty-first century world a place that reflects this psychospiritual awakening to our true Selves. We will all be better for it.

*Editor's Note: For the reader's convenience we have included a complete version of Dickens' classic tale* A Christmas Carol *as Part Two of this book—a book within a book. All page numbers from* A Christmas Carol *given within* Transforming Scrooge *are in reference to the version in Part Two. We suggest reading it after you have finished* Transforming Scrooge. *A complete bibliography and index for* Transforming Scrooge *follows Part Two.*

## CHAPTER ONE

# Dickens, Scrooge, & Our Scrooge Within

Until February 1994, I had never actually read Charles Dickens' immortal novella, *A Christmas Carol*. I have seen four movie versions of it, some more than once. Viewing the 1938 Reginald Owen version with my wife and kids has become an essential annual holiday tradition the week before Christmas. During our late December "Night of Lights," we gather and light every candle and oil lantern in the house, drink hot cocoa, and pop in the video.

My wife and I once attended a musical adaptation of "The Carol" at a local college. As a child, I vaguely remember watching the Mr. Magoo cartoon version, and in recent years, I have watched the Disney animation with my daughter. But, to reiterate, I had never read the original story. Concerning the modern-day reading public, my instincts inform me that very few people actually have read the book. An informal survey conducted to test my belief leads me to conclude that less than ten percent of all people have read Dickens' classic in its original form.

When I did read it, I was stunned by its power. Despite its quaint, period-piece feel, I realized that Dickens was writing much, much more than a holiday fairy tale. It overwhelmed me with its relevance and immediacy to our twentieth-century lives. In my estimation, *A Christmas Carol* is an incredibly accurate, if not wisely subtle, fictional account of the myriad ramifications of unresolved childhood trauma. Scrooge's wounded inner child was easy to locate. The defense mechanisms he freely used in adulthood to protect himself from further pain, although life-killing, were the predictable result of unresolved childhood trauma.

There is no doubt that the three dream-ghosts were performing intensive, brief, experiential psychospiritual therapy to free him from the bonds of the past. Scrooge's "three day" trek through his unconscious mind perfectly follows the classic mythological structure known as the hero's journey, in that he experienced the following sequential elements: departure, attainment through ordeal, and return with altered knowledge. After his reclamation, Scrooge immediately and obviously demonstrated spiritualized behavior by his ability to productively live and relate to his other "fellow-passengers" (7) of the world in a totally loving way.

Additionally, it is clear that Scrooge experienced what we would today call a combination alien abduction/near-death experience, which activated a physical phenomenon known as the *kundalini* syndrome. This occurrence caused a permanent and fortunate psychobiological shift in his physical system, not unlike many who currently report having undergone a near-death experience or an alien abduction encounter. Parallel to these experiencers, upon his return, Scrooge also demonstrated a new-found spiritual attitude about his own life and caring concern for the general welfare of the planet.

By writing *A Christmas Carol*, Dickens' main message was to inform us about our own urgent need for positive, permanent change, which he illustrated through the extreme example of overnight transformation experienced by Scrooge. The traumatic evolutionary leap Scrooge successfully completed underscores Dickens' point about the possibility of change in our lives: if Scrooge, as old and as overtly cold and unfeeling as he was, could experience this positive, lifesaving shift, then we, too, in our own individualistic and idiosyncratic ways, can experience it. Dickens is telling us that just as Scrooge died to his

former dysfunctional self and was born anew physically, psychologically, and spiritually, so can we.

In "The Carol," Dickens also issued a stern warning about our
shamefully pervasive mistreatment of children. He clearly prophesied
that if we don't heed his warning to change this situation, as a society,
we will all suffer from the dire consequences that will inevitably result
from this shameful neglect. Unfortunately and appallingly, what he
foretold has already, to a large degree, come to pass. So far, we have
survived these horrors. If we do not wake up to his warning soon, however, we will not be able to survive the chaos and destruction our mass
denial engenders.

## Dickens' Dilemma

It has been strongly suggested by several of Dickens' biographers that
his main motivation for writing *A Christmas Carol* was to make a quick
monetary "killing." He had just released the book *Martin Chuzzlewit* in
installment form; sales were not at all what were expected by his publisher. Because of this, he felt pressure to quickly come up with something to bolster his less than adequate cash flow and faltering reputa-
tion. His publisher was threatening to significantly reduce his month-
ly royalties (Davis 1990). In order to cut expenses, he even anguished
over a decision to move his family out of its London home, lease it out,
and move to a less expensive residence.

In short, Dickens felt he needed to produce something quickly to
support the complicated life he was leading. He needed something to
mollify the growing monetary demands of his nuclear and extended
families. He needed something to bolster his waning literary reputa-
tion. As a result of this pressure, he felt threatened.

This stressful situation caused the unresolved pain and fear from
Dickens' own damaged childhood to surface. He feared the financial
collapse that befell his own father, John, who eventually landed in

debtor's prison. He reexperienced the intolerable pain of being taken out of school at age ten, then physically separated from his once financially secure family at the age of twelve for more than a year in order to work. He reexperienced the anxiety of not really knowing when, or even if, he would ever be restored to the family home.

He felt the humiliation of having to labor manually in a rat-infested boot-black warehouse, seventy-two hours, six days a week, during this time. He relived the shame that he undoubtedly felt when his parents, as Leonard Shengold (1989) tells us in *Soul Murder*, sent him as:

> *[A] small boy in precarious health, to do menial work—a 'young gentleman' thrown among common, lower-class boys with no future who jeered him for his way of speaking and being.*

He felt the intensification of his life-long resentment toward his mother for actively lobbying her husband, who had by now gained release from prison after receiving an unexpected inheritance, to keep Charles laboring at the factory.

Fearing his current situation and fueled by these unresolved old feelings, Dickens wrote *A Christmas Carol* during a frenzied six weeks during the late fall of 1843. In order to take full advantage of its seasonal sales appeal, he desperately needed to compose the story, write it, publish it, and deliver it to book stores before late December.

He furiously walked the streets of London for up to eight hours at a time, often covering upwards of fifteen miles per journey. During these treks, which would take him into the lower-class parts of London (where he was further reminded of his traumatic childhood year in exile), he would laugh and cry out loud, all the while composing the story line and fleshing out the characters in his head. Many have concluded that he invested more raw visceral emotion in the writing of *A Christmas Carol* than in any other literary undertaking during his long, prolific career.

Going on sale less than a week before Christmas 1843, "The Carol" was a rousing popular and literary success for Dickens. The first

printing completely sold out by Christmas Day, and the second printing had a large advance order.

Unfortunately, because of inadequate copyright laws, the story was
almost instantaneously ripped off and adapted by other writers, who
began to produce a variety of inexpensive written renditions and stage
plays within weeks.

Despite the fact that Dickens quickly won court cases to stop the
literary robbery, the cost of these litigations and the inability of the
defendants to pay damages negated any initial profits he had just
begun to realize. Ironically, because of "The Carol's" publication, he
actually lost money during the time period that he felt the urgent need
to greatly increase his cash flow.

In spite of the myriad problems associated with the initial publication of the book, Dickens survived the crisis. There may be truth to
the money motive as his main conscious catalyst for the writing of
"The Carol." I believe, however, that powerful unresolved subconscious forces quite literally overtook him during the creative process.
These imperatives, compressed by the constraints of time, actually
directed the production of this literary endeavor.

In "The Carol," Dickens was not just writing an entertaining
Christmas tale; he was writing a cathartic story that welled up from the
depths of his troubled soul. In the story, he grappled with his own life-
long, deeply embedded childhood abandonment wounds that haunted
him throughout his adult life, never assuaged by money or success.

We know it to be true that as an adult Dickens was often deeply
affected and troubled by this childhood trauma. Concerning his
ordeal, he wrote:

> The deep remembrance of the sense I had of being utterly neglected
> and hopeless; of the shame I felt in my position; of the misery of it
> was to my young heart to believe that, day by day, what I had
> learned, and thought, and delighted in, and raised my fancy and
> my emulation up by, was passing away from me, never to be

*brought back any more, cannot be written. My whole nature was*
*so penetrated with the grief and humiliation of such considerations,*
*that even now, famous and caressed and happy, I often forget in my*
*dreams that I have a dear wife and children; even that I am a man;*
*and wander desolately back to that time of my life (Wilson 1941).*

Dickens never completely recovered from this period of extended abandonment. He never got over how his father, whom he deeply loved and respected, and described as being totally devoted to the family, could uncharacteristically generate no interest whatsoever toward his plight for such an extended period of time:

*But, in the case of his temper, and the straitness of his means, he*
*appeared to have lost utterly at this time the idea of educating me at*
*all, and to have utterly put from him the notion that I had any*
*claim upon him, in that regard, whatever (Wilson 1941).*

According to Edmund Wilson (1941), Dickens was never able to forgive his mother for her behavior during this dark time: "I never afterwards forgot. I never shall forget, I never can forget."

In response to his unresolved pain, Shengold (1989) tells us that as an adult:

*Dickens became determined never again to suffer such helplessness*
*and misery; the trauma fed an intense ambition. But he was left*
*with terrible conflicts: he needed both to idealize his parents and*
*accuse them, which made for splits in his inner images of his par-*
*ents and his own identity that can be seen projected into his fiction,*
*particularly in* Little Dorrit *(1855-57), written when Dickens*
*was in his early forties.*

It is my contention that he also very clearly projected these issues into Ebenezer Scrooge. Like his creator, this character carried submerged internal conflicts and intense ambition into his adulthood.

Like his infamous character Scrooge, Wilson made it clear that Dickens himself was also capable of "great hardness and cruelty," not only to those hangers-on whom he had some real cause to feel ill-will toward, but also to friends and family alike. One of his daughters would eventually write that she loved her father "for his faults,"adding that he could be "a wicked man—a very wicked man."

# Reframe of the Pain

Despite this, we should rejoice at Dickens' financial woes and unhappy state of mind in 1843. Just as the Cratchit family initially balked at, but reluctantly toasted the heartless Scrooge as the founder of their meager Christmas feast, we also need to celebrate the unhappy circumstances surrounding the author's creation of this masterpiece. As we know, Scrooge ultimately transformed and served as a boon to the Cratchits. Likewise, Dickens' little book, despite its troubled inception and less than auspicious start, survives today as a gift for the ages. Out of the darkness, comes the light. The necessity for suffering gives way to the glory of resurrection.

From my perspective, the major dilemma that we have with the story has been one of identification. Most of us identify with Bob Cratchit, Scrooge's work place victim, or with Scrooge's nephew, Fred, his family victim, or with Tiny Tim, Scrooge's physical victim. Because most of us were initially exposed to A Christmas Carol as children, we have not taken the time to meditate maturely upon the story as adults. In order to understand and feel the full impact of the message, we need to let go of our fairy tale preconceptions of the story, derived from and filtered through a variety of media, and read it as serious adult psychology and mythology. Dickens always intended his story to inform us about our own lives.

Therefore, it is imperative for each and every one of us to come to identify primarily with Scrooge himself. Dickens himself did; to a very real degree, he was Scrooge. We need to understand and to come to grips with our own personal versions of the pretransformed Scrooge, which lurk within (and around) each and every one of us, so that we can be in position to experience our own permanent transformation, just as he did. The more we deny the shadow of Scrooge within ourselves, the more we guarantee his existence in our lives. It is our responsibility to seek him out from the dark recesses of our unconscious minds, deal with him, understand him, and come to love and accept him. By doing so, we free and transform ourselves.

This is not easy to accept. We do not want to believe that our lives in any way remotely parallel the obviously harsh, cold behavior exhibited by Scrooge. Scrooge did not see his life as lacking, or dysfunctional. He believed himself to be a good man running a successful business, one who dutifully (if begrudgingly) paid his taxes and minded his own affairs. He did not go searching for trouble; he merely wished to be left alone. All he did was protect himself from those who he believed "unjustly" invaded his life. He truly believed, as almost all of us do, that he was a hard-working, law-abiding, responsible citizen who pulled his own weight in society. He believed that he had no problems. Other people had problems, but not him.

He would deny the hurt, isolation, coldness, defensiveness, and tremendous fear he obviously operated under, which controlled his life each and every day. In fact, quite literally, he was not aware of these feelings and behaviors, because they were banished from his conscious mind. He would have rejected Thoreau's notion that he, like most people, was leading a life of quiet desperation. His fierce defense mechanisms, which surfaced while he was young, were firmly in place and operating strongly by early adulthood. Their ghostly presence in his adult life did not allow him to have awareness of his pain until these defenses began to weaken in the waning years of his life. Until, of course, he was forced to face them in his Christmas Eve ordeal.

This denial gives us a major clue as to the severity of the abandonment he suffered as a child, only briefly and subtly alluded to during the story by Dickens, who provided few clues to explain the situation. (I will have much more to say later about the implications behind his

wisely understated treatment of Scrooge's childhood abandonment.)
The strength of his denial also helps us to realize the titanic magnitude
of his unique transformation experience. As the old cliché goes, the
bigger they are, the harder they fall.

The important thing to keep in mind is that within Scrooge and all
people, the potential for the permanent change he experienced is
always possible. We are never really abandoned; we are never too old,
and it is never too late. The birth of a spiritual life, represented by the
tiny, vulnerable Christ child on Christmas morning, is present all year
long, during any season of our lives.

Paul Davis' (1990) comprehensive book, *The Lives and Times of
Ebenezer Scrooge*, includes this elegant quote from turn-of-the-century literary critic Edwin Charles concerning Charles Dickens' story:

> *I regard* A Christmas Carol *as a sacred subject, and I believe
> there are thousands of other Dickens worshippers who think with
> me in that respect. It is a sermon, amplifying and exemplifying
> Holy Writ itself, telling as in a practical and material manner of
> the newer and holier duties of man to man which Christ came down
> on earth to teach. It is a work to be read over quietly and pondered
> over seriously, so that its glorious lesson of Charity to men may
> sink into the heart.*

This passage, written in 1909, is truer today than ever. It is my hope that
this current endeavor will help to keep *A Christmas Carol* alive in the sacred
and serious sense originally intended by Dickens in 1843.

## CHAPTER TWO

# Scrooge's Wounded Inner-Child

Today, many people consider John Bradshaw, the nationally known and widely acclaimed therapist, author, and lecturer, to be the single person who has done more than anyone to bring into present-day popular consciousness the truth and heartbreak of the wounded inner-child. His work makes clear the untold number of people who, in adulthood, continue to suffer the consequences of the terrible parental abandonment they were subjected to in a wide variety of ways as children.

He discusses the inevitable development of the "false self," which surfaces as a direct result of parental abandonment. It attempts to mask the intense inner pain and loneliness of the neglected "true Self," or wounded inner-child. The false self eventually leads people to become either "more than human" by taking on the role of the abuser, or "less than human" by taking on the role of the abused. Bradshaw's teaching gift and the various facets of his extensive therapeutic endeavors have had a positive and lasting effect on thousands of people.

He has synthesized, in a clearly understandable manner, a great mass of physiological, sociological, psychological, and spiritual theories, studies, and treatment modalities to aid people on their journeys within to heal childhood wounds.

Because of his work, and the work of many notable others, thousands of people have learned to cognitively understand the systemic connection of the past to the present. They have learned to work through their various childhood injuries, which ultimately gives them the knowledge, the choice, and the tools to stop relying on a plethora of dysfunctional adaptations in compensation for these injuries. As a result, more and more people are becoming liberated from the iron shackles of their childhood wounds.

Inner-child work is designed to help people stop blaming themselves and/or others for their present problems and to take sole responsibility for their lives. By taking care of their real needs first, by learning to parent and nurture themselves, and by finding ways to relate to their concept of God in healthy ways, they learn to live authentically. This important personal work gives people the freedom to relate to the world in a loving, or what Bradshaw calls, "soulful" manner.

Historians know that those who do not understand history are doomed to repeat it. This concept applies to the field of psychology as well: individuals who do not understand their own dysfunctional histories are also doomed to repeat them. Conversely, those who do understand their own personal histories are set free to make functional decisions. By doing so, the vicious cycle known as the "multigenerational transmission of dysfunctional behaviors," which plagues our present day world, can be stopped. We do not have to keep passing our unresolved problems down the generational line to damage our children.

# Dickens & the Poisonous Pedagogy

Turning our attention to the nineteenth century, it is clear that Charles Dickens, more than any other literary author, should be considered an important antecedent to our present-day child-centered movement. He was a child advocate at the same time when the patriarchal system, operating under the rules Alice Miller (1990) has identified as the "poisonous pedagogy," was at its inception. In *The Family*, Bradshaw (1988) provided a list of the child domination rules as delineated by Miller:

1. Adults are the masters of the dependent children.
2. Adults determine in a godlike fashion what is right and wrong.
3. The child is held responsible for the anger of adults.
4. Parents must always be shielded.
5. The child's life-affirming feelings pose a threat to the autocratic parent.
6. The child's will must be "broken" as soon as possible.
7. All this must happen at a very early age so the child "won't notice" and will not be able to expose the adults.

In *A Christmas Carol* and throughout the vast collection of Dickens' writings, it is evident that he continually dealt with the poisonous pedagogy and the victimization of children. Through his fictional characters, it is patently clear that he was communicating the horrors of his own unresolved personal childhood abandonment experiences and their ramifications upon his adult life.

## Scrooge as Wounded Child

In "The Carol," Tiny Tim was the quintessential child victim. Bob Cratchit, Tim's father, was an adult victim, albeit a less obvious one. Equally valid as victim was Ebenezer Scrooge himself, the paragon of abusive behavior in adulthood. Unlike those of Tiny Tim, Scrooge's childhood wounds were not visually observable; unlike Bob, he took on the abuser's role as an adult. This doesn't mean that the early wounds he suffered weren't just as grievous in their own way; they just were not as readily apparent. It is much harder to feel empathy for him because of the particularly abusive dysfunctional adaptations that emerged to hide these childhood hurts.

The major clue we have that Scrooge was victimized as a child is that, like Dickens, he was completely abandoned for a period of time by his parents. As stated in Chapter One, this is only subtly referred to by the author, almost as if he were intentionally glossing over it. All we really learn is that Scrooge was sent away to a run-down boarding school late in his childhood and that he was not allowed to come home for at least one holiday season. We also learn from his sister Fan that their father had become "so much kinder than he used to be" (38), and that after repeated requests, he ultimately allowed her to bring her big brother, Ebenezer, home for Christmas before he was to begin an apprenticeship, and given the opportunity "to be a man" (38).

Without careful reading and deep reflection, it is rather easy to miss the implications and full import of this vital information in *A Christmas Carol*. Furthermore, it is certain that many people today do not realize the important ramifications of this section of the story upon Scrooge's development. In fact, Davis (1990) included this 1968 quote from the president of Screen Gems, who once considered making a film version of the story:

> *Dickens is a terrible writer. In the original, Scrooge was mean and stingy, but you never know why. We're giving him a mother and father, an unhappy childhood, a whole background which will motivate him.*

Dickens was not a terrible writer. Scrooge was mean and stingy, but it is not true that we never know why. He did have parents, and there is a background that explains his adult motivations. We just aren't clubbed over the head with the details. We must learn to decipher Dickens' shorthand style in this section of the story. We have to work a little bit to connect Scrooge's adult behaviors with his traumatic childhood experiences, which was presented with understatement.

Perhaps Dickens downplayed Scrooge's abandonment because he was extremely ashamed of his own traumatic childhood separation experience. In *The Wind and the Bough*, Edmund Wilson (1941) made it clear that Dickens completely hid the truth about this horrible time in his life from his own family. In fact, they did not learn of it until after the information appeared in John Forster's exhaustive authorized biography, and only after Dickens' death.

More important than this possibility, however, Paul Davis (1990) feels, and I wholeheartedly concur, that whatever Dickens' real motivation for glossing over the details of Scrooge's childhood abandonment in this section, he is giving us the opportunity to allow "the specifics to be imaginatively filled in by individual readers." This makes A Christmas Carol "a vicarious framework on which to fit a multitude of life stories." By doing so, we are given the chance to imagine vividly the horrors that Scrooge was subjected to as a child.

We are also given the golden opportunity to project our own unresolved childhood traumas onto his blank screen, or we can project the painful pasts of significant others in our lives onto this screen. By doing so, we can learn to identify with and begin to understand our own wounded Scrooges within. And we can learn to understand those wounded Scrooges surrounding us who have either negatively affected our lives in our pasts, or those who continue to dysfunctionally affect our lives today. At any rate, the main point is we are not to gloss over this subtly presented information; we are to reflect on the profundity and severity of it, perhaps even own it.

If we don't dwell deeply on this part of the story, we will never make sense of why Scrooge turned out the way he did. We know he spent the Christmas holiday with his family and that eventually he was placed with the benevolent master Fezziwig, from whom he learned his trade. We also know that for a time he fell deeply in love with Belle, a poor but caring young woman he was engaged to marry. Despite these positive developments in his life, it is obvious that he was becoming deeply disturbed, and that these life-affirming events were not enough to counteract the effects of his childhood trauma.

We know that when given the opportunity by Belle, who became alarmed by his greed and desire for monetary "gain," to back out of his marriage promise, Scrooge agreed to do so with only token resistance. Unlike his mentor, Fezziwig, Scrooge eventually became a hard, severe master to his singular employee, Bob Cratchit. He all but denied his family ties to his nephew Fred, the only child of his once beloved, now deceased sister, Fan. He also flatly and rudely rejected the humble entreaty of two men soliciting for "slight provisions" for the poor during the holidays.

These are not the expected behaviors of a well-integrated man. These behaviors reflect the ramifications of the largely unarticulated hurts Dickens leaves for us to ponder, still operating in Scrooge's damaged psyche, pervasively controlling his moods and behaviors.

What were these hurts? Was he the victim of an alcoholic family system? Did he suffer from physical abuse, or emotional abuse, or possibly even sexual abuse? We will never know in absolute terms, but we surely know that his injuries were indeed deep for him to turn out the way he did. We should never be fooled by Scrooge's, our own, or by other people's defenses and fear-driven attempts to appear strong. The more a person has need for power, control, and domination, the more obvious it is that person is living out of fear. *A Course in Miracles* (Foundation for Inner Peace 1992) tells us that "No one who lives in fear is really alive." Belle saw this clearly and said to him at their breakup:

> *You fear the world too much....All your other hopes have merged*
> *into the hope of being beyond the chance of its sordid reproach (46).*

# Scrooge as "More Than Human"

In *Creating Love*, Bradshaw (1992) stated that people who adapt to their childhood traumas in this way behave in a "more than human" fashion. Through their thoughts and actions, they come across as "shameless." The behavioral characteristics associated with this type of dysfunctional life adaptation includes these false self needs:

1. perfection
2. control
3. power
4. patronizing attitude
5. critical attitude
6. judgmentalism, blaming behavior
7. self-righteousness
8. driven, superachieving behavior
9. superior attitude

Pretransformed Scrooge fit these characteristics perfectly. He was a consummate workaholic, who chastised Bob Cratchit for not wanting to work past closing time on Christmas Eve and who resented his wanting Christmas Day off with pay. He refused to exchange holiday greetings with his nephew Fred and castigated him for marrying out of love. In addition, he told Fred that he would rather go to hell than dine with him and his wife on Christmas Day.

He sarcastically queried the men collecting for charity about the continued existence of poor houses and jails, stating that he had already contributed his "fair share" to the poor to help meet their needs through these "useful" institutions—then abruptly dismissed them. In terms of the poor, he showed little sympathy for their plight, suggesting that they could die, and "decrease the surplus population" (10), if that was their wish. Furthermore, he told the collectors that he only thought of his business and that he had neither time nor interest in other people's problems.

## Scrooge's Cultic Family Background

Working backward from the premise that Scrooge developed this particular personality type, we can deduce that he was shaped by and the product of what Bradshaw (1992) termed a "cultic" family system. He stated that:

> *The whole system is based on a rigid control over its members'*
> *thoughts, feelings, and desires. The whole system is based on a rigid*
> *ideology which is considered sacred. The system with its ideology*
> *is more important than any of the individual cult members.*

Again, we can't be sure exactly what cultic ideology the Scrooge family followed, but very likely it was based on a particularly harsh strain of the Puritan work ethic. It might be surmised that their ideology was a "religion" of hard work and superachievment in the business world, especially for males.

Perhaps young Ebenezer was banished to a boarding school because he wasn't applying himself to the rigid educational standards and strict work ethic of his father. Maybe he was being punished for being a dreamer, therefore a family embarrassment. Perhaps this banishment was his father's brutal attempt to let him know that he had better learn to conform and achieve, or suffer the consequences by being completely abandoned.

From the story, we learn that young Scrooge was very fond of, and eventually developed an intense relationship with fanciful childhood literature. During the dream conducted by the Ghost of Christmas Past, Scrooge expounded emotionally on a variety of literary characters who vividly kept him company during his deep isolation at the boarding school. Dickens wrote:

> *To hear Scrooge expending all the earnestness of his nature on such*
> *subjects, in a most extraordinary voice between laughing and cry-*
> *ing; and to see his heightened and excited face; would have been a*
> *surprise to his business friends in the city, indeed (36).*

This obvious love of and intense involvement with creative literature certainly was not useful in the hard, cold world of "bottom-line" business. Perhaps Scrooge's father knew this and sent his son away in a harsh attempt to tear this frivolity and wastefulness out of his young soul.

We know that Scrooge's father changed at some point, and became, according to his sister Fan, "so much kinder than he used to be." This change is indicated when Fan stated that she asked him (once again) for the return of Ebenezer after he had spoken particularly gently to her one night, causing her fear of him to abate. She told her brother that compared to the past, "home's like Heaven"(38). We are never told why the father changed, we just know that it happened.

Due to this change, apparently he modified his rigid cultic family philosophy and softened his severe stance, at least to a degree. Unfortunately, the damage from the past had already been done. The father and the system rules changed, but this did not imply in any way that the damages already inflicted upon his son, or any other individual family member, would be automatically erased. In order for that goal to be achieved, Scrooge would have to suffer through his own life-saving ordeal, which he eventually did.

Perhaps the father's abrupt change may be viewed as a model, or literary foreshadowing, predictive of the overnight transformation that would eventually occur in his son. The main point we need to keep in mind, however, is that the father's change did little or nothing to alleviate his son's unresolved pain while he was a child.

## Scrooge's "Snapping" Phenomenon

Bradshaw (1992) informs us that in cultic family systems, there is a heavy price to be paid by at least some of the individual members. It is obvious that young Ebenezer paid that price. Bradshaw stated the following about this particular family type:

> The purity of doctrine with its demand for blind obedience leads to a phenomena called 'snapping.' Psychologists Flo Conway and Jim Siegelman describe 'snapping' as 'the process of shutting off the mind, of not thinking.' The process leaves the people numb to their own feelings and the world around them. When you 'snap,' you have become a nonthinking part of the family cult.

It is evident that Ebenezer had snapped during the time he was banished to the boarding school by his father. The total isolation he experienced while forced to spend a holiday in exile more than likely precipitated this phenomenon. Like many prisoners of war, cut off from all others, he was psychologically broken.

Dickens clearly indicated that snapping had occurred by including an incredible scene showing young Scrooge actually projecting Ali Baba, and a variety of other fictional literary characters, into his physical environment. The adult Scrooge, while watching his former self, told the Ghost of the Past the following:

> 'One Christmas time, when yonder solitary child was left here alone, he [Ali Baba] did come, for the first time, just like that' (36).

Young Scrooge snapped in order to stop thinking consciously about his unbearable isolation, therefore numbing himself to his incredible mental anguish. He completely tuned out the real world. From that point forward, no family changes affected his personality formation. The pain of the boarding school experience, and any other previous parental damage inflicted upon him, still existed. When he snapped, however, this pain became repressed, totally walled off from his conscious mind. At this point, he began to live life totally out of his false self.

## Scrooge's Repression & Loss of True Self

In *Giving Back the Pain*, Robert Bleck (1993) stated that "repressed feelings never die, nor do they fade away with laughter. They linger and turn into poison within a person's soul." This statement is especially apropos, in light of the fact that a careful reading of "The Carol" shows that Scrooge possessed, and occasionally flashed, a cynical "humor." For example, after sarcastically dueling with the gentle solicitors about a holiday offering for the poor, Dickens wrote that:

> *Scrooge returned to his labours with an improved opinion of him-*
> *self, and in a more facetious temper than was usual with him (11).*

In other words, after the confrontation, not only did he feel even more superior about himself than usual, he also felt an increase in his warped jocularity. This "humor," as Bleck advises, did nothing to alleviate the pain associated with his deeply repressed childhood hurts.

In terms of deeply buried hurts, Bleck (1993) goes on to say that:

> *Our subconscious literally wants to 'vomit' this stuff out.*
> *However, the conscious part of us wants desperately not to feel any*
> *pain and tries to deny these feelings at any costs.*

The psychospiritual tome *A Course in Miracles* further enlightens us to the mechanics involved in pain avoidance. It states that human beings can live in only two distinct ways: out of fear or out of love. When we live our lives out of our fear centers, we are separated from our love center and from God. The Holy Spirit, God's mediator within each person, is potentially ready to aid us in our necessary psychospiritual growth.

The key is that this spiritual help must be consciously called forth; it only emerges into our presence when we actively seek it out. To attain love, we must drop the illusion that we have control of our lives and get in touch with the Holy Spirit within, accomplished through prayer and meditation. The Alcoholics Anonymous maxim "Let go and let God" gives the sense of what needs to happen. Only then will God emerge fully into our lives to engulf and defeat the fear with love.

The problem for Scrooge, and for most of us, is that he was forced to live out of his fearful, or ego-controlled, false self personality. This fear-driven state of mind emerged in response to his childhood abandonment trauma. Many therapists, most notably the child advocate Alice Miller, state that actual physical survival of these unfortunately very common early traumas would not be possible if it were not for a shutting down of the true Self. In Scrooge, this was indicated by the snapping which occurred because he was banished from his family.

Snapping was a heavy but necessary price he had to pay in order to survive. It left its mark on his life, as it does on all people's lives, from that point forward.

It put Scrooge, as it puts all of us, in a terrible double bind. In order to survive, he had to completely stop living out of love, as God intended. He was forced to give up totally his loving true Self, and began living out of his fearful, ego-controlled, false self. He had no choice in the matter; it was mandatory for his very existence. Once this occurred, it became impossible for him to recognize his pain; therefore, it never crossed his mind to actively call forth help from the Holy Spirit within.

## Scrooge's Development of Adult Defense Mechanisms

Unless these early traumas are resolved during childhood, a highly unlikely proposition, they eventually lead to the development of adult defense mechanisms. The more severe the childhood traumas were, the more fiercely the adult defense mechanisms operate.

It is clear that Scrooge feared abandonment more than anything else because of his unwanted removal from his family and the incredible shame and pain involved in it. There is nothing inherently wrong about going away to school; thousands of people willingly do so every year. For him, however, the reasons for it and his experience of it were devastating. Imagine his public shame at Christmas when all the other boys left for home while he was left behind, completely isolated, totally alone in the morose environment of the ever-deteriorating school he was forced against his will to attend.

Scrooge's eventual array of "more than human" defense mechanisms, originally set in motion when he snapped in order to survive and be fully operational by his early adulthood, were on guard to keep him from feeling a repeat of the pain and horror of that original abandonment experience. These defenses included severity, coldness, attainment of power, and accumulation of money. These behaviors and drives were designed to keep all others at a "safe" distance.

To repeat, these unconsciously driven defenses existed to ensure him that he would never again feel the unbearable pain of abandonment. Because of this irrational but ever-present fear, however, it also precluded him from investing in the necessary emotional risks required for real connections with others. If people were never allowed in, they could never do him any harm. If they were never allowed in, however, he could never experience the warmth and love he so desperately wanted and missed during his childhood.

In fact, the only person he ever "joined up" with in any sense during his adult life was Jacob Marley, his mirror image and emotional double. Dickens wrote that after his death:

> Scrooge never painted out Old Marley's name. There it stood,
> years afterwards, above the warehouse door: Scrooge and Marley.
> The firm was known as Scrooge and Marley. Sometimes people
> new to the business called Scrooge Scrooge, and sometimes Marley,
> but he answered to both names. It was all the same to him (2).

Marley was no threat to Scrooge. Their relationship, in reality, was no more than a business deal. It did not imply any sort of emotional investment. It was predictable, safe, and in Bradshaw's (1988) term, "famil(y)iar." Therefore, it was non-threatening to Scrooge's fragile psyche.

The major problem with defense mechanisms is that they are not needed and serve no useful purpose. In fact, they only exist as the outgrowth and unfortunate remnants of the sad but mandatory childhood compromise, essential at that time to survive intolerable trauma. Ironically, all they do in adult life is to ensure a different form of unnecessary misery and separation from others. The unavoidable compromise that leads to their development now only serves to keep people shut down from experiencing life in its full range of wonders and glories. Scrooge's life serves as a perennial reminder to us of what happens when they operate unchecked, as if they are still vitally necessary.

In *A Return to Love*, Marianne Williamson (1992) tells us it is the ego's intention to deny us this important truth. Once the ego comes into being, it takes on a life of its own, leeching off us in order to exist. It does not want to die. It informs us in no uncertain terms and in an almost infinite number of ways that by giving up our dysfunctional behaviors, we will perish. It lies to us to save itself. It acts like our best friend, when in reality, it is our worst enemy.

## Scrooge's Defeat of the Ego

According to *The Course in Miracles*, only by fearlessly facing our pasts in an act of atonement, as Scrooge ultimately did, and turning to the Holy Spirit for guidance and support, can we overcome this state of being. This is not an easy task. Remember, the ego will not let go without a major fight. It would prefer keeping the original pain walled off from consciousness in order to avoid a fight. It will do everything it possibly can to stop us from living out of love. It tries with all of its power to keep us from knowing that we are "living lives of quiet desperation."

That is the reason why the therapeutic process is so difficult, even for people who are aware enough of their pain to enter into counseling. Clients often feel horrible, both mentally and physically, for a period of time when they connect up with their repressed memories and work through them. In a sense, they are going through an exorcism of the ego. That is exactly what Scrooge endured.

They often feel like they are falling into a black hole. They certainly do not want to go into this unknown territory, and they have no idea of how it is possible to live a life different than the one they know. Most people courageous enough to seek out therapy in the first place know that they were miserable before they made the decision to go into the black hole, but many seriously question the decision once the ego gets down to its very dirty business. It will yield the necessary information, but very grudgingly and often very painfully. It makes people believe that they were better off leaving well enough alone. The trip into love is not for the faint-hearted. It is the most courageous and important journey one can make.

Scrooge lived life out of his fear-driven ego state from the time of early adulthood. Until, of course, that fateful Christmas Eve, when he finally and reluctantly faced up to his dreaded fear from his childhood trauma in the form of a series of dreams: past, present, and future. His ego always caused him to consciously avoid the journey into this repressed information from his personal past. It made him believe that dealing with it would be so painful and so devastating, that confronting it could cause his death. When given the opportunity, represented by Marley's apparition, for a "chance and hope" (25), Scrooge initially responded, "I—I think I'd rather not" (25). Indeed, even when he finally was able to deal with this repressed information, he quite literally felt he was at death's door.

His ego made his transformation extremely painful, even to the point that he ends the dream sequence staring directly at his own grave, not sure if he would be given a second chance at life or not. In his reasoning mind, he knew that the dreams were intended to bring about his spiritual awakening, his reclamation. Despite this knowledge, he greatly feared that it was too late. His ego, intending to maintain its existence until the bitter end, made it appear that Scrooge was the one who would die, not it. The glory of the situation is that Scrooge successfully went through his fear, into the light of his new life:

> Holding up his hands in a last prayer to have his fate reversed, he
> saw an alteration in the Phantom's hood and dress. It shrunk, col-
> lapsed, and dwindled down into a bedpost (110).

Staring directly into his own grave, he did not succumb to this ego-induced fear. Instead, Scrooge prayed, asking his Holy Spirit within, for the first time in his adult life, to help him in a way he had always so desperately needed.

His prayer, like all properly motivated prayers, was answered. His ego was defeated, once and for all. At that point, he died to his old self and was reborn spiritually. He was ready to begin his new life, living out of love instead of fear.

Ego-driven defense mechanisms are unfortunate remnants from our troubled pasts. Their existence causes us, or others we love, to miss out on a spiritually awakened life in the present. Despite this, we can choose to look at them in a positive light. If they do exist in our lives, we are being given wondrous clues to indicate that our pasts must be deeply affecting us. They are providing us with the choice to go on an archeological search into our personal pasts. They are giving us the life-saving opportunity to cull out and deal with the repressed original painful traumas that led to their existence. We need to remember that the reason for their ultimate existence and unnecessary control over our lives today once served the most noble purpose of protecting us from physically dying.

Ponder Scrooge's life. How much of his valuable time on Earth was unnecessarily wasted by being spiritually asleep? Remember that his personal defense mechanisms kept him from getting what he always really wanted: closeness with others. Perversely, all they guaranteed was that he could never get the closeness he desired by ensuring a separation from others, accomplished by keeping him apart from his loving, true Self.

## Wake Up to Your Spiritual Opportunities

Scrooge was lucky; not everyone is given the type of last-chance, instantaneous transformation experience he got. Fortunately, Scrooge's ego was not quite strong enough to ruin his God-intended life of love.

In *The Untouched Key*, Alice Miller (1990) tells us that in order to awaken, it is important to have had at least one advocate during childhood who valued our existence and who loved us unconditionally. For Scrooge, his little sister Fan served this substantial role. Although she could not directly rescue him from his ultimate adult fate, she was able to show him deep, authentic love during the time he was being rejected and isolated by his father. After he snapped, Scrooge's knowledge of her advocacy was repressed. Fortunately, it resurfaced subconsciously on that fateful Christmas Eve in the figure of her only child and his nephew, Fred.

Despite Scrooge's outrageous rejection of his visit, of his dinner invitation, and of him as a person, Fred did not reject back in return. In fact, he said:

> *'I am sorry, with all my heart, to find you so resolute. We have never had any quarrel, to which I have been a party. But I have made the trial in homage to Christmas, and I'll keep my Christmas humour to the last. So A Merry Christmas, uncle!' (8).*

Dickens wrote that Fred left his uncle's office "without an angry word, notwithstanding" (8), despite the verbal abuse and rejection to which he was subjected. In a Christ-like manner, he turned the other cheek.

Fred unknowingly "fanned" the dying embers of his cold uncle's hidden love during this holiday visit by subconsciously reminding him of his beloved, long-deceased sister Fan. Through his selfless show of love, he somehow bypassed his uncle's defenses. By doing so, he synchronistically helped to trigger the chain reaction which ultimately led to the demise of his uncle's ego, which to that point held a decades-long stranglehold on the repressed abandonment information. Love, indeed, does conquer all.

Marianne Williamson (1992) tells us that we should not react adversely or defensively to the fearful, abusive, defense-driven attempts of others to push us away. Through her interpretation of *The*

*Course in Miracles*, she teaches us that our show of love, despite the negative reactions of others, is good for us, and that it can possibly lead to the miracle of the awakening of their loving, soulful side. We can't make it happen directly, but we can react differently to make it possible for them to accomplish only what they alone are capable of doing.

## Treat Every Chance to Change as if It Is Your Last

By introducing Jacob Marley's memory to Scrooge on that specific Christmas Eve day, Dickens draws upon a legal concept to indicate that Scrooge's time for transformation was within a scant few hours of expiring. Scrooge tells the charity solicitors that "Mr. Marley has been dead these seven years....He died seven years ago, this very night" (9). Marley's re-emergence into Scrooge's consciousness, like Fan's, served to lead him into his dream journey. We all know that seven years is the traditional limit to file a legal claim. Scrooge's true Self filed this "eleventh hour" claim, appealing to the Holy Spirit within to help him avoid the dire fate of his dysfunctional "twin," Marley.

While the clock struck one to signal the beginning of Scrooge's first two dreams, we learn that the last dream began at the stroke of midnight, the well-known bewitching hour. This was the "death" dream, conducted in the form of Christmas Yet to Come. Once again, Dickens was indicating that Scrooge's time to change was up. It was do or die time.

These two pieces of information are important to us. They imply that our time to change is quickly running out, and if we do not take the necessary proactive measures to begin the transformation process, eventually we do run out of time. It is never too late to begin; do not let your clock strike midnight.

# Resurrection and Rebirth from Darkness to Light

Despite the fact that all of Scrooge's dreams occurred in one night, the reclamation process felt to him like it took place over a three day period. This was no literary coincidence. Christ's resurrection took three days, and Scrooge's rebirth felt as if it took three days. Dickens was letting us know that this is not really just a Christmas story. More importantly, it is an Easter story, one of resurrection. Davis (1990) suggested that Dickens, in all of his Christmas stories, viewed and treated the two holidays as part of a singular continuum.

The calendar timing of Christmas, properly understood, is an elegant representation and yearly reminder of the possible return of God's light, or love, into our lives. It occurs, not coincidentally, just after the winter solstice, the very darkest time of the year. We all know that it is darkest before dawn. The infant Christ is the symbolic tiny "light of the world," giving us the smallest amount of hope at the onset of the coldest time of the year. To understand the titanic transformation that took place in Scrooge's wretchedly cold, dark life is to understand the power of even a minuscule amount of Christ's true light when it is allowed to enter our lives.

It made all the difference for Scrooge. When he awoke from his sleep, both actually and spiritually, and discovered that he had not missed Christmas, he said, "I'm quite a baby. Never mind. I don't care. I'd rather be a baby" (112). In an article about reclaiming his own inner-child, or true Self, Matousek (1994) stated the following:

> Contrary to what the ego believes, it's the childmind—not the yogi, magus, priest, or martyr—that holds the keys to enlightenment. . . . we become the hidden children of God, and find a new life within us.

Christ stated that we must become like children to enter into the kingdom of heaven. Having defeated his ego, Scrooge reclaimed his inner-child, entered the kingdom, and lived within it for the duration of his physical existence.

Can you say the same? It is never too late. Like Scrooge, take a Twelve-Step-inspired, fearless, moral inventory of your life in order to begin the process to defeat your ego. Go through your pain. You will come out on the other side, like Scrooge did, and enter into the life of the soul, resurrected right here and right now. Then and only then will you live the true-Self life God always intended for you. Your inner-child will be reclaimed.

## CHAPTER THREE

# Scrooge's Ghosts as Metaphor for Change

As a science, modern psychology is widely believed to have begun in 1879, when Wilhelm Wundt, commonly regarded as the discipline's founding father, began the first established laboratory. Sigmund Freud, the first major social scientist to propose a unified theory to understand and explain human behavior, began his theorizing and research in the latter part of the nineteenth century. Out of the huge mass of his very controversial work came some very important and viable concepts useful to this day, including that of the unconscious mind, with its attendant effects upon our adult lives, and of the role defense mechanisms play to irrationally protect us from our past hurts.

For our purposes, the main point is that psychology, much less psychotherapy, did not exist in any standardized, accepted form at the time Charles Dickens wrote *A Christmas Carol* in 1843. Yet, through the metaphor of Marley and the three ghosts, he astonishingly detailed the necessary elements of a perfectly accurate modern psychospiritual therapeutic recovery process during Scrooge's night of transformation. It was a compressed process, to be sure, but all the essential elements were included.

## Scrooge's Wake-up Call

In *The Untouched Key*, Alice Miller (1990) tells us that as we age, our defense mechanisms naturally begin to loosen their iron grip on our lives. Because of this, we get brief glimpses into our repressed pain, as it fleetingly breaks through the ego's barriers. Many people begin the counseling process after their defense mechanisms weaken and they begin to sense that something is very wrong in the way they are living their lives.

Because of the charitable solicitors' chance reintroduction of Marley into Scrooge's conscious mind, fortunately, he experienced this phenomenon. The memory of Marley served to ignite a subtle but powerful uneasiness into his physical system. Later that evening, his long-suppressed stress erupted, triggering the appearance of Marley's specter. Through the dire warnings he received from the ghost, Scrooge realized that the life he was leading, like the one Marley had led, was doomed. In response, he began his therapy process.

## Uncovering the Past—Inner-child Work

At the very onset of the dream-therapy process, through the Spirit of Christmas Past, Scrooge was immediately taken back into his childhood, specifically to the time period of his boarding school exile. For the first time in his adult life, he allowed himself to think about his excruciatingly painful childhood abandonment. This confrontation was intensely emotional for him, and he "wept to see his poor forgotten self as he used to be" (35). He encountered his true Self just before the time he snapped, when he was forced to completely shut down emotionally in order to physically survive his plight. Through this memory, and through his tears, he began the painful grief process for his wounded inner-child.

## Ramifications of Snapping

Because he snapped, Scrooge saw how he learned to rely heavily on reading and an intense fantasy life in order to survive this trauma. He remembered how he populated his lonely world with fanciful fictional characters, among them Ali Baba, and projected them into the physical world to keep him company and to occupy his deeply troubled mind during the trauma:

> *The Spirit touched him on the arm, and pointed to his younger self, intent upon his reading. Suddenly a man, [Ali Baba] in foreign garments: wonderfully real and distinct to look at: stood outside the window, with an axe stuck in his belt, and leading by the bridle an ass laden with wood (36).*

## Realistic Appraisal of Family Members

Continuing the process, he clearly allowed into his conscious mind the reality of the cruel abandonment behavior of his father. He also realized the deep love that his little sister, Fan, had for him. He remembered that it was through her repeated efforts that he was finally released from further childhood isolation. He could not contradict the Spirit that she was indeed a large-hearted person.

## Remembering Fezziwig's Benevolence

Through scenes involving his benevolent master, Fezziwig, Scrooge remembered a brief period of good times in his early adulthood and how he viewed his master's kindness before his insidious defense mechanisms overwhelmed him. Conversing with the Spirit, Scrooge, "speaking unconsciously like his former, not his latter self," said of Fezziwig:

> *'He has the power to render us happy or unhappy; to make our service light or burdensome; a pleasure or a toil. Say that his power lies in words and looks; in things so slight and insignificant that it is impossible to add and count them up: what then? The happiness he gives, is quite as great as if it cost a fortune' (45).*

## Unsnapping as a Result of the Recovery Process

By remembering his childhood and grieving for his abuse, and by objectively remembering his father's cruelty, his sister's love, and Fezziwig's kindness, we can deduce that Scrooge began the vital "unsnapping" process at this point in his therapy. All of this long-repressed information came back to him with such emotional force that he was now able to cry about it for the first time in his life. This significant information from his past was no longer "warehoused" away, as Stettbacher (1991) teaches us it can be, cut off from all feeling: "Many memories, particularly those arising in childhood, are stored not as conscious experiences but as simply having happened."

These memories were now fully integrated in his mind, animated with the full range of feelings that were always intended to accompany them. From *The Gospel of Thomas** we learn that this uncovering eventually leads to a life of spiritual awakening and rebirth:

> *Jesus said, 'Know what is within your sight, and what is hidden from you will become clear to you. For there is nothing hidden that will not be revealed.'*

## Understanding the Effects of Adult Defense Mechanisms

During his therapy delving into the past, Scrooge was able to pinpoint the precise time his defense mechanisms, which directly resulted from his unresolved childhood trauma, began to overwhelm him in adulthood. He fully realized that their onset caused him to lose Belle, his one true love. He finally realized why Belle said the following to him when she broke off their engagement:

> *'You may—the memory of what is past half makes me hope you will—have pain in this. A very, very brief time, and you will*

---

* Included in Meyer's 1984 *The Secret Teachings of Jesus*, a translation of the Gnostic Gospels.

*dismiss the recollection of it, gladly, as an unprofitable dream,*
*from which it happened well that you awoke' (48).*

Scrooge now understood that Belle unequivocally realized he had fallen deeply asleep to his true Self. He knew she clearly realized that because of his desire to control his fears, he would interpret his defenses in a falsely positive way. He knew she patently realized that he would staunchly defend his defenses as justifiable, mature measures needed to deal with the harsh realities of life. He finally understood why she released him to his fate.

He was even able to deduce, with probable accuracy, how wonderfully well Belle's life had turned out. He visualized her surrounded by a large and loving family, despite the fact that there is no indication in "The Carol" that he had direct, factual knowledge of this truth. It is possible that Scrooge had secretly followed her life, but there is no indication of this in the story. It is as if he finally had the ability to fathom that because of her nature, she could have only married a fully functional husband, one who truly had the capacity to love himself and her in a way that was good for both of them, and for their children.

During this part of his therapeutic work, Scrooge felt sadness and remorse when he finally expressed desire for a child of his own, one who "might have called him father, and been a spring-time in the haggard winter of his life" (50). This is an important clue concerning his level of awakening by this point in his therapy process. Despite the fact that Scrooge was connecting with his feelings for the first time, and that he desired a child of his own as a result of this process, he was still thinking dysfunctionally.

It is never appropriate to dependently count on a child to save a parent from a "haggard" old age. Scrooge's use of the word "haggard" in conjunction with the aging process implied that he still fully expected this time in his life to be contracted with fatigue or inner stress. Even though Scrooge was beginning to feel, he still could not envision a different life for himself other than the wretched one he was currently leading.

He was still subconsciously wishing to be rescued from his own fate, much in the way Fan was forced to save him when he was a child—when she was an even younger child. At this point in his process, he was still denying the full responsibility he would finally need to accept in order to be the true master of his own life.

## Too Much Pain; the Reemergence of the Ego

Scrooge became highly agitated at this point in his uncovery process. When he realized that he sat alone in his office while Marley, his "partner," lay on his death bed, he boldly commanded the Spirit to stop the memories: " 'Remove me!' Scrooge exclaimed. 'I cannot bear it!' " (51). He finally knew how little compassion he showed to the dying Marley, and how instead of being with him, he "solemnised" the event "with an undoubted [business] bargain" (2). This full realization of how alone he was in the world, once again, took him back directly to the intense pain associated with the isolation and loneliness he experienced at the boarding school.

His ego, which always served to keep him from feeling this intense pain, strongly reasserted itself at this time. It told Scrooge that the sum of all these truths he now consciously remembered was far too much for him to handle. Using angry emotion, which always served to push others away to defend himself in adulthood, and physical force, Scrooge stopped the Spirit. This attempt at control and denial, however, did not reverse the connections he had already made with his full range of feelings. Most importantly, it did not stop his necessary recovery process.

Many clients going through original pain work often need a much deserved period of rest before they can continue the therapy process. During this time, they may attempt to shut down again, and they often think about quitting the process. But after taking this valuable time out, they usually realize they have learned an important lesson. They become fully cognizant of the fact they have been shut down for the whole of their adult lives, and they now know, in no uncertain terms, how this repressed information has negatively affected them. Once the incredible pain associated with the release of this huge mass of life-long, pent-up energy has time to settle, they are free to move forward. There is always calm after a storm.

# Connecting in the Here and Now

After his brief time out, represented in "The Carol" as a "heavy sleep" (53), Scrooge freely chose to continue the therapy process, accompanied for this leg of his journey by the vibrant form of the Spirit of Christmas Present. Because he was now consciously connected with his pain from the past, he became much less inwardly directed, and more outwardly oriented. He was now open enough to realistically evaluate his life from other than his own ego-driven perspective. With full import, he was also able to clearly realize the effect his fear-driven defense mechanisms were having on the lives of many other people. Tacitly, he was able to accurately "know" their current attitudes and feelings toward him.

## Recognizing Personal Effect upon
## Others in the Present

Scrooge visualized how Fred, his wife, and their friends, despite showing frustration and pity while discussing his behaviors, were still able to have fun in his name and in spite of his rejection of them:

> 'He has given us plenty of merriment, I am sure,' said Fred, 'and it would be ungrateful not to drink to his health. Here is a glass of mulled wine ready to our hand at the moment; and I say, Uncle Scrooge.' 'Well. Uncle Scrooge!' they cried (84).

He was able to see how the Cratchit family, as modestly as they were forced to live due to his parsimony, was still able to enjoy the holiday. He saw that despite Mrs. Cratchit's objections, they still half-heartedly toasted him as the founder of their Christmas feast, and quickly got over the intrusion of his existence into their celebration:

> It was the first of their proceedings which had no heartiness. Tiny
> Tim drank it last of all, but he didn't care twopence for it. Scrooge
> was the Ogre of the family. The mention of his name cast a dark
> shadow on the party, which was not dispelled for full five minutes
> (72).

## Recognition of Happiness Despite Trouble

He awoke to the knowledge that his philosophy of attending solely to his personal business was an inauthentic, pathetically isolated way to live. He realized that many others unknown to him had the ability to truly rejoice in life together, despite their poor, remote, isolated conditions:

> Much they saw, and far they went, and many homes they visited,
> but always with a happy end. The Spirit stood beside sick beds,
> and they were cheerful; on foreign lands, and they were close at
> home; by struggling men, and they were patient in their greater
> hope; by poverty, and it was rich. In almshouse, hospital, and jail,
> in misery's every refuge, where vain man in his little brief authori-
> ty had not made fast the door and barred the Spirit out, he left his
> blessing, and taught Scrooge his precepts (85).

## Recognition of Impersonal Negative Effect Upon Children

He also allowed himself to think about the innocent children of the world who were being brutally affected by institutionalized neglect, of which he was an integral part. These anonymous children were being victimized by forces beyond their control, having no real chance for survival, given no love, broken in spirit, perverted from the life intended for them. The Spirit opened his robe, showing Scrooge something he had not previously allowed himself to realize:

> *They were a boy and girl. Yellow, meagre, ragged, scowling, wolfish; but prostrate, too, in their humility. Where graceful youth should have filled their features out, and touched them with its freshest tints, a stale and shriveled hand, like that of age, had pinched, and twisted them, and pulled them into shreds. Where angels might have sat enthroned, devils lurked, and glared out menacing. No change, no degradation, no perversion of humanity, in any grade, through all the mysteries of wonderful creation, has monsters half so horrible and dread (86).*

# Projecting in the Future

Immediately after completing his here-and-now therapy work, Scrooge continued to press forward, now accompanied by the dark, formless Spirit of Christmas Yet to Come. At this point, however, it is important to realize that he was still in major denial. Notwithstanding his good work, he still refused to accept the death of his ego, greatly fearing that its death would cause his physical demise.

Despite this fear, he was still able to predict accurately the wide ranging negative ramifications that his life's dysfunctional pitch would result in if he persisted to think and behave in fear-driven ways. Regardless, he was still searching for an easy way out, still fantasizing about a rescue, still looking for a compromise. He did not want to come face to face with death in order to live spiritually. Elizabeth Kubler-Ross (1969) has taught that no one truly lives until death has been fully accepted as a part of life; Scrooge was no exception to this truth. It is important to remember that throughout the following scenes, Scrooge would not admit to himself that the dead man shown to him by the Ghost of the Future was himself.

## Realization of Peers' Reactions to His Death

Regarding his future death, he could accurately picture how his business associates would callously take the news. He could project how they would discuss the nuisance of attending his funeral, putting their own concerns first. He imagined that a particular colleague would say:

> 'Well, I am the most disinterested among you, after all,' said the
> first speaker, 'for I never wear black gloves, and I never eat lunch.
> But I'll offer to go, if anybody else will. When I come to think of it,
> I'm not at all sure that I wasn't his most particular friend; for we
> used to stop and speak whenever we met. Bye, bye' (92).

## Realization of Servants' Reaction to His Death

He saw how his housekeeper, Mrs. Dilber; his laundress; and the "undertaker's man" would mirror back the same lack of respect he had shown them. He predicted they would steal and sell off many of his personal effects, including the very burial shirt off his corpse. He conjured up what the laundress would say to sum up their collective feelings about their theft and his situation:

> 'If he wanted to keep them after he was dead, a wicked old screw,'
> pursued the woman, 'why wasn't he natural in his lifetime? If he
> had been, he'd have had somebody to look after him when he was
> struck with Death, instead of lying gasping out his last there, alone
> by himself' (96).

## Realization of Clients' Reaction to His Death

When he searched his mind in the form of asking the Phantom to show him an example of anyone "who feels emotion" (101) because of his death, he was given no relief. In a darkly ironic scene, he imagined a husband and wife actually experiencing great relief because of it. His death meant they got a fortuitous postponement in repayment of a business debt immediately due to him. Of the wife, Dickens wrote:

*She was a mild and patient creature if her face spoke truth; but she was thankful in her soul to hear it, and she said so, with clasped hands. She prayed forgiveness the next moment, and was sorry; but the first was the emotion of her heart (102).*

## Realization of Authentic Sympathy

When Scrooge next asked to be shown "some tenderness connected with a death" (103), he conjured up his nephew, Fred. He now realized that because of Fred's loving manner toward him, despite his show of coldness and rejection in return, his nephew would be the person best able to show authentic, heartfelt sympathy. He was—not for his uncle's future death, however, but instead for the imagined death of Tiny Tim. Note Bob Cratchit's reaction to Fred's compassion while telling of it to his family:

> *'Now, it wasn't,' cried Bob, 'for the sake of anything he might be able to do for us, so much as for his kind way, that this was quite delightful. It really seemed as if he had known our Tiny Tim, and felt with us' (106).*

## Identification with the Death of Tiny Tim

Throughout all this, Scrooge continued staunchly denying that it was his death that was being shown to him. Until, that is, he realized that his own unresolved painful childhood trauma, and his own adult dysfunctional abandonment and neglect, were intimately linked to the death of the wounded child, Tiny Tim. Immediately after he made this compassionate connection, Scrooge finally was prepared to confront the realization of his own death. At this point, he freely requested for this painful truth to surface to his conscious mind:

> *'Spectre,' said Scrooge, 'something informs me that our parting moment is at hand. I know it, but I know not how. Tell me what man that was whom we saw lying dead' (107).*

# Painful Death of the Ego

The Phantom/therapist made it unmistakably clear to Scrooge that he was, indeed, the wretched man they observed lying dead. Now in a neglected churchyard, he pointed "from the grave to him, and back again" (109). Even with this harsh therapeutic confrontation, Scrooge was only able to just begin breaking through his thick wall of death denial. In reaction, he said:

> 'I am not the man I was. I will not be the man I must have been but for this intercourse' (109).

Despite the fact that the Phantom/therapist began to relent somewhat, indicated by the fact that "For the first time, the hand appeared to shake" (109), Dickens also indicated that Scrooge showed denial. By his use of the word "must," Scrooge demonstrated that he still neither completely accepted nor took full responsibility for his life's foul bent.

At this point in the process, Scrooge's ego broke down further. Yet, he begged the Phantom for a guarantee that he would be saved from this fate if he changed:

> 'Good Spirit,' he pursued, as down upon the ground he fell before it: 'Your nature intercedes for me, and pities me. Assure me that I yet may change these shadows you have shown me, by an altered life' (109).

As all therapists know, there are no guarantees in life, and Scrooge received none, despite his promises to repent. But the Spirit recognized his progress, and relented further: "The kind hand trembled" (110).

Scrooge pressed on, despite his failed bargaining attempts, vowing the following:

> 'I will honour Christmas in my heart, and try to keep it all the year. I will live in the Past, the Present, and the Future. The Spirits of all Three shall strive within me. I will not shut out the lessons that they teach' (110).

John Bradshaw once said that trying is not the same as doing. Even with that heartfelt pledge, the Phantom/therapist was not finished with his work.

In response to Scrooge's agonized attempt to hold onto his hand, "The Spirit, stronger yet, repulsed him" (110). This indicates that there can be no hand-holding when it comes to change. Compassion is important in therapy, and the Spirit showed it. In *Awareness*, Anthony deMello (1990) said the following:

> [C]ompassion can be very hard. Compassion can be very rude, compassion can jolt you, compassion can roll up its sleeves and operate on you. Compassion is all kinds of things.

The truth about the defeat of the ego is that it must be done alone. The Phantom did what he had to do to free Scrooge from his bondage.

Scrooge did not completely defeat his ego and achieve absolute resolution until he finally reached spiritually within himself and held "up his hands in a last prayer to have his fate reversed" (110). With this, he finally stood alone in life, and turned to God. His ego was finally defeated, and the Phantom/therapist released him from the process: "It shrunk, collapsed, and dwindled down into a bedpost" (110).

# Summary of the Psychospiritual Process

The full psychospiritual therapy process was now complete. Scrooge went back into his past and got in touch with his original pain. He realized it was caused by his father's harsh abandonment. He did not blame him; he just realized the truth of it. He remembered his sister's love and knew that she was his only childhood advocate. He began to remember some good times, but he also realized that his defense mechanisms overtook him. He saw their multiple effects on his life, from early adulthood to the present, and realized how he kept people away in futile attempts to protect himself from further abandonment.

He understood the myriad missed opportunities in his life because of these life-denying mechanisms, and mourned these losses.

He was able to break out of his rigid thinking style to the point where he could project the outcome of his life if he persisted along his dysfunctional path. Through Tiny Tim's death, he learned compassion for others. After several bargaining attempts, he ultimately confronted his fear of death, realized his aloneness in the world, learned to pray, and was reborn spiritually. Finally freed from the bondage of his fear-driven ego, he truly connected with those around him in a variety of loving ways, no longer bitter and asleep because of his childhood abandonment.

## Therapist as "S.O.B. with a Heart"

As stated by Gravitz and Bowden (1985), a good therapist is one "who can be an 'S.O.B. with a heart,' " when necessary. That was the precise role all of the Phantoms assumed, especially the Ghost of the Future, to give Scrooge the independence he needed to defeat his persistent ego. Clients must be guided into areas they would rather avoid in order to confront and grieve their hurts, and they must have enough trust in their therapists to safely lead them to these dread places. Painful truths and life-killing denials must be confronted and released to clear the path leading to true spiritual freedom and loving connection with others. For Scrooge, this was not an easy process; yet he trusted his guides, confronted these issues, and overcame his earthly fears.

## Willingness to Experience Pain

The night before His ordeal, Jesus, out of human fear, pleaded with the Father to take the "cup" of the crucifixion from him. Yet, with free will, realizing that this incredibly painful act was necessary for the resurrection of all true believers after Him, He retracted the request, and stated His willingness to allow God to do His will.

He was showing us that we must willingly confront our pain and die to our old false selves in order to be reborn into the truly spiritual life of mature adulthood. We have to let go of our ego-driven desires, and with the help of the Holy Spirit, allow the will of God to shine through us. Psychospiritual therapy, like the process conducted by Marley and the three ghosts of Christmas within Scrooge, provides us with the opportunity to attain this glorious state of spiritual being.

Scrooge tried to avoid this unavoidably painful journey into a loving, spiritual life. Initially, he told Marley that he would rather not go through the ordeal. And with the Ghost of Christmas Past, when the totality of his past pain became particularly unbearable, Scrooge unsuccessfully attempted to stop the process by covering up the Spirit's bright light of truth and love when "he seized the extinguisher-cap, and by a sudden action pressed it down upon its head" (52). Dickens continued:

> *The Spirit dropped beneath it, so that the extinguisher covered its*
> *whole form; but though Scrooge pressed it down with all his force,*
> *he could not hide the light, which streamed from under it, in an*
> *unbroken flood upon the ground* (52).

Dickens is informing us that once we have been truly exposed to the burning light of psychospiritual awareness, it cannot be stopped. Scrooge knew this, and despite his pain, voluntarily went forward with the Ghost of Christmas Present:

> *'Spirit,' said Scrooge submissively, 'conduct me where you will. I*
> *went forth last night on compulsion, and I learnt a lesson which is*
> *working now. To-night, if you have aught to teach me, let me prof-*
> *it by it'* (59).

He understood what Jesus meant when He said, "Whoever is close to me is close to the fire" (Meyer, 1984).

Despite his initial fear, Scrooge went forward. Despite his denial until the very last, he charged ahead. When confronted with wave after wave of pain sent up by the ego in an attempt to halt the process, he did not quit. Instead, he "let go—and let God" set him free from the bondage of his denial; his ego was defeated. In *The Gospel of Thomas* (Meyer, 1984), Jesus said:

> *'Let one who seeks not stop seeking until one finds. When one finds, one will be disturbed. When one is disturbed, one will be amazed, and will reign over all.'*

## Reframing Scrooge: From Infamy to Glory

Scrooge is primarily remembered as a notorious literary character; we dwell almost completely on his pre-transformed personality. Instead, he should be honored as a rare role model of one who had the courage to go through the difficult psychospiritual therapy process we all need to go through in order to fully awaken to our true, spiritual Selves. Properly understood, we should be honored, not insulted, when referred to as "a Scrooge." Remember, Dickens said that:

> *He became as good a friend, as good a master, and as good a man, as the good old city knew, or any other good old city, town, or borough, in the good old world. Some people laughed to see the alteration in him, but he let them laugh, and little heeded them; for he was wise enough to know that nothing ever happened on this globe, for good, at which some people did not have their fill of laughter in the outset; and knowing that such as these would be blind anyway, he thought it quite as well that they should wrinkle up their eyes in grins, as have the malady in less attractive forms. His own heart laughed: and that was quite enough for him (120-121).*

In this paragraph, Dickens repeats the word "good" seven times. He was telling us that Scrooge's seven particularly painful years since the death of Marley ultimately yielded to seven good, or God, ways that Scrooge was remembered in the story. He went through his compressed therapy ordeal, awoke to the truth, and showed no attachment to what others thought. He was finally freed from the past, finally his own person, finally able to live fully in the here and now—finally able to give freely to others.

## Free at Last

Scrooge did not become what M. Scott Peck calls "therapeutically depressed" after his awakening. His new-found awareness did not lead him back into loneliness and isolation after going through therapy, which Peck reports many newly conscious people often feel today. He stated in an interview in Common Boundary (Simpkinson, 1993) that these feelings arise partly because "few social institutions support one's new inner awareness," due to:

> [O]ur cultural value system that promotes excessive individualism
> and discourages a respectful, ethical behavior between and among
> individuals.

Scrooge no longer showed concern for the prevailing value system of his time; he realized that the attainment of true individualism always leads one to a sense of bondedness and community. He was now a spiritual man, who "loved his neighbors as he loved himself." He found himself, let go, and found the kingdom of God—right here, right now. He understood what Jesus intended in *The Gospel of Thomas* (Meyer, 1984) when he said of the kingdom:

> "It will not come by looking for it. Nor will it do to say, 'Behold,
> over here!' or 'Behold, over there!' Rather, the kingdom of the Father
> is spread out on earth, but people do not see it."

Scrooge finally woke up and saw that the kingdom was always there. We all need to wake up to this same truth and see it.

## CHAPTER FOUR

# The Dysfunctional Chakras of Scrooge

In *Kundalini Awakening*, John Selby (1992) tells us that some four thousand years ago in India, Hindus began to develop a varied system of yogic spiritual beliefs and practices, which included physical movements and postures, breathing exercises, community devotional acts, chanting, and meditation. In addition, a specific body of techniques was developed to focus on improving the flow of basic life-force, or kundalini, in the human body. Selby says that kundalini, or "coiled serpent," refers to:

> [T]he latent power of spiritual realization buried deep down in the human body, perpetually under pressure to rise up and manifest its ultimate truths, power, and bliss.

This spiritual energy, represented by the symbolic "coiled serpent," resides at the base of the spine, basically lying dormant until activated. A variety of kundalini meditations exist to focus attention on subtle yet specific centers, or chakras, located at various points along the spine and head. These yogic techniques are employed to induce this spiritual energy to travel up the spine to the particular chakra being fixated upon, thus releasing its unique energy.

The names and approximate physical locations of the seven chakras, or "wheels," are:

1. Earth Chakra: base of spine
2. Sex Chakra: in reproductive organs
3. Power Chakra: between navel and solar plexus
4. Heart Chakra: center of chest
5. Throat Chakra: in and around larynx
6. Intuitive Chakra: between eyebrows
7. Mystic Chakra: top of the head

Selby clearly states that these specific energy centers are more than metaphors; they are "definite energetic happenings inside each of our bodies—whether we're aware of them or not."

He goes on to say that every human being has kundalini energy. It is active in all of us to varying degrees, but the important thing to remember is that not very much is needed to maintain life.

Selby informs us that for a variety of reasons, this spiritual energy is largely blocked from traveling freely throughout our bodies. We can consciously increase its flow through a variety of breathing and other meditative techniques. And at times, it becomes activated without our direct awareness. During sexual intercourse, for example, energy located in the genital area is obviously stimulated and released. We recognize the pleasant physical sensation, but probably do not recognize the increased spiritual energy associated with this chakra center.

As Selby stated earlier, kundalini energy is "perpetually under pressure to rise up and manifest its ultimate truths, power, and bliss." In spite of this, it can and does become thwarted. Ebenezer Scrooge is a classic example of a man whose kundalini energy was largely blocked early in life, and who subsisted on a paucity of this potential spiritual energy throughout his adult life. Until, of course, it broke through spontaneously in a titanic upsurge, altering his life forever.

Uncannily, Dickens' *A Christmas Carol* perfectly illustrates what can happen to a person when kundalini energy is hampered for a lifetime, then suddenly released. It is hard to fathom that this Western writer knew of this Eastern system of belief, and intentionally wrote the story in homage to it, but it is remotely possible. We know England and India are linked historically; Dickens may have been exposed to it because of this connection. It can even be conjectured that he picked up knowledge of kundalini through obscure Western religions. Selby states that:

> In Western antiquity quite a number of esoteric societies, such as the Knights of Templar, the Freemasons, and the Gnostic Christian cults, dealt at very high levels with chakra systems and the use of Christ consciousness for attaining kundalini awakening.

We also know from Hearn (1976) that Dickens was associated with Unitarianism during the 1840s. Again, it is possible that he may have learned of it through the open-minded spiritualism exhibited by this religion.

And it is possible that Dickens knew nothing directly of kundalini. It could be that because he was writing the story from the very depths of his own troubled soul, he tapped into the universal theme and Jungian archetypes which embody the truths described in kundalini. Essentially, then, the story could have poured out from him, customized by his local slant and personal issues, but it could have been told by another quality writer tacitly grappling with the same basic truths, from any other culture. The melody of the song remains the same; only the lyrics change.

## Scrooge's Dysfunctional Earth (Root) Chakra

Joseph Campbell (Flowers, 1988) informs us that the Earth chakra, also known as the "root" chakra, located at the very base of the spine, is closely associated with "the rectum, representing alimentation, the basic, life-sustaining function." He states that in order to live, we are required to eat. And if we do not eat, we die. About the Earth chakra, Selby states the following:

> This chakra strongly connects you to your childhood past and to the entire world of physical phenomenon. It therefore is of vital importance in your life. This chakra energized your physical development up through puberty, and maintains your basic sense of physical contact with the planet.

He goes on to say that it "grounds us into our instinctive, animal, earthly needs and desires, and that it ensures our survival."

It is obvious that the energy associated with and flowing to Scrooge's first, or Earth chakra, became severely compromised during his childhood because of the abandonment ordeal he suffered. At the point when he was forced to snap in order to physically survive the boarding school isolation experience, the kundalini energy flowing to this chakra reduced to a bare minimum. This snapping ensured his survival, but the quality of his life force was drastically degraded. He was left cold as an adult because of this reduction, carrying "his own low temperature" (3).

Even before he snapped, Dickens makes it clear that young Ebenezer was not being sustained properly. Describing the dilapidated boarding school to which he was exiled, he wrote:

> There was an earthy savour in the air, a chilly bareness in the place, which associated itself somehow with too much getting up by candle-light, and not too much to eat (35).

Imagine the young Scrooge, waking up in the middle of a cold, dark night, his stomach hurting from hunger, looking for something to eat, not finding much.

After he snapped, when Fan arrived at the school to rescue her brother from familial exile, Hearn (1976) tells us that the customary wine and cakes were served by the masters before a final departure.

Dickens described these "treats" as having a curious taste. Even the driver taking the Scrooge children home from the school rejected an offered drink, based on a previous knowledge of its bad quality.

We are shown the better time in Scrooge's young life, after he snapped and before his adult mechanisms completely overwhelmed him. At Fezziwig's Christmas Eve party, Dickens describes the holiday spread:

> [T]here was cake, and there was negus, and there was a great piece
> of Cold Roast, and there was a great piece of Cold Boiled, and
> there were mince-pies, and plenty of beer (43).

He does not clearly indicate whether the apprentice Scrooge partook in the feast or not, but we do know it was available to him. The description of the celebration indicates that while Scrooge was there and exhibited excitement, we are left with the distinct impression that he was more of a passive observer than an active participant—like an outsider looking in. Other than spiritedly helping convert the warehouse into a ballroom, Scrooge is never described by the author as directly taking part in the celebratory action in terms of games, dance, or food.

Dickens clearly demonstrates the long-term energy reduction to Scrooge's Earth Chakra once his adult defense mechanisms completely took over by including several examples of his paltry food intake and outright refusal of food. For example, when Fred invited his uncle to Christmas dinner, Scrooge replied that he would see him in hell before he would eat with him. Later on that Christmas Eve, we learn he ate "his melancholy dinner in his usual melancholy tavern" (13). Even later that same night, because "Scrooge had a cold in his head" (16), he sat before his meager fire to eat a small amount of gruel. Hearn (1976) tells us that gruel is a very thin cereal, often served "in the prisons and workhouses" of England. The dictionary yields the following chiefly British, and very relevant, definition for gruel: punishment.

It is clear that Scrooge was subconsciously self-administering imprisonment and punishment by sadly eating bad food alone, in the cold, much like he was forced to as a child. No dysfunctional parent or school was necessary at this point in his life to deprive him. Once his Earth Chakra energy barely trickled, minimally sustaining him in his adulthood, he adapted to this state of being by compulsively repeating the deprivation scenario from his childhood. Throughout his adult life he merely subsisted; his root life force energy barely pulsed.

In the scene with the apparition Marley, it is obvious that Scrooge did not even trust food. While boldly arguing with the ghost about his reality, Scrooge stated the following about basic sustenance and how it can affect the physical senses:

> 'A slight disorder of the stomach makes them cheats. You may be an undigested bit of beef, a blot of mustard, a crumb of cheese, a fragment of an underdone potato. There's more of gravy than of grave about you, whatever you are!' (20).

How awful it must have been for Scrooge not be able to trust his bodily senses because of a lack of Earth Chakra energy. He never developed a reliable connection with the physical phenomena around him. It is no wonder he limited his food intake; he feared its affect upon him as much as he feared life in general.

## Scrooge's Dysfunctional Sex Chakra

Selby tells us that the spiritual energy of the second chakra, or the Sex Chakra, is located in the sex organs, and is activated:

> Once the work of the first chakra is completed at puberty. Through the awakening of this chakra you move from being a creation of your parents to becoming a creative being who in turn creates the new generation.

Scrooge did turn out to be a creation of his parents: a dysfunctional being lacking spiritual energy. Because of this, he was not able to complete the work of the Earth Chakra by puberty, instead having to wait until the latter years of his adult life, when it spontaneously and forcefully broke through on that fateful Christmas Eve. This work was indefinitely delayed because of the trauma caused by his unwitting exile to the pitiful boarding school by his father. He took this action to eradicate young Ebenezer's "irrelevant" childhood love of creative literature and to prepare him for the "manly" rigors of the hard, cold business world. Both of these goals were accomplished, but more importantly, when Scrooge snapped due to his childhood abandonment, the flow of kundalini energy to the essential Earth Chakra shut down.

This blockage, in turn, led to a suppression of spiritual energy to Scrooge's Sex Chakra, and the remaining five chakras. Selby states that the Earth Chakra:

> [I]s the energetic gateway between the organic world of Mother Earth beneath you and the mental and spiritual worlds that can be awakened step-by-step up your spine.

Once the kundalini energy flow to his Earth Chakra had been muted, it guaranteed that all of Scrooge's chakras would merely subsist on a minimal amount of sustaining life-force. It severely limited his ability to awaken to his spiritual Self.

Fezziwig's Christmas Eve party once again provides us evidence of Scrooge's early chakratic suppression. In terms of his Sex Chakra dysfunction, we learn that despite the fact that his master's three "beaming and lovable" (42) daughters were at the party, Scrooge, probably in the earlier part of his adolescence at this time, showed no particular interest in them. Dickens does let us know that these girls generated a lot of amorous interest, evidenced by the "six young followers whose hearts they broke" (42). Six's Latin root is sex. So the sexual interest they engendered in many other young men at the party did not manifest in young Scrooge. As with his Earth Chakra, the opportunity was there to partake, but he was on the sidelines of life, not an active participant.

Despite his childhood snapping, which led to the creation of his fear-based ego and the defense mechanisms, there was a temporarily increased flow of kundalini energy to Scrooge's Sex Chakra during his early adulthood. Evidenced by his falling in love with Belle, we know this energy did break through for a short period of time, despite the early trauma. In *The Road Less Traveled*, M. Scott Peck (1978) provides us with the mechanics of this phenomenon:

> [T]he temporary collapse of ego boundaries that constitutes falling in love is a stereotypic response of human beings to a configuration of internal sexual drives and external sexual stimuli, which serves to increase the probability of sexual paring and bonding so as to enhance the survival of the species.

Peck is telling us that there is an incredibly strong natural impulse to pair up in order to produce children, which is what nature demands in order to ensure the continuation of the species. In its most basic form, nature impels us to produce a large quantity of offspring. Bradshaw (1988) informs us that we are, first and foremost, sexual creatures. And Scrooge, like all people, had to deal with this powerful instinctual drive, despite his dysfunctional Sex Chakra. In response to this phenomenon, Scrooge's fear-based ego boundaries collapsed for a period of time and he fell in love with the delightful young woman, Belle. This was supposed to lead to their marriage and the eventual production of children, but it did not.

Despite the fact that they were engaged, the relationship began to fall apart. Scrooge's adult defense mechanisms emerged full force during their extended engagement, when his dysfunctional need for "gain" replaced her as his "idol," or object of love. In other words, Scrooge's biological imperative to fall in love waned, and the energy flowing to his Sex Chakra dwindled. It was superseded by a surge of dysfunctional energy to his third, or Power Chakra, the next energy center up the spine.

This energy flowing from the Sex Chakra to the Power Chakra was redirected to support his now fully emerged defense mechanisms.

They provided him with a false sense of security. For Scrooge, the love of and need for the production of money (false power) took the place of the need for Belle's love and the production of children born out of that love. Having realized this change in Scrooge, she released him from his marriage promise:

> 'But if you were free to-day, to-morrow, yesterday, can even I believe that you would choose a dowerless girl—you who, in your very confidence with her, weigh everything by Gain: or, choosing her, if for a moment you were false enough to your one guiding principle to do so, do I not know that your repentance and regret would surely follow? I do....' (47-48).

Belle realized that Scrooge had lost the spiritual flow of energy to his Sex Chakra, and that he no longer felt sustainable love for her. She understood she had been replaced as his love object by a sick love for power and money, the by-products of his defense mechanisms. Note Dickens' description of Scrooge by the point in his life:

> He was older now, a man in the prime of life. His face had not the harsh and rigid lines of later years but it had begun to wear the signs of care and avarice. There was an eager, greedy, restless motion in the eye, which showed the passion that had taken root, and where the shadow of the growing tree would fall (45-46).

She did not want to marry him under this condition. Even if Scrooge still wanted to marry her, she knew she would be nothing more than a sex object to him, and that he would eventually regret the union. Any children they would have together would not be conceived out of a mutual love.

In her youthful wisdom, she knew there wasn't enough spiritualized Sex Chakra energy flowing within him to sustain their marriage in a meaningful way. She knew that he would never be able to freely participate in the evolution of their marriage. She knew that he would not be able to develop what Peck (1978) calls "long-term relational love" once the natural sexual urges of their youth began to wane.

When Fred came to his elder uncle on Christmas Eve and invited him to dinner on Christmas Day, Scrooge harshly rejected the offer. When Fred asked why, Scrooge answered with this question: "Why did you get married?" (7). When Fred replied he did because he fell in love, Dickens related the following:

> 'Because you fell in love!' growled Scrooge, as if that were the only
> one thing in the world more ridiculous than a merry Christmas (7).

We can see by this interchange and his attitude that he does not understand the higher order, spiritual reason for marriage. Marrying out of love for another is not a business proposition; it is sexual and spiritual union. Because his spiritualized sexual energy flowed inadequately, he could not relate to a partnership based on love.

In fact, it might be argued that this energy flow was so constricted, there exists the distinct possibility that he was rendered sexually impotent. In other words, not only was the spiritual flow to this chakra non-existent, but the physical flow may also have been below the threshold for any sexualized feelings. Dickens provided no indication in the story that Scrooge ever attempted another relationship after Belle. Apparently, he partnered with no one else during his life, save for the economic one he formed with his dysfunctional "twin," Marley.

Obviously, Scrooge did not have any children of his own. During his Christmas Eve dreams, however, he does show remorse for not having taken part in the creation of life. He fantasized about a daughter of his own who "might have called him father, and been a spring-time in the haggard winter of his life" (50). At this point in his awakening process, however, he still does not understand his role as creator. He still expected his old age to the thin and constricted. If his spiritual chakra energies were flowing uninhibited, he would not have thought he would be haggard in old age, and he certainly would not expect a child to "save" him from this condition.

# Scrooge's Dysfunctional Power Chakra

This chakra center, located between the navel and the solar plexus, is mainly associated with the element of fire. Selby states that "It is the energy of the solar system radiating in our personal lives, and like the sun, creates energy for us to burn."

He states that our raw, uncommitted willpower resides in this third chakra. Furthermore, he adds the following:

> *Whether we send this energy down into brute sexuality and worldly dominance, or up into the heart to be used for personal transformation, determines if we use this energy in malevolent or positive ways.*

It is obvious that throughout most of Scrooge's adult life, his Power Chakra energy was not used in positive ways, but rather followed the dark path of malevolent, worldly dominance. The energy associated with this chakra was used as the mandatory fuel needed to power the actualization of his adult defense mechanisms. The malignant power he manifested was used in a vain attempt to keep him safe from his ego-driven fear state.

Scrooge's strong need for the attainment of significant monetary accumulation and his associated greediness provided him with an illusionary power base. The ultimate purpose for this "gain" was to give him a sense of physical security and to protect him from the threat of further exile. Through the holding of vast wealth, he would always have enough money to provide for himself; no one would ever be able to remove him from his "home." He would never again be at the mercy of others, like he was in his powerless childhood, when he was sent away.

Scrooge's coldness and harshness with others became the dysfunctional, ego-driven protective devices that gave him a sense of emotional security. It served to protect him from the pain of human abandonment. If he could keep others at a distance and did not care about them or their personal plights, then he would not have to feel. Deep down, he feared becoming close to others. From his childhood, he learned that those he loved were capable of rejection; they could and did emotionally and physically abandon him. To avoid this dreadful possibility and its associated unbearable pain ever again, he would reject and abandon people first. This negative use of Power Chakra energy was designed to keep him in control of his life, to give him the power to keep himself "safe."

Selby states, "some of us are overly fixated on this willpower chakra, acting as manipulators instead of participants in life's intimate, social, and business realms." It is clear that of all the seven chakras, the adult Scrooge fixated primarily on the Power Chakra in a dysfunctional manner. During his adolescence at Fezziwig's party, the beginnings of his inability to relate to others intimately and socially was suggested by Dickens, evidenced by his lack of interest in his master's attractive daughters and by his indirect participation in the gaiety of the celebration.

By early adulthood, Scrooge could not participate intimately with Belle, whose character demanded more than he was able to give to her, but he had not yet learned how to manipulate her to his advantage. Because of this, she refused to allow herself to be joined with him in a marriage of social convenience. Later in his life, however, he had become a consummate manipulator. He rejected the solicitors' request of him to make a small "social" contribution to the poor, but only after he sarcastically manipulated the conversation to lecture them about his contribution through taxation. He flatly turned down his nephew's family and social invitation, again after he manipulated the bent of the conversation with the intent to deprecate Fred for marrying out of love.

In the business world, Scrooge was able to manipulate in an unfettered manner. Even on the very day of Marley's death, he was able to secure "an undoubted [business] bargain" (2). In his counting house setting, he controlled the physical environment to the point that his sole employee, Bob Cratchit, spent the winter months wearing a "comforter" to help ward off the frigid cold. He verbally castigated and shamed Cratchit for wanting Christmas Day off, the only recognized business holiday of the year at that time. And he controlled Cratchit's pay to the point where his family barely eked by, having to compromise regularly in terms of food, clothing, and in Tim's case, medical attention. In short, Scrooge spent the bulk of his adult life manipulating and controlling others for his individual purposes rather than participating with them for their mutual benefit.

## Lack of the Element Fire

As stated earlier, the Power Chakra is associated with the earthly element fire. Dickens provides numerous examples throughout *A Christmas Carol* to clearly show that there was no fire in Scrooge's adult life. Instead, it was permeated with fire's opposite, cold.

Going back to his childhood, we see that he was physically deprived of the warmth of heat before he snapped in response to his abandonment. Describing the boarding school, Dickens tells us that it was "cold, and vast," and that the boy read "near a feeble fire" (35). More importantly, we know that his father had to have been exceedingly cold toward his son to have exiled him to that environment in the first place, and to have eventually ended up "so much kinder than he used to be" (38).

Note Dickens' physical and character description of the adult Scrooge:

> *The cold within him froze his old features, nipped his pointed nose, shrivelled his cheek, stiffened his gait; made his eyes red, his thin lips blue; and spoke out shrewdly in his grating voice. A frosty rime was on his head, and on his eyebrows, and his wiry chin. He carried his own low temperature always about with him; he iced his office in the dogdays; and didn't thaw it one degree at Christmas* (3).

Before his transformation, the adult Scrooge treated everyone he encountered coldly: from strangers on the street, to Cratchit, to his nephew, to the charitable solicitors, to the poor, to the young

Christmas caroler singing through his warehouse keyhole. We learn that Scrooge kept a very low fire in his suite of rooms, "nothing on such a bitter night," and that he ate his gruel sitting close to the fire because he "had a cold in his head" (16). Even when confronted by Marley's phantom, Dickens gives this account of his incredibly brazen initial reaction to this manifestation: "'How now!' said Scrooge, caustic and cold as ever" (19).

The only "fire" Scrooge had in his life, fueled by a fear-based ego and its concomitant defense mechanisms, was his burning desire to distance himself from others. This subconscious combustion process, intended to protect him from the possibility of further rejection, isolation, and abandonment, paradoxically only guaranteed that he would be walled off from the human warmth he so desperately desired. No heat from this roaring implosion ever escaped; it left Scrooge cold, both internally and externally.

## Physical Ramifications of the Power Chakra

Selby tells us that our Power Chakra energy greatly influences the pancreas glands. He states that "digestion, therefore, will be directly influenced by our third-chakra condition." From this, we can deduce that Scrooge had trouble with his pancreas glands, indicated by his odd explanation to the specter Marley, relating how his sensitive digestive process could account for a sensory hallucination. He even goes on to detail what would happen if were to ingest a single toothpick:

> 'I have to but swallow this, and be for the rest of my days persecuted by a legion of goblins, all of my own creation' (21).

## Use of Power Chakra Energy for Social Destruction

Selby indicts the negative use of Power Chakra energy as a major cause of the mass manipulation of people for very destructive reasons. On the macroscopic social level, he counts Hitler and a variety of other later twentieth-century dictators among those who "have heartlessly damaged or destroyed the lives of countless millions of people." In smaller settings, people like Jim Jones, David Koresh, and Charles Manson have exacted the use of this destructive power upon the lives of numerous others.

On the microscopic social level, countless individuals, wielding this same dysfunctional Power Chakra energy, cause extreme damage in their own family systems and in their communities at large. It can be argued that collectively, these individuals have perpetrated more damage and destruction throughout history than macroscopic megalomaniacs have perpetrated during their relatively short reigns. Unnamed millions of people throughout the ages have been manipulated, controlled, abused, tortured, and murdered because of these small, silent "Hitlers." Alice Miller (1990) argues that unresolved childhood abandonment and abuse leads to the adult rage that is projected onto others in society. In his own limited way, the pre-transformed Scrooge was a member of this very destructive group.

## Scrooge's Lack of Heart Chakra Energy

The kundalini energy associated with the all-important Heart Chakra, located in the center of the chest, is necessary in order to live a spiritual life. Of this vital chakra, Selby writes:

> The Heart Chakra is equidistant between the first and the seventh chakra, between heaven and earth. It is the centerpoint of the primary emotional energy of the universe, which we call love. It balances the chakras above with the chakras below, all of equal importance.

In *The Power of Myth* (Flowers, 1988) and other writings, Joseph Campbell informs us that the lower three chakras are primarily of our animal nature. Throughout the entirety of our lives, all of us have to consume at least a minimal amount of food in order to survive, to contend with our sexuality in some way, and either to manifest or to deny power in some way.

Campbell goes on to tell us that the highest three chakras are primarily associated with our spiritual nature. The fifth chakra holds our potential for authentic communication of deep, innermost feelings with others. The sixth chakra holds our potential for the development of intuition and wisdom. And the seventh chakra holds our potential, at least occasionally, for the direct experience of mystical and undefinable union with God.

He tells us that until we experience an opening up at the level of the heart, we can never hope to open the flow of spiritual energy to the highest three chakras. In other words, not until our lives have been infused with spiritual love can we hope to "move out of the field of animal action into a field that is properly animal and human." He is telling us, as does Selby, that all seven chakras will not become permeated with spirituality until the energy of the Heart Chakra has been released.

It is patently obvious that Scrooge did not have any Heart Chakra energy available to him throughout the majority of his adult life. He lived, as it were, almost completely out of his non-spiritual animal nature. Dickens lets us know in no uncertain terms he thought of the pre-transformed Scrooge as an animal. At his nephew's Christmas party, a game called "Yes and No" was begun; the participants, through asking a series of questions, had to guess the identity of a hidden subject Fred had chosen. We find out that:

> [H]e was thinking of an animal, a live animal, rather a disagreeable animal, a savage animal, an animal that growled and grunted sometimes, and talked sometimes, and lived in London, and walked about the streets, and wasn't made a show of, and wasn't led by anybody, and didn't live in a menagerie, and was never killed in a market, and was not a horse, or an ass, or a cow, or a bull, or a tiger, or a dog, or a pig, or a cat, or a bear (83).

The secret animal Fred chose, and a guest finally identified correctly, of course, was Scrooge himself.

The blockage of Heart Chakra energy in Scrooge started at the time he snapped during his childhood in order to survive the abandonment trauma. This deprivation continued through that wondrous night relatively late in his adult life, when it finally burst through, transforming him instantaneously and forever. Until that point in time, almost all of his available energy was centered in his non-spiritualized Power Chakra, used to support the existence of his ego-induced defense mechanisms. He lived out of fear rather than out of love.

The Heart Chakra is associated with the  element air. A basic rule of physics teaches us that for combustion to occur, air is necessary. We know that Scrooge had no spiritual third chakra fire burning in his life, which rendered him cold and lifeless. This is because he had no fourth chakra air available for combustion purposes. He could not warm up; consequently, there was no light in his wretched life.

# Scrooge's Dysfunctional Communication Chakra

Located in the throat, the fifth chakra is known as the Communication Chakra. Selby relates that when infused with kundalini energy, it "is the center of communication, of talking, of expressing our inner depths of feeling in words that the people around us can understand." The important part of this statement has to do with expression in words people understand. When lacking in spiritual energy, the verbal emanations from this chakra center become merely a masking of the truth.

A lack of self-awareness makes authentic communication with others impossible. Through deciphering and interpretation, only the most perceptive of people will be able to "read" the important unstated content of verbal communication and understand its true meaning.

Whether the speaker is consciously aware of it or not, unresolved childhood pain is always being communicated when left unresolved.

Through his physical appearance, his non-verbal actions, and primarily, through his cold words, Scrooge was hiding, instead of expressing, his inner depths of feeling, both from himself and from others. Concerning the actual sound of Scrooge's adult voice, Dickens tells us that it had a "grating" quality, clearly indicating that it was disagreeable to the ear. He also relates that "he spoke out shrewdly" (3). An obsolete meaning for shrewd indicates that Dickens' intention was to let us know Scrooge was scolding and abusive when he spoke, rather than clever and perceptive. In other words, both in how he spoke and what he said, Scrooge put people off. By going on the verbal offensive, the negative energy of Scrooge's dysfunctional Communication Chakra was "successfully" used to keep people at a distance, thus protecting himself from any possibility of reexperiencing the deep hurt he endured in childhood.

Unfortunately, his grating vocal vibrations also served to prevent him from the possibility of harmonizing with others. Selby tells us of the phenomenon of physics known as "entrainment," "the tendency of two vibrational sources to resonate at the same or harmonic vibrations." He goes on to say that if our own vibratory system is disharmonious, if our chakras are fighting against each other and not surrendering to the entrainment principle, then everywhere we go will be spread with disharmony.

There is no doubt that Scrooge's audible vibrations were indicative of the disharmony within him, which blocked his chances for harmony with others surrounding him.

Apparently, no one around Scrooge completely understood why he behaved the way he did. Belle understood that her young fiancée was motivated by fear, and Fred realized that his uncle's inner thoughts must not be very pleasant, but no character in the story connected his scolding, abusive verbalizations with his childhood past. Only the three non-material spirits within Scrooge directly challenged him with this long hidden truth, no matter what he verbally protested. Through this confrontation he was able to harmonize, or balance, his chakra system, freeing him to allow entrainment to occur. Ultimately, he was free to become one with those he had formerly so desperately pushed away. Finally, he was free to broadcast his inner feelings.

## Fifth Chakra Dreams

Selby tells us that the fifth chakra "is also the center for dreaming and imagination activity." From Scrooge's childhood, we know he had a very active imagination. He could visualize fanciful literary characters and even project them into the physical world. In terms of dreams, the Christmas Eve transformation experience seems to have originally emanated from this non-spiritualized chakra:

> In the more esoteric dimensions of fifth-chakra experience, we encounter the magical and sometimes horrifying dimension where dreams seem to be real, where ghosts leap out at us and challenge us to call them figments of our hyperactive imaginations (Selby).

To Scrooge, these dreams did have the quality of reality, and affected him as if they were of the material world.

## Physical Problems Associated with the Fifth Chakra

Finally, Selby tells us that the Communication Chakra controls the thyroid and the parathyroid. He states that when this chakra is not in balance, "people tend to have chronic colds." We do not know if Scrooge had chronic colds, but we do know he was chronically cold, and that he was battling a head cold on the very night of his transformation.

# Scrooge's Dysfunctional Intuitive Chakra

Selby tells us this sixth chakra, located "right behind and above your eyes," is also known as "The Third Eye." This chakra center holds the energy associated with wisdom. Of it, he relates the following:

*Now, with this chakra, we reach the point where we are conscious-*
*ly focusing on the part of the body that in fact is doing the con-*
*scious focusing: the mind is finally looking directly at itself.*

Immediately, two things are apparent concerning Scrooge. First, throughout most of his adult life, he demonstrated no wisdom in terms of how he conducted himself or in how he treated others. Second, this lack of wisdom was a direct result and inevitable outcome of the childhood trauma he suffered. The necessary snapping, which occurred to help him endure and physically survive his childhood abandonment, blocked him from metacognition—the ability to mentally step back from himself, to think about what he was thinking. Therefore, he could neither reflect on the pain of his childhood nor understand its implications upon his present day thoughts, verbalizations, and actions.

## Embraced by the Darkness

Light is intimately associated with the Intuition Chakra. Selby tells us:

*[W]hen we reflect upon the sixth chakra, we are reflecting upon*
*our relationship with the center of our solar system—the sun itself.*

When the Intuition Chakra is not spiritualized with kundalini energy, we are left "in the dark." Devoid of the light needed for intuition, enlightenment is not possible.

Dickens made it clear throughout *A Christmas Carol* that Scrooge's adult mind and the world, as he experienced it, lacked light. Because he had no relationship with the "sun/son of God," known as the "light of the world," he was trapped in the darkness of a non-spiritual existence.

From the onset, the physical setting of the story was permeated with darkness. Note the dreary description Dickens provides as the story begins at Scrooge's counting house:

*The city clocks had only just gone three, but it was quite dark*
*already—it had not been light all day—and candles were flaring*
*in the windows of the neighbouring offices, like ruddy smears upon*
*the palpable brown air (4).*

After Scrooge had his confrontations with Fred and the charitable solicitors, Dickens tells us that "the fog and darkness thickened," and a bit later it was "Foggier yet" (11,12).

Upon Scrooge's arrival to his house, we are informed that:

> *The yard was so dark that even Scrooge, who knew its every stone,*
> *was fain to grope with his hands. The fog and frost so hung about*
> *the black old gateway of the house, that it seemed as if the Genius*
> *of the Weather sat in mournful meditation on the threshold (14).*

As Scrooge climbed the stairs to his suite of rooms, we learn that it is so dark that "Half a dozen gas-lamps out of the street wouldn't have lighted the entry too well" (16). Despite this dreariness, Dickens wrote:

> *Up Scrooge went, not caring a button for that. Darkness is cheap,*
> *and Scrooge liked it. (16)*

The author is informing us that even though darkness had pervaded the entirety of Scrooge's life, like many abused people, he was comfortable with it. It was all he had ever known as an adult; he had learned to adapt to it and comfort himself with it. In Bradshaw's (1988) words, he had learned to "bond with the perpetrator."

After Marley's apparition confronted Scrooge, he fell asleep. Note Dickens' description of the situation after he awoke, just before the appearance of the first spirit:

> *When Scrooge awoke, it was so dark, that looking out of bed, he*
> *could scarcely distinguish the transparent window from the opaque*
> *walls of his chamber. He was endeavouring to pierce the darkness*
> *with his ferret eyes... (29).*

Once again, we are left with the distinct knowledge that Dickens thought of his character in animal terms, living out of his lower three, non-spiritualized chakras. More importantly, however, the author is relating to us the absolute darkness in Scrooge's life at this time. It had become so totally immersed in darkness that he could no longer distinguish between transparent and opaque.

Dickens is telling us that Scrooge had finally hit bottom, that there was no other place for him to go. Just after the winter solstice, the very darkest time of the calendar year, he had come to the very darkest time of his life. At this point, he could choose to live it out completely shrouded by darkness, or he could go on the painful journey to psychospiritual enlightenment.

It is always darkest before the emergence of light. When the clock struck one, the Ghost of Christmas Past entered and "Lights flashed up in the room upon the instant, and the curtains of the bed were drawn" (30). Despite his fear and the veil of darkness surrounding him, Scrooge opened to the challenge and the prospect of allowing spiritual light to emerge and transform him.

## Scrooge's Dysfunctional Crown Chakra

The Crown Chakra, or seventh chakra, is located at the top of the head. Selby states that an understanding of "the true nature of the seventh chakra is beyond human comprehension." He goes on to say the following:

> Sometimes in Western culture, the awakening of the seventh chakra is called "receiving Christ consciousness." But even this label tends to stand between a person and seventh-chakra experience. Christ Consciousness is a transcendent concept, but still is a concept, which ultimately must be put aside…in order to move into both sixth and seventh-chakra awakening.

Joseph Campbell (Flowers, 1988) supports this concept by informing us that to experience the awakening and bliss associated with the seventh chakra, we must allow ourselves to be taken past all conscious knowledge and limiting definitions of Christ and God. He states the dilemma involved with these cognitive confinements:

> *The mystery has been reduced to a set of concepts and ideas, and emphasizing these concepts and ideas can short-circuit the transcendent, connoted experience. An intense experience of mystery is what one has to regard as the ultimate religious experience.*

Campbell agrees with interviewer Bill Moyers in *The Power of Myth* that to achieve this experience and to "find out who Jesus is, you have to go past the Christian faith, past the Christian doctrine, past the Christian Church." In other words, to truly experience God within the depths of our souls, we have to give up our pre-established cognitive frames of God, which only serve to preclude us from directly experiencing the undefinable bliss of being at one with God.

Despite this, Selby warns never to consciously fixate attention upon the Crown Chakra for long periods of time, or overstimulate it, in the attempt to experience the bliss involved with it. He informs us that:

> *This experience will come to you when your nervous system fully is prepared for such infinite realization and union with the creative force of the universe.*

He does, however, advocate directly focusing on it for short periods, in order to achieve kundalini energy balance and to open up "to the inflow of energy from above."

It goes without saying that for a vast majority of Scrooge's adult life, no spiritualized energy was coursing through him, and certainly none was available either for the balancing of his chakratic system or for the releasing of it to radiate downward from above. Not until, of course, that Christmas Eve, when its pent-up energy finally unleashed, sending spiritual shock waves throughout his entire chakratic system, ultimately leading to "the inflow of energy from above."

When this finally occurred, Scrooge achieved an animal and human balance in a way he had never known before as an adult. He was no longer just a "Man of the worldly mind" (21), as Marley had called him, but a man with a spiritualized mind, finally able to "see the light" with his fully functioning Third Eye of wisdom.

CHAPTER FIVE

# Scrooge's Fully Functioning Chakras

Every human being is born with the potential for a life continuously filled with the flow of spiritual energy. Very few people, however, can honestly say that they have been in touch with this flow throughout their entire lives. To an extent, many people experience the flow of kundalini energy during the earliest part of their lives; some even have fond, vivid adult memories of being truly alive and at one with the universe during childhood. Selby (1992) says the following about this phenomenon:

> Unless you grew up in an especially repressive family environment, you almost certainly entered quite often into a diffuse type of kundalini consciousness, especially when you were engaged in free play.

For a large percentage of people raised in repressive families, however, even if they did experience this early spiritual flow, it can barely be recalled. And for millions of people, because they did grow up in "especially repressive family environments," there is absolutely no remembrance of any experiences associated with this wondrous, life-enhancing flow because it shut down and was taken away before they consciously knew it existed.

The horror of the "poisonous pedagogy" (see Chapter 2), as delineated by Alice Miller, is the major reason for the killing off of this energy. John Bradshaw refers to it as "soul murder." The methodical, socially-sanctioned application of these life-killing parenting rules, under which almost all people are raised, only serves to subjugate children and to suppress their natural curiosity and love of life. The almost universal use of these rules blocks countless numbers of people from developing their unique personalities. It causes them to be subjected to a life devoid of natural zest; it leads to a life overwhelmed with the darkness of fear.

When left largely intact and available, this energy shepherds people to the highest levels of personal actualization and universal love. The movie *Forrest Gump* perfectly illustrates the possibility of this important truth. Despite the fact that Gump was born physically and mentally challenged, his mother made sure that he was given every possible opportunity to develop to the fullest of his human potential; she did nothing to block the flow of kundalini energy available to him. Gump's miraculous achievements serve as a fictional paean to the potential within all of us.

His life is contrasted throughout the movie with that of his lifelong love, Jenny. It is clear that because of the sexual abuse she suffered as a young child at the hands of her alcoholic father, the flow of kundalini energy to her system was severely constricted. As a result, she spent the vast majority of her life consumed in situations and relationships that only served to repeat her early abuse. In spite of the fact that she was finally able to wake up and begin to deal with her problems at mid-life, it was too late; by that time she had contracted and ultimately died from AIDS.

Certainly, Scrooge can be counted among those vast numbers of victims whose early-life kundalini energy was constantly threatened and ultimately critically compromised before he reached puberty. We know that his father was a cold man during Ebenezer's youth, and we know that he snapped in order to survive during the latter part of his childhood, during the time he was cast out of the family and exiled to the boarding school.

Other than that information, Dickens supplied no direct details to fully inform the reader of the early abuse to which young Scrooge was subjected. Circumstantially, however, Dickens did provide us a very telling piece of information. After Scrooge encountered Marley's ghostly face on the door knocker, the author stated the following:

> To say that he was not startled, or that his blood was not conscious of a terrible sensation to which it had been a stranger from infancy, would be untrue (15).

Obviously, the "terrible sensation" Scrooge experienced at this encounter was the release of kundalini energy, deeply suppressed since his infancy, and almost completely blocked since his late childhood. Selby addresses this unexplainable rise of energy in the following manner:

> One of the true mysteries and blessings of humanity is that our kundalini energy often spontaneously surges up through our various energy centers, encouraging a new awakening into more expansive levels of consciousness.

What Scrooge experienced as a "terrible sensation," Selby describes as a blessing. It is completely reasonable that the adult Scrooge would experience the awakening of this kundalini flow as a "terrible sensation." There is no doubt that it felt utterly foreign to him. It was something within him that he had never been consciously aware of before this time, and it felt "terrible" because its reemergence was out of his immediate control. And conscious control, as we know, is what Scrooge needed to make himself feel safe from his deep-seated fears.

In his book *Making Sense of Suffering* (1991), J. Konrad Stettbacher wrote that in myriad ways, as early as birth itself, an infant can become traumatized to the point that if never resolved, these unconscious but very damaging experiences will have far-reaching negative consequences throughout the duration of its life. Of this situation, he wrote:

*When those primal needs are not met, a child will become unsure of itself. If its tears or calls for help go unheeded, it will increasingly become a helpless prey to fear and pain. Unfortunately, the child will interpret this as a product of its own inadequacy. To realize that it is being neglected in the moment of its need is for the child insupportable. If the situation then continues, the child will, out of self-defense, become nonfeeling and nonsensing. Otherwise, it would suffer physical harm or even die. The child will notice that something is wrong with its self-preservation system. But because its appeals to its environment go entirely or partially unheeded, because no help is forthcoming, its ability to form relationships will become increasingly impaired. Ultimately, it will become disturbed.*

Scrooge may or may not have noticed that his need for and ability to project fictional characters into his physical world to ward off the intense pain of his childhood abandonment was informing him that something was deeply wrong with his self-preservation system. He may or may not have realized that by late adolescence and early adulthood, he was less and less able to form meaningful relationships with other people in his environment. By adulthood, however, it is certain that he was not consciously aware of how increasingly disturbed he had become, and how totally disturbed he ultimately became by the seventh year after the death of his emotional "twin," Marley.

The neglect that started in Scrooge's infancy, and culminated at the time of his total abandonment in late childhood, caused him to snap, which in turn led to an almost complete shutdown of kundalini energy to his system. He survived by subsisting on this very minimal flow of energy, its trickle not nearly strong enough to open up the latent spiritual energy locked away in any of his seven chakras. In turn, the void created by this lack of loving energy allowed for the opening of his negative energy flood gates; this caused his system and his life ultimately to be permeated by the needs of his fearful false self.

As taught in *The Course in Miracles,* the development and mainte-
nance of the ego is always a result of living out of fear instead of living
out of love. Selby states that "Fear is the great enemy of spiritual
growth." He continues:

> *A basic psychological fact is that consciousness contracts in fear,*
> *and relaxes and expands in peace. When we feel threatened by*
> *something, we shut it out, we close down our awareness. When we*
> *feel secure and receptive, we expand.*

Certainly, Ebenezer Scrooge's chakratic system contracted because
he was forced very early in life to live in fear. Its lack resulted in the
development of his adult defense mechanisms, which served to keep
him free from consciously feeling the fear that permeated his life since
childhood. It safeguarded him from the dangers involved with getting
too close to others, and guaranteed him that he would never again be
placed in a position to be hurt or abandoned. This kundalini constriction cut off vital life force energy, which led to the bitterly cold and
isolated life he led as an adult.

The "terrible sensation" Scrooge experienced at the reintroduction
of spiritualized energy into his system was the ego's attempt to keep
him from changing. Remember that the fear-driven ego can't allow feelings of love to enter or establish themselves if it is to continue its existence. It will do whatever is necessary to block the positive; it caused
Scrooge to mistrust this loving sensation. Selby states that:

> *If we don't deep down trust in the spiritual universe, if we don't*
> *make contact with our inner Master, and feel we are being guided*
> *in positive directions, then we won't be able to open ourselves to*
> *kundalini awakening—because who knows what we might*
> *encounter as we let go of the known past and venture into genuine-*
> *ly new territory within us.*

Despite this sensation-distorting attempt by the ego, which caused
Scrooge to interpret this new energy negatively, there was enough

spiritual flow spontaneously introduced into his system to allow him to continue the transformation process. By no means was he a willing participant in the uncovering of the repressed information at the onset. Even when he finally consciously chose to continue in this process after remembering and feeling his childhood pain during his time with the Ghost of Christmas Past, he still had a very difficult time completely freeing himself from his ego-driven defense mechanisms. He still greatly feared what was hidden in the black hole, deep within him.

## The Opening of Scrooge's Heart Chakra

The Heart Chakra is the mid-point of the seven-level chakratic system and it is the focal point of kundalini awakening. Selby says "It is the centerpoint of the primary emotional energy of the universe, which we call love." By using the word "heart" or derivatives of it over forty times in *A Christmas Carol*, there is no doubt that Dickens clearly understood that the release of Heart Chakra energy was the very core of human transformation. Scrooge began the story as an extremely cold-hearted person, but at the end of it, he was "glowing" and "His own heart laughed" (121).

Scrooge was able to begin the process of completely unblocking his flow of kundalini energy only after he opened up at the level of the heart by courageously confronting his own mortality. This occurred immediately after the death of Tiny Tim, the present-day wounded child. Dickens clearly shows us this conscious decision at that time:

> 'Spectre,' said Scrooge, 'something informs me that our parting moment is at hand. I know it, but I know not how. Tell me what man that was whom we saw lying dead' (107).

Only after identifying with Tiny Tim's death did Scrooge have the courage to delve into the depths of his own life-killing denial. Scrooge was able to compassionately comprehend that Tim's physical demise was a result of the childhood "death" of his own flow of kundalini life force energy. He connected the suffering of his emotionally wounded inner-child to the suffering he was causing the physically wounded child. He finally realized that the dysfunctional pitch of his life would end up killing both of them.

To pinpoint this identification even further, we can deduce that as a child, Scrooge was deeply wounded, specifically in his Heart Chakra. Selby informs us that:

> *If you got hurt in the realms of the heart as a child, your Heart Chakra will remain blocked as an adult—until you face this blockage and risk allowing energy to flow through that chakra again.*

By identifying with Tiny Tim and confronting the very real prospect that his heart would soon be mortally wounded and that he would die, Scrooge finally faced up to the critical blockage of life force energy to his own severely malfunctioning emotional heart. By doing so, he risked allowing "energy to flow through that chakra again."

More than anything else, this realization concerning Tim lead Scrooge to his complete spiritual awakening. This heartfelt connection finally infused his Heart Chakra with kundalini energy. Joseph Campbell (Flowers, 1988) said the following:

> *When the center of the heart is touched, and a sense of compassion [is] awakened with another person or creature, and you realize that you and that other are in some sense creatures of the one life in being, a whole new stage of life in the spirit opens out. The opening of the heart to the world is what is symbolized mythologically as the virgin birth. It signifies the birth of a spiritual life in what was formerly an elementary human animal.*

The opening of Scrooge's Heart Chakra led to the liberation of his soul. It also set in motion the spiritual balancing of his entire chakratic system. The strongly dysfunctional and destructive will of his Power Chakra, intimately influenced by the negative verbalizations emanating from his non-spiritual Communication Chakra, was immediately transformed once the power of love from the Heart Chakra burst forth. Selby writes:

> Love that can act in the world, which can express itself in compassionate interaction with other human beings, needs a great deal of power to overcome the inertia of habitual self-centered behavioral and emotional patterns. Love transforms will, and will empowers love. This interaction of these two polarities is one of the most beautiful dynamics of our chakratic system.

By identifying with and showing compassion for Tiny Tim, Scrooge broke the mental bonds that kept him chained to his fear-driven ego. Once unshackled, he opened up his heart to love. In Campbell's (Flowers, 1988) words:

> It happens when you awaken at the level of the heart to compassion, com-passion, shared suffering: experienced participation in the suffering of another person. That's the beginning of humanity.

This identification with Tim, followed by the willingness to confront his own death-denial, ultimately allowed Scrooge to follow his nephew's sentiments about Christmas and "to think of people ... as if they really were fellow passengers to the grave, and not another race of creatures bound on other journeys" (7).

Once Scrooge's Heart Chakra opened, instantaneously his pent-up kundalini energy surged downward, releasing the latent spiritual energy locked in his animal chakra centers. He was no longer doomed to his pre-transformed existence, living life in fear, restricted by self-centered coldness, completely shutting others out. Now saturated with spiritual energy and love, Scrooge learned to live life fully, demonstrating this by freely and joyfully participating with others.

Scrooge was no longer doomed to the fate of his now former "twin," Marley. Dickens gave a startlingly clear chakratic description of the lower-level "animal" life that Marley led through this visual description of the specter:

> Marley, in his pigtail, usual waistcoat, tights and boots; the tassels on the latter bristling, like his pigtail, and his coat-skirts, and the hair upon his head. The chain he drew was clasped about his middle. It was long, and wound about him like a tail; and it was made (for Scrooge observed it closely) of cash-boxes, keys, padlocks, ledgers, deeds, and heavy purses wrought in steel (18).

First, there are three rather obvious references in this short excerpt concerning pigtails and a tail, clearly indicating that the author thought of Marley as an animal. Second, through word play Dickens is telling us that Marley's life was a "chronic waste" by telling us he was wearing his "usual waistcoat." Third, he is telling us that he was severely constricted at the midsection of his body, which was bound with a chain and weighed down by numerous other heavy metal objects. There is no doubt that Dickens was giving us a clue that Marley's existence was a waste, animal in nature, and cut off from spiritual energy because he was bound "about his middle," just below the level of the heart.

These truths are further supported by an observation of the transparent Marley by Scrooge. Through his thoughts, we learn that it had often been rumored that during life, Marley had "no bowels" (18). Scrooge confirmed that this suspicion was true. Bowels, or intestines, are intimately related to the Earth, or Root, Chakra of alimentation. Dickens is telling us that Marley lacked this essential part of the alimentary canal. In other words, he was indicating that in life, he was even less than an animal.

Despite all of this, through Scrooge, the ghost himself tells us he now realizes, although too late in this lifetime, that he was responsible for his ultimate fate:

> 'I wear the chain I forged in life,' replied the Ghost. 'I made it link by link, and yard by yard; I girded it on of my own free will, and of my own free will I wore it' (22).

Dickens is informing us that like Scrooge, Marley certainly had opportunities for a kundalini awakening. Like Scrooge, the original life-killing, spiritually restricting childhood circumstances which led to Marley's dysfunctional life were most certainly also out of his immediate control. No child can ever be held responsible for the abuse heaped upon it by any adult, under any circumstances.

Dickens is teaching us that as an adult, however, it was Marley's ultimate responsibility to take the necessary and painful actions needed to wake up and free himself from the noxious abuses inflicted upon him during his childhood. It was his responsibility to break the other-inflicted early bonds, and the far worse self-inflicted adult shackles that were deeply disturbing him. Marley did not heed the challenge; consequently, he died—stuck in his lower three animal chakras. He did not recognize what Marianne Williamson (1992) tells us in *A Return to Love*:

> *Although experiences such as childhood trauma can lead us to deviate from our true nature, the truth itself is held in trust for us by the Holy Spirit until we choose to return.*

Scrooge, on the other hand, did heed the challenge. He narrowly escaped Marley's fate by journeying all the way through the black hole that contained his pain and came through into the light. Finally freed from the past, he was ultimately able to give up his fear-driven defense mechanisms and live in the present with an unfettered flow of kundalini energy. His entire physical system was unshackled from his "ponderous chain" (22), a full seven years older, longer, and heavier than Marley's, which was also binding him below the Heart Chakra; his life became spiritualized.

# Scrooge's "Big Bang" Awakening

The opening of Scrooge's Heart Chakra and the death of his doggedly determined ego was followed by an unprecedented surge of kundalini energy coursing through his chakratic system with tremendous force. Note Selby's description of this phenomenon, which he calls the "big bang theory of spiritual awakening":

> It is true, as I have known from working with a number of clients in my psychological practice, that sudden spontaneous kundalini awakening, especially in already unstable personalities, can be chaotic, frightening—even shattering to a person's normal life. Imagine what it's like to suddenly experience a hundred times more energy flowing through your body without any preparation or warning. This extreme is certainly not a desired aim of kundalini awakening.

Although Scrooge's particular type of awakening may not have been desirable, its extremity certainly matched his dire circumstances. No other change attempt could have produced the radical conditions necessary to finally break through his firmly entrenched ego. The intensity of the breakthrough equaled the desperation of his situation. While both were dangerous to him, only the traumatic awakening precipitated by this inordinate flow of initial energy could have saved Scrooge from an empty life of total denial.

This sudden surge of spiritual energy certainly shattered Scrooge's former dysfunctional life, altering it from that point forward in a positive way. Before this initial onslaught of energy evened out, we know that he had been in a state of extreme fright and chaos. Dickens tells us that after waking up, "He had been sobbing violently in his conflict with the Spirit, and his face was wet with tears" (111), no doubt from the abject fear he experienced at his own grave.

Once Scrooge realized that "the shadows of the things that would have been, may be dispelled" (111), Dickens spent time detailing the initial chaos that Scrooge experienced. Note the randomness of his actions concerning his attempt to put on clothes:

> *His hands were busy with his garments all this time; turning them*
> *inside out, putting them on upside down, tearing them, mislaying*
> *them, make them parties to every kind of extravagance (112).*

Mixing laughter and tears, Scrooge exclaimed, "I don't know what to do" (112) because of his confused state.

Dickens continued delineating Scrooge's chaotic state in the following passage:

> *'I don't know what day of the month it is,' said Scrooge. 'I don't*
> *know how long I've been among the Spirits. I don't know anything.*
> *I'm quite a baby. Never mind. I don't care. I'd rather be a baby.*
> *Hallo! Whoop! Hallo there!' (112).*

During this physical and emotional exertion of energy, we learn that he became "perfectly winded" (112). We also find out that when he tried to write (116) and later to shave, he experienced difficulty, "for his hands continued to shake very much," and that he "chuckled till he cried" (115).

Selby informs us that a sudden infusion of kundalini energy can be very risky:

> *If too much of this energy flows through us too fast, our nervous*
> *system, unprepared, reacts much like an electrical system that*
> *receives too powerful an electrical upsurge. This is the serious dan-*
> *ger of uncontrolled kundalini awakening.*

There is no doubt that Scrooge walked this precarious tightrope. Although it caused him great fright and chaos and shook him emotionally, he was able to stay under the threshold where it did more damage than good.

It appears very likely that Scrooge's once cynical sense of humor, housed in his Power Chakra, may have saved him when the massive amount of energy released by the Heart Chakra transformed it. Selby informs us that all great spiritual Masters believe that to have "great personal power," it is essential to have the ability to laugh greatly. Dickens clearly indicated that Scrooge began laughing during the transformation and that his very first laugh was "The father of a long, long line of brilliant laughs" (112). Selby tells us that "This is the trick of the Masters—to be able to laugh when the pressure of kundalini realization becomes too great." Through laughter, Scrooge weathered the dangerously wonderful storm of initial kundalini energy flow after the long-closed floodgates to his spiritual system flew wide open.

# From Negative to Positive Energy

In *The Inner Reaches of Outer Space*, Joseph Campbell (1986) tells of the kundalini phenomenon known as the "turning about of the energy." The implication behind this statement is that once the spiritual energy contained in the Heart Chakra has released, and kundalini energy is finally flowing downward to the lower three animal chakras, the focus of this energy is no longer pitched totally outward, in a vain attempt to aggressively control the world. Instead, it becomes pitched inward, to defeat "attachment to physical desires and the fear of physical death."

By turning this energy in on himself, Scrooge let go of his animal way of life and became spiritualized. He stopped trying to control his outward world in an attempt to ward off his inward fears, and he conquered his fear of death. In *The Gospel of Thomas* (Meyer, 1984), the following passage is attributed to Jesus:

> '[T]he kingdom is inside you and outside you. When you know yourselves, then you will be known, and will understand that you are the children of the living Father. But if you do not know yourselves, then you live in poverty, and embody poverty.'

By turning inward and knowing himself for the first time, Scrooge became a child of God. By stating, "I'm quite a baby" (112) on Christmas morning, he understood he was spiritually reborn. Dickens matched his spiritual birth with the physical birth of Jesus. And Scrooge's life became rich in a way his vast monetary holdings couldn't buy.

## Chakratic Transfer of Kundalini Energy

Once Scrooge's kundalini energy began streaming downward from his Heart Chakra to his dysfunctional lower three chakras, it spiritualized the way he dealt with his animal needs of food, sex, and power. With this influx, the lower chakras freely sent energy back through the Heart Chakra into the upper three energy chakras to activate their power. Both Selby and Campbell (1986) give the following specific energy connections that are forged between lower and upper chakras:

Earth Chakra (1) and Crown Chakra (7)
Sex Chakra (2) and Intuition Chakra (6)
Power Chakra (3) and Communication Chakra (5)

In addition, Selby tells us that each of the chakras is either male or female in nature. Note the following list:

1. Earth Chakra: male
2. Sex Chakra: female
3. Power Chakra: male
4. Heart Chakra: female
5. Communication Chakra: male
6. Intuition Chakra: female
7. Crown Chakra: male

The awakening of the female Heart Chakra serves as the catalyst to balance and spiritualize the entire system. Through its activation, it connects one with seven, two with six, and three with five, thus equalizing the flow. When the Heart Chakra is in control, there is no gender domination of the chakras.

Selby says that by putting the Heart Chakra in charge of the entire chakratic system, "we regain a perfect balance between masculine and feminine, between above and below, between strong and yielding—between yang and yin."

In *The Gospel of Thomas* (Meyer, 1984), when asked how to enter the kingdom of God, Jesus replied:

> *'When you make the two into one, when you make the inner like the outer and the outer like the inner, and the upper like the lower, when you make male and female into a single one, so that the male will not be male and the female will not be female, when you make eyes replacing an eye, a hand replacing a hand, a foot replacing a foot, and an image replacing an image, then you will enter the kingdom.'*

In His own way, He is saying that when kundalini balance is achieved, the kingdom of God is at hand, right here and right now. Scrooge entered it by spritualizing and balancing himself; his whole being transformed.

## Scrooge's Functional Earth Chakra

Infused with kundalini energy, Scrooge's Earth Chakra energy released and transformed his behavior associated with it. Selby tells us that:

> *Fear, for instance, is considered a first-chakra emotion. So are greed and possessiveness. In fact, we speak of people as being 'tight-assed' if they are afraid to lose their physical possessions that ensure their security.*

We know that by mustering the courage to confront his physical death, Scrooge conquered his fear. We also know that he demonstrated his loss of greed by liberally tipping the boy who ran an errand for him early on Christmas morning. Later that same morning, he was praised by one of the charitable solicitors (one of the two he had rebuked the day before) for his monetary "munificence" when he promised a substantial contribution to the poor, which included "A great many back-payments" (116). And the day after Christmas, he continued exhibiting this change by his declaration to Bob Cratchit, "I am about to raise your salary" (120).

Scrooge's gift of a large prize turkey to the Cratchit family served a double Earth Chakra purpose. First, it tells us that he no longer was possessive; he was giving things away. Second, it directly relates to alimentation, or food, the hallmark of the Earth Chakra. By this gesture, he was providing plentifully for others at this basic, or root level, instead of depriving them as he had previously done.

In addition, by showing up unannounced at Fred's Christmas celebration, Scrooge was demonstrating that he was also dealing positively with his personal alimentation needs. Note the precise words Dickens used: "It's I. Your uncle Scrooge. I have come to dinner. Will you let me in, Fred?" (118). Dickens wrote that "Nothing could be heartier" (118) as he joined Fred, his wife, and their guests for good food and good company.

When Scrooge announced to Bob Cratchit that he was going to raise his salary and help his family, Dickens wrote that on Scrooge's request, the two would sit down later that day and discuss the details "over a Christmas bowl of smoking bishop" (120), which Hearn (1976) tells us was a traditional drink of the holiday season. Once again, Scrooge was taking care of his Earth Chakra needs in community with another. Note the vast difference between this behavior and the behavior he manifested before the transformation, when he ate bad food alone, and did not care either about the needs of others or for the company of others.

Scrooge showed great spiritual growth during the manifestation of these Earth Chakra changes. By anonymously sending the prize turkey to the Cratchits, and by whispering the amount he wished to contribute to help the poor, he demonstrated the quality of true giving by quietly going about his business of helping mankind. Joel Goldsmith (1986) teaches us that heartfelt prayer and contribution should always be done very privately, even secretly. Scrooge did not trumpet his change; he did it humbly.

He also showed great courage during this process. When he encountered one of the gentlemen solicitors, Dickens wrote of Scrooge:

> *It sent a pang across his heart to think how this old gentleman would look upon him when they met; but he knew what path lay straight before him, and he took it (116).*

Now aware of other's feelings, Scrooge knew that the old gentleman most likely would not think well of him, based upon the encounter from the day before. Despite this, he conquered his fear, made straight for him, and amended for his previous actions.

When Scrooge decided to accept Fred's Christmas dinner invitation, once again he had to grapple with the possibility of rejection, the thing he formerly feared the most. Again, Dickens let us know that Scrooge conquered it:

> *He passed the door a dozen times, before he had the courage to go up and knock. But he made a dash, and did it (117).*

To drive the point home, the author had him finally confront his fear on the thirteenth pass; superstition informs us that this is the unluckiest number. Despite both, Scrooge went through his fear, and was accepted warmly.

## Scrooge's Functional Sex Chakra

Selby writes that the life-force energy released from an activated Sex Chakra doesn't have to be "a dramatic sexual charge at all." The energy released in Scrooge's Sex Chakra did not manifest itself in an obviously sexual way. Dickens does not have his character go feverishly in search of his long lost love, Belle.

He does, however, subtly suggest that Scrooge has powerfully regained the energy of this chakra in the following excerpt, which occurred during the initial stage of his chaotic awakening:

*He was checked in his transports by the churches ringing out of the lustiest peals he had ever heard. Clash, clash, hammer; ding, dong, bell. Bell, dong, ding; hammer, clang, clash. Oh, glorious, glorious* (113).

The not-so-veiled linguistic references to Belle, the object of his youthful sexual desire, and to the awakening of his raw sexual energy, are obviously implied.

By going to Fred and his wife's house for dinner, Scrooge did not just demonstrate Earth Chakra energy, he also displayed intimate Sex Chakra energy. Embedded within his journey to their house was the meaning that he finally condoned the marriage he formerly condemned, a marriage born out of romantic love. By his actions, he blessed the marriage, joined their family, and as Dickens wrote, "He was at home in five minutes" (118).

During his dream with the Ghost of Christmas Past, Scrooge fantasized having a child of his own, one that would have "been a springtime in the haggard winter of his life" (50). As previously noted, he clearly indicated dysfunction at this point in his reclamation by his expectation that the child would take care of him. By the end of the story, however, we learn that "to Tiny Tim, who did not die, he was a second father" (120). Scrooge no longer expected any child to take care of his needs; he realized it was his job to take care of the needs of the child. By becoming fatherly to Tim, Scrooge once again demonstrated a form of Sex Chakra energy.

By becoming "as good a friend, as good a master, and as good a man as the good old city knew" (120), it is clear that Scrooge actively did his individual part to take care of the family of humanity. In his way, he became an anonymous father to all the children of London saddled by the labels "Ignorance" and "Want" (88). He no longer tried to deny them and pawn them off as belonging to the Ghost of Christmas Present; he took ownership of them. Once again, his actions showed the presence of spiritual Sex Chakra energy.

# Scrooge's Functional Power Chakra

The major transformation that took place with the unlocking of kundalini energy to Scrooge's Power chakra was his loss of the need to manipulate and dominate people in service to his own dysfunctional purposes. With the death of his ego, he now became a joyful participant "in life's intimate, social, and business realms" (Selby). He no longer used his willpower for malevolent purposes, but instead for benevolent purposes.

Selby tells us that the Power Chakra "is associated with fire, with combustion, with anger, joy, and laughter." It is obvious that Scrooge's third chakra was activated immediately during his transformation. Dickens wrote that:

> He was so fluttered and so glowing with his good intentions, that
> his broken voice would scarcely answer to his call (111).

This glow emanated from the warmth now combusting from a source deep within him. Sam Keen, the popular men's movement psychologist, would agree that Scrooge now manifested what he refers to as a "fire in the belly."

Early in the story, before his awakening, Dickens wrote that Scrooge was affected very little by external heat and cold, and "He carried his own low temperature" (3). In addition to being internally aglow, he also became sensitive to the external environment. As he opened the window on Christmas morning, we learn he was fully aware there was:

> No fog, no mist; clear, bright, jovial, stirring, cold; cold, piping
> for the blood to dance to; Golden sunlight; Heavenly sky; sweet
> fresh air (113).

The cold now actually roused him, and caused his formerly torpid blood to course through him. By getting in touch with himself, he connected with his natural environment, and felt the warmth of the sun as it mingled with worldly cold.

Selby notes the following about the release of Power Chakra
warmth:

> *The sun is the explosion that brings new life into being. And the*
> *third chakra is the energy center that brings the power of the sun*
> *into our lives.*

It is apparent that Dickens is also saying exactly the same thing. On
Christmas morning, the sun broke through the gloom, fog, and cold that
dominated London on Christmas Eve. And the birth of the son of God
broke through the dark and cold that permeated Scrooge's adult existence. By praying, Scrooge finally saw the "light of the world"; it brought
him the spiritual warmth he so desperately lacked for most of his life.

During Scrooge's encounter with Bob Cratchit on the day after
Christmas, not only did he raise his salary, but he also made the following third chakra declaration:

> *"Make up the fires, and buy another coal-scuttle before you dot*
> *another 'i,' Bob Cratchit"* (120).

With this act, we learn that in addition to the fact that Scrooge now
generated his own internal heat and that he had connected with the
natural environment, he had also taken the responsibility to bring
facets of warmth directly into his own business environment.

In *The Gospel of Thomas* (Meyer, 1984), Jesus told a story of a person
who prepared a feast, and instructed his servant to go out and invite
the guests. Every one of them turned down the invitation, citing business needs that precluded them from attending. When informed of
this, the host directed the servant to go out and invite anyone who had
the willingness to attend. Jesus then said: "Business people and merchants will not enter the realm of my Father." By awakening, Scrooge
finally put into action in life what Marley only came to realize in
Scrooge's dreams:

> *'Mankind was my business. The common welfare was my busi-*
> *ness; charity, mercy, forbearance, and benevolence, were, all, my*

*business. The dealings of my trade were but a drop of water in the*
*comprehensive ocean of my business!' (24).*

Scrooge entered the kingdom of God when he understood that the real business of life was infinitely more important than the insignificant trade carried on in his "money-changing hole" (22). With this realization, he spiritualized his trade, and made it a place where the authentic business of life would be conducted. In summary, the whole of Scrooge's life became infused with warmth when his Power Chakra became energized.

In the process of Scrooge's awakening, he ceased directing anger at others, both indirectly and directly. With the death of his fear-driven ego, this defense mechanism, used to keep people at a distance in order to safeguard himself from further rejection and abandonment, was no longer needed. On his Christmas morning stroll, Dickens wrote that while:

> *[W]alking with his hands behind him, Scrooge regarded every one*
> *with a delighted smile. He looked so irresistibly pleasant, in a*
> *word, that three or four good-humoured fellows said, 'Good morn-*
> *ing, sir. A merry Christmas to you.' And Scrooge said often after-*
> *wards, that of all the blithe sounds he ever heard, those were the*
> *blithest in his ears (115).*

Thus disarmed to the world, his friendly mode of ambulation clearly indicated that Scrooge no longer projected the same fear-producing, angry aura that formerly, even blind men's dogs sensed and helped their vulnerable masters to avoid.

Scrooge even exhibited playfulness with his former anger. On the day after Christmas, Bob Cratchit arrived to work somewhat late. The awakened Scrooge acted as if he was angry at him:

> *'Hallo,' growled Scrooge, in his accustomed voice, as near as he*
> *could feign it. 'What do you mean by coming here at this time of*
> *day?' (118).*

He kept up the farce for a while, stating, "I am not going to stand this sort of thing any longer" (119), before excitedly announcing to Bob that he was going to give him a raise.

In *A Return to Love*, Marianne Williamson (1992) writes that it is perfectly acceptable for a spiritual person to show intense feelings. Her belief is that fear and anger should be expressed, but never in service to a personal attack upon another. In his book *Awareness*, Anthony deMello (1990) concurs. He states that the goal is to not personalize the anger, where our emotions become entangled, thus rendering us ineffective in dealing with injustice.

By defeating his ego, Scrooge was able to release the personal anger he was feeling in his dysfunctional Power Chakra. It was replaced with lively spiritual energy, available to take positive action in the correction of his personal wrongs, and to help correct the wrongs of society at large. Instead of showing coldness and anger, he was able to feel joy intensely and to laugh brilliantly while doing the work of God.

## Scrooge's Functional Heart Chakra

Selby provides an excellent way to physically locate the position of the Heart Chakra, the spiritual center of the chakratic system:

> *The Christian cross offers a perfect way to locate this center. All you have to do is to raise your arms out to each side and tune experientially in to the point where the vertical intersects with the horizontal. There you have your heart center.*

At the time Scrooge encountered his "plundered" (100) corpse on his death bed, he had not yet located his own Heart Chakra. Despite his desperate attempt to avoid looking at the corpse, and to deny his own death, a voice within him revealed that he was not among those who would be "loved, revered, and honoured" (100). But the voice informed him that his fate could be different if:

> *[T]he hand was open, generous, and true; the heart brave, warm,*
> *and tender; and the pulse a man's. Strike, Shadow, strike. And see*
> *his good deeds springing from the wound, to sow the world with life*
> *immortal (100).*

The voice was urging him to stop denying his childhood wounds, to come to grips directly with the pain buried deep within his own shadow. The voice was that of the Holy Spirit, attempting to get Scrooge to let go of his fear-driven ego.

In *The Power of Myth*, Joseph Campbell informs us that Jesus Christ's death on the cross was an act of willing and loving atonement:

> *Abelard's idea was that Christ came to be crucified to evoke in*
> *man's heart the sentiment of compassion for the suffering of life and*
> *so to remove man's mind from blind commitment to the goods of this*
> *world. It is in compassion with Christ that we turn to Christ, and*
> *the injured one becomes our savior.*

During his spiritual awakening, Scrooge ultimately identified with the past suffering of his childhood, and he identified with the present suffering of Tiny Tim. He finally faced up to his own death. When he held "up his hands in a last prayer to have his fate reversed" (110), he finally turned to and identified with the suffering of Christ.

With this act of turning to the wounded savior, Scrooge found his spiritual center. He fully realized the meaning of the arc of Christ's life, from the beginnings of hope represented by His birth at Christmas, to the full expression of His love for all of humanity by His brutal death on the cross at Easter. Scrooge's Heart Chakra opened wide. Immediately, he was released from the incredible pain he had stubbornly denied since childhood. It had been an excruciating process, and the death of his ego made him feel as if he was being "boiled with his own pudding, and buried with a stake of holly through his heart" (6).

No literary character other than Ebenezer Scrooge has been so intimately and universally connected with a dysfunctional enslavement

to material goods; he was the paragon of greed. By turning to the suffering of Christ, the savior freed Scrooge from his mindless bondage to
gross materialism. The constricting fear lodged in his ego was defeated
and the love of God poured abundantly into his life from a limitless
font. He died to his animal self and was reborn to his spiritual Self.

Dickens wrote that when Scrooge opened the window on
Christmas morning, the air, which had been brown and densely foggy
the day before, was now "sweet" and "fresh" (113). The Heart Chakra
is represented by the element air. Selby says that "there is no fire, no
combustion without oxygen." Once Scrooge's spiritual center opened,
the pent-up "air" associated with it blasted downward. Immediately, the
fire of the Power Chakra ignited, and in a glorious chain reaction, his
Sex and Earth Chakras were vitalized with kundalini energy.

## Scrooge's Functional Communication Chakra

The spiritual energy that flowed downward almost simultaneously
began coursing upward. Now infused with kundalini energy emanating
from the Heart Chakra, Scrooge's Communication Chakra opened up.
As Selby predicted, he was now able to express his "inner depths of
feelings in words that people around him" could understand.

After his spiritual awakening, not one person had trouble understanding that Scrooge's change was authentic. Even Bob Cratchit, who
at first thought that Scrooge had lost his mind when he announced he
was going to raise his salary, and began to make a move to defend himself from possible physical injury, quickly realized that it was a sincere
declaration:

> 'A merry Christmas, Bob,' said Scrooge, with an earnestness that
> could not be mistaken, as he clapped him on the back. 'A merrier
> Christmas, Bob, my good fellow, than I have given you for many
> a year' (120).

Once Scrooge dropped his defensive mask, his need to obfuscate disappeared; with this, it was easy for people to clearly understand the benevolence of his spiritual intentions.

As stated in Chapter Four, the fifth chakra controls the thyroid and parathyroid. When this gland is not functioning properly, it can lead to chronic colds. We know that Scrooge had a head cold on Christmas Eve, and that he treated it by eating gruel. After his transformation, it is clear that the cold no longer had an effect on him. It was not mentioned, and his joyous actions clearly indicated that it was not bothering him.

This is not to imply that his cold magically disappeared. In *Awareness*, Anthony deMello (1990) states the following:

> *Before enlightenment, I used to be depressed: after enlightenment, I continue to be depressed. But there's a difference: I don't identify with it anymore. Do you see what a big difference that is?*

Scrooge still had his cold, but because of his awakening, he no longer identified with it. It can be conjectured that with the advent of kundalini energy flowing to his Communication Chakra, his thyroid and parathyroid would function more efficiently from that point forward. But the important point is that after the psychospiritual transformation, he no longer allowed the cold to interfere.

# Scrooge's Functional Intuition Chakra

There is no doubt that with the flow of spiritual energy to Scrooge's sixth chakra, his "Third Eye" activated. Now he had the ability to think metacognitively—he could think about what he was thinking about. In touch with his intuition, he opened up to enlightenment, or wisdom.

Scrooge knew that the drastic change in him would not be understood by many people who did not directly "know" him:

*Some people laughed to see the alteration in him, but he let them laugh, and little heeded them; for he was wise enough to know that nothing ever happened on this globe, for good, at which some people did not have their fill of laughter in the onset; and knowing that such as these would be blind anyway, he thought it quite as well that they should wrinkle up their eyes in grins, as have the malady in less attractive forms. His own heart laughed: and that was quite enough for him (120-121).*

Having once been "incorrigible" and bitterly cynical himself, Scrooge had the wisdom to know that there were people in this world who would scoff at him and would never accept the change he had experienced as authentic.

Scrooge was now in the world, but no longer of the world. It did not matter what others thought of him because he no longer feared what they might possibly do to harm him. In *A Return to Love*, Marianne Williamson (1992) says:

*If we wait for the world's permission to shine, we will never receive it. The ego doesn't give that permission. Only God does, and He has already done so. He has sent you here as His personal representative and is asking you to channel His love into the world. Are you waiting for a more important job? There isn't one.*

By not reacting to the blind cynicism of the world, Scrooge demonstrated the spiritual consciousness to change those things he could, and to let go of those things he could not. He had developed the wisdom to know the difference.

Selby tells us that "the sixth chakra is the chakra of light." He encourages people "to venture into light, but also embrace darkness." Joseph Campbell (Flowers, 1988) wrote of this concept in the following terms:

*The bodhisattva represents the principle of compassion, which is the healing principle that makes life possible. Life is pain, but compas-*

*sion is what gives it the possibility of continuing. The bodhisattva*
*is one who has achieved the realization of immortality yet volun-*
*tarily participates in the sorrows of the world.*

By becoming compassionate to his own painful past and to the
pain of Tiny Tim in the present, Scrooge's Heart Chakra filled with the
"Golden sunlight" (113) of Christ Consciousness. By becoming as
good a friend, a master, and a man as society ever knew, he embodied
the life of the bodhisattva. He did not deny the darkness of the world
with his enlightenment; instead, he joined the world and worked to
cultivate the light in spite of it. He saw "his good deeds springing from
the wound, to sow the world with life immortal" (100). He became a
beacon of spiritual light in the midst of an ego-controlled world largely shrouded in darkness.

## Scrooge's Functional Crown Chakra

Just after Scrooge awoke from his dreams, he experienced a rare state
of bliss consciousness. Selby informs us that when this phenomenon
occurs:

*[A] remarkable sense of light and energy will flow into your body,*
*filling each chakra with bliss, and healing personal imbalances*
*with the universal power of love.*

There is no doubt that in the first few hours after his awakening,
Scrooge's chakras were filled with bliss, and that his lifelong imbalances were healed. His entire body was energized: he laughed and
cried, his "grating" (3) voice broke, and his hands shook almost uncon-
trollably. We know that he felt as if the weight of the world was lifted
from his shoulders when he declared:

*'I am as light as a feather, I am as happy as an angel, I am as*
*merry as a schoolboy. I am as giddy as a drunken man' (112).*

In a letter reprinted in *Parabola* (1987) from Carl Jung to Bill Wilson, the founder of Alcoholics Anonymous, Jung stated the following:

> *You see, 'alcohol' in Latin is* spiritus, *and you use the same word for the highest religious experience as well as for the most depraving poison.*

Dickens is telling us that Scrooge had consciously achieved the ultimate spiritual bliss experience that alcoholics often attempt to attain through drinking, but always in vain. Alcohol always leads to unconsciousness, whereas Scrooge's awakening led the ultimate experience of total awareness.

Once the kundalini energy had traveled all the way up through Scrooge's chakratic system to the Crown Chakra, it activated the pineal gland in his brain. Selby states:

> *Medicine claims that this mysterious gland is defunct. But Yogis for thousands of years have come to know intimately from the inside out that the pineal gland is awakened through kundalini energy and begins secreting only when we become spiritually awakened. In fact, biochemically, it is possible to talk about enlightenment as a state where the pineal gland is regularly secreting special hormones into the body's lower glandular system.*

In other words, once Scrooge's pineal gland had been vitalized, it activated a downward flow of hormonal spiritual energy that worked in bidirectional unison with his upward flow of kundalini energy.

Mark Twain wrote a short story called "Lost in the Snow." In it, three travelers were caught in an unexpected blizzard while traveling at night. The storm became so intense and they got so lost, they assumed they would die. In separate, desperate bargains with God, all three vowed to give up their vices of smoking, drinking, and card playing if only they would be allowed to survive. They did survive, and to their surprise, discovered they were but a very short distance from the safe haven of a stagehouse. Within scant hours, all three went back on their bargains, and resumed the habits they solemnly vowed to break.

This is not the kind of transformation experience Scrooge underwent. Because his kundalini energy flowed downward from his Heart Chakra, then back upward through what Dickens called the "the organ of benevolence" (40) to his Crown Chakra, his mysteriously spiritual pineal gland activated. This total experience guaranteed that the transformation he endured was not temporary, but rather, permanent.

It spiritualized him and altered his life forever. Scrooge finally came "home" to his true Self, to the "home" his little sister repeatedly promised he would return to when she rescued him as a youth. He finally found the "om" embedded in the word. He realized the healing power of this great chant, and found what Selby calls the "pathway into the great white light and beyond, and of course back again as well."

Very few people will be fortunate enough to be given the drastic kundalini awakening opportunity that Scrooge experienced. We have to realize, right now, that we can awaken this energy by actively pursuing it. We have to accept the challenge, allow ourselves to feel the pain of our shadows, and learn to live life fully, one day at a time.

## CHAPTER SIX

# Scrooge's Near-Death Experience & Abduction

In recent decades, medicine has developed the capability to resuscitate people who, previous to these technological developments, would have remained dead. Kenneth Ring, author of *Life at Death*, *Heading toward Omega*, and *The Omega Project*, reports that of those who have been successfully brought back to life through the application of these life-saving techniques, one in three experiences what has come to be known as the near-death experience.

Not all people who report having had this experience, however, were actually clinically dead; this phenomenon can be triggered by a variety of crises and situations, some of which have little or nothing to do with actual medical emergencies. In the mid 1970s, Raymond Moody began to write extensively about near-death experiences. In his book *Reflections on Life after Life* (1978), he said the following:

> *Many people have told me of out-of-body experiences which took place spontaneously. The persons involved were not "dead" or even ill or in jeopardy. Further, in most cases these experiences were not being sought out in any way. They came as complete surprises.*

He conjectured that "stresses, etc." could possibly trigger the sending of a false message to the body, resulting in the premature release of the soul from the body. According to Moody, this "malfunction" could account for the genesis of the near-death experience without the threat of physical death present. Although not typical, this particular type of experience does get reported on occasion.

Moody's investigations yielded the existence of a typical pattern of events embedded within the uniqueness of each near-death experience. At the onset, a sense of well-being and a quiet peace may envelop the person. Next, a sense of separation from the physical body may occur, where the person can look down upon the physical realm, as if floating from above. At this point, the person may be drawn into a dark tunnel; once in it, a "presence" precipitates a quick, panoramic examination covering the entirety of the experiencer's life.

The person may then journey deeper into the tunnel toward a brilliant light, which is full of love, warmth, and understanding. At this time, an encounter with a deceased loved one or loved ones may be experienced. At some point, the person is either commanded against his or her will to return to life, or chooses freely to return. The rejoining to the body is instantaneous and the mechanics of the reunion often cannot be accounted for. After the return, the person may be reticent to discuss the event, either because it is nearly impossible to put into words, or because of the fear of being thought of as crazy. Despite this, the pleasantly disturbing near-death experience usually has a profound and lasting effect upon the person's life.

# Alien Encounter & Abduction Experiences

In the foreword to Kenneth Ring's The Omega Project (1992), Whitley Strieber states that by the late 1940s, concurrent with the dawn of the Nuclear Age, widespread UFO sightings, alien encounters, and alien abductions began to be reported internationally. Strieber himself was an experiencer of a traumatic alien abduction. The story recounting the particulars of his "close encounter of the fourth kind" was chronicled in his best-selling book, *Communion*.

Parallel to the near-death experience, Ring informs us that although the particular content of each reported sighting, encounter, or abduction is unique, "there is still a distinctive and undeniably meaningful patterning to these experiences." This does not imply that the near-death experience and the alien encounter are equivalent in content. In fact, they are polar opposite in terms of what actually unfolds experientially and what is felt emotionally.

In terms of the alien encounter pattern, there is an initial sighting by the person, who is drawn almost hypnotically to "a riveting light in the sky," which may be followed by the appearance of a "wondrously multicolored craft" (Ring). Next, an alien or aliens may appear and abduct the person to the spacecraft, where he or she is more than likely subjected to a variety of bizarre and painful physical examinations and other probing medical procedures, very often sexual in content. The subject may be warned by the aliens about the fallibility of human behavior and about human insensitivity to environmental issues. After this excruciating ordeal, the dazed person is usually returned to the very same site from which he or she was abducted.

According to Ring, this experience can be very traumatizing, leaving the person in a state "often marked by feelings of confusion, disorientation, time loss, and memory impairment." Despite the terror associated with this phenomenon, he relates that the experiencer of a "fourth kind encounter," akin to the person who has had a near-death experience, is left with an undeniable sense that in some way, whatever has transpired will leave a profound and lasting effect upon his or her life.

The internally consistent details and patterns derived from countless reports for each of these surreal experiences does not suggest or imply absolute proof of the physical reality of their occurrence. In truth, it does not matter; what does matter is that these experiences often produce undeniable, life-changing, positive effects upon the people who have undergone them. The impact of the meaning of these phenomena upon the experiencers' lives is far more important than any ironclad proof that they did indeed physically occur in any scientifically provable sense.

## Similar Patterns

Ring realized that in addition to the vastly different surface details and the internally consistent patterns manifested during the near-death experience and the alien encounter experience, they both follow the exact same archetypal structure. He informs us that in mythology, this is known as the initiatory ordeal, which is "marked by the classic states of separation, ordeal, and return."

This is precisely what Joseph Campbell characterized (first in *The Hero with a Thousand Faces*, and later in *The Power of Myth*) as the hero's journey, where the sometimes not-so-willing hero goes through a cycle of departure, attainment, and return. The adventurer returns from the trip with valuable experience that leads to a dramatic personal metamorphosis. If this knowledge is imparted to others, it can result in a benefit, or "boon," to society at large. As we will see, experiencers of both the near-death experience and the alien encounter often return to effect positive changes in their lives and, systemically, in the lives of those around them.

In addition to the identification of this structural similarity, Ring gathered and administered a variety of self-report inventories to four distinct groups: near-death experiencers, alien encounter experiencers, those only interested in near-death experiences, and those only interested in alien encounters. This study was published as the book, *The Omega Project*. The statistical analysis of the collected data indicated numerous astonishing and mathematically significant similarities between the experiencers of these two seemingly disparate phenomena.

# Ring's Omega Project

Through the "childhood experience inventory," a childhood sensitivity to perceive "alternate realities" for both near-death experiencers and alien encounter experiencers was discovered:

> *UFOers, and to a somewhat lesser extent NDErs, were much more likely than respondents in our control groups to affirm that as children they were already sensitive to these alternate realities. Indeed, our statistical analysis revealed a huge difference in this respect between our experiential and control groups.*

This sensitivity to alternate realities means that as children, the respondents reported the ability to project non-real entities into the physical plane. This suggests that they were aware of nonphysical beings, they could perceive other realities that others didn't seem to be aware of, and they could "see what some people call fairies or 'the little people.'"

Ring also learned that as children, both of the experiencer groups lived in "the presence of relatively high levels of childhood abuse and trauma and possibly other forms of stress." They reported maltreatment in the following areas:

1. physical abuse and punishment
2. psychological abuse
3. sexual abuse
4. neglect
5. negative home atmosphere

From his analysis of the data collected from the "home environment inventory," Ring concluded "that these two categories of experiential respondents may well have had similarly troubled childhoods."

The "psychological inventory" report of the Omega Project was designed to measure the tendency to dissociate. According to John Bradshaw (1988), dissociation is the ability to "instantly numb." Abuse victims often "numb out" when they are placed in intolerably abusive situations that are emotional, sexual, or physical in nature. This ability to "mentally leave" the abuse is a defense mechanism used to survive the severe mistreatment. All people dissociate to some degree; high levels of it, however, appear to indicate exposure to abuse and trauma. Ring reported the following: "Overall, individuals who report UFO encounters and NDErs appear to have a greater likelihood to showing dissociation tendencies in their psychological functioning."

In terms of the profound and lasting life changes alluded to earlier for both near-death experiencers and alien encounter experiencers, Ring included a "psychophysical inventory" in the Omega Project. The areas covered were:
1. physical sensitivities
2. physiological and neurological functioning
3. psychoenergetic functioning
4. emotional functioning
5. expanded mental awareness
6. paranormal functioning

From the results of this inventory used to indicate bodily and emotional changes, he concluded that:

> If these self-report data are valid, it is clear that at face value they suggest that there may be something about these encounters that may actually reprogram an experiencer's physiological and nervous system so as to make that individual inwardly and environmentally more sensitive.

The Omega Project also included a "life changes inventory" to help test for statistically significant indications of life values shifts for both groups of experiencers. Ring included the following nine value cluster subsets within the inventory:
1. appreciation for life
2. self-acceptance
3. concern for others
4. concern for impressing others

5. materialism

6. concern with social/planetary issues

7. quest for meaning

8. spirituality

9. religiousness

He summarized his findings for this category in the following way:

*1. In general, all groups report becoming more altruistic, having greater social concern, and increasing in spirituality.*

*2. In general, these changes are somewhat more evident for our experiential respondents and are significantly greater for the following value clusters: appreciation for life, self-acceptance, concern for others, materialism (decrease), quest for meaning and spirituality.*

*3. In general, the NDE sample shows a greater shift than the UFO sample on altruistic (increase) and materialism (decrease) values. Specifically, the changes are statistically significant for concern for others, impressing others (decrease), and materialism (decrease).*

# Historical Indications of These Phenomena

While appearing to be intimately tied to the technological advancements of the twentieth century, the near-death experience is not new. It is true that major advances in medical resuscitation techniques have resulted in many more people being brought back from clinical death. Of those people, significant numbers have reported the occurrence of this experience more now than at any other time in history. Despite this increase, in his book *Reflections on Life after Life*, Raymond Moody wrote that although at one time he thought there were no historical examples of these events, reports of them have always existed:

*Since then it has become obvious that there is a wealth of accounts*
*of near-death experiences available in writings from earlier times.*

To support this fact, Moody wrote that the Venerable Bede included an account of a near-death experience in his eighth-century book, *A*
*History of the English Church and People*. He provided an account of one
from the works of the English writer, Thomas De Quincy (1785-1859).
He related that C. G. Jung experienced one and chronicled it in his
book *Memories, Dreams, and Reflections*. In addition, he wrote that Ernest
Hemingway, in his book *A Farewell to Arms*, and Leo Tolstoy, in *The Death*
*of Ivan Ilyich*, both provided legitimate literary examples of the experience. Moody concluded that "Far from being a new phenomenon, near-
death experiences have been with us for a long, long time."

In terms of UFO sightings, alien encounters, and alien abductions,
again it appears that these phenomena seem to be tied closely to the
latter half of this century. In *The Demon-Haunted World* (1995), however,
Carl Sagan helped to dispelled this notion. He stated that throughout
the centuries, people have reported strange sightings, encounters, and
abductions by a variety of creatures. Note the following example
Sagan gave:

> *In 1645 a Cornish teenager, Anne Jeffries, was found groggy,*
> *crumpled on the floor. Much later, she recalled being attacked by*
> *half-a-dozen little men, carried paralyzed to a castle in the air,*
> *seduced, and returned home. She called the little men fairies....*
> *They returned to torment her.... Fairies traditionally have magi-*
> *cal powers, and can cause paralysis by the merest touch. The ordi-*
> *nary passage of time is slowed in fairyland. Fairies are reproduc-*
> *tively impaired, so they have sex with humans and carry off babies*
> *from their cradles.... If Anne Jeffries had grown up in a culture*
> *touting aliens rather than fairies, and UFOs rather than castles in*
> *the air, would her story have been distinguishable in any signig-*
> *cant respect from the ones 'abductees' tell?*

Along Sagan's same historical perspective line of thinking, Ring stated the following:

> During the medieval period, for example, unexplained celestial events might be seen as 'dragons flying through the sky' or some other kind of fiery supernatural object or portent. If apparitional beings were sighted, they were likely to be thought of as angels, witches, demons, or perhaps sylphs of the air.

He continued by noting that these encounters seem to be "viewed and interpreted in terms of the prevailing belief and conceptual systems of the times." Ring believes that with the advent of the nuclear age and the popularization of science fiction, it is no wonder that today's UFO experiences are clearly related to these current motifs.

It appears, then, that neither the near-death experience nor the alien encounter is new. For a variety of reasons, these events are more prevalent today than ever before. Sheer numbers of people on the face of the earth has something to do with it; more people leads to more reported experiences. Advances in medical technology certainly has proportionally increased the percentage of people reporting having had near-death experiences. Finally, increased mass media coverage of these events has served to widely disseminate information concerning both types of events to millions upon millions of people via television, radio, newspapers, films, books, magazines, and even the Internet.

## What Does This Have to Do with Scrooge? Childhood Antecedents

There is no doubt that Scrooge's childhood background undoubtedly predisposed him to be sensitive enough to experience either of these phenomena. We know that as a child, he was fond of fantasy literature. Ring tells us that while "fantasy proneness" itself does not predict openness to these experiences, the ability to slip into "alternate realities" does. We learned that Scrooge used fantasy literature to go into a mental state where he actually projected fictional characters into the physical world.

During his time with the Ghost of Christmas Past, Scrooge encountered himself alone at the boarding school as a child, reading. Note Dickens' account of what happened as they observed the scene:

> *Suddenly a man, in foreign garments: wonderfully real and distinct*
> *to look at: stood outside the window, with an axe stuck in his belt,*
> *and leading by the bridle an ass laden with wood (36).*

Scrooge informed the Spirit that "One Christmastime, when yonder solitary child was left here all alone, he [Ali Baba] did come, for the first time, just like that"(36).

During this scene, Scrooge also witnessed a myriad of other non-ordinary characters, including Robinson Crusoe, that he had projected onto the physical plane as a child. Dickens informed us that "The man thought he was dreaming, but he wasn't" (37). From this, it is clear that the youthful Scrooge indeed slipped into alternate realities on more than one occasion, and that the adult Scrooge was able to corroborate this truth.

As Ring noted earlier, experiencers of both NDEs and CE-IVs (close encounters of the fourth kind) lived in "the presence of relatively high levels of childhood abuse and trauma and possibly other forms of stress." Doubtlessly, Scrooge's background was very much in line with this finding. We know that he was abandoned to the dilapidated boarding school, where he was forced to remain completely isolated for at least one full holiday season. This neglect took its toll upon Scrooge.

There is also distinct evidence of ongoing abuse in the Scrooge household, perpetrated by his father during Ebenezer's childhood. Dickens let us know of this by Fan's statement that their father had eventually become "so much kinder that he used to be" (38). Whatever damage inflicted upon Scrooge by that time, however, had already psychologically marred him.

Ring discovered that individuals reporting near-death experiences and alien encounters "appear to have a greater likelihood of showing dissociation tendencies in their psychological functioning." It has already been clearly demonstrated that Scrooge snapped during his childhood in order to survive the abandonment he experienced. This shutting-down behavior was his way to remove himself from the horror of the situation, and to survive the trauma so that he could continue to physically exist. Dissociation often leads to the development of adult defense mechanisms, of which Scrooge had many.

All three of these factors put Scrooge's background in close alignment with those who report near-death experiences and alien abductions. Ring states that a person with this specific background qualifies for what he calls "the encounter-prone personality." He continues:

> We have now in effect set the development stage for an extraordinary encounter—either an NDE or a UFO. To summarize our theory to this point, we have as a prototype an individual who, coming from a history of childhood abuse and trauma, has developed dissociative tendencies as well as a capacity to become deeply absorbed in alternate realities. Indeed, we can assume that such an individual, by virtue of this kind of psychological conditioning, is well accustomed to such unusual states of consciousness since he has often had recourse to enter them.

When Scrooge had his Christmas Eve encounter, this background set him up, according to Ring, to "'flip' into that state of consciousness, which, like a special lens, affords a glimpse of these remarkable occurrences."

## Mixed Motif Encounter

While Scrooge was in no real danger of imminent physical death, upon close examination, much of what he underwent on Christmas

Eve appears to be closely related to a near-death experience. And while Scrooge's nocturnal journey did not relate closely to most of the elements expected in alien abductions, some of his experiences are strikingly similar to those of that phenomenon.

It is clear that Scrooge had a nineteenth-century version of what Ring terms a " 'mixed motif' case," one that intermingles elements of both the near-death experience and the alien abduction. In his studies, Ring reports that while this particular type of event is not common, "as the phrase implies, it is not the only one in my files." So while the mixed motif occurrence is not particularly clear-cut or exceedingly common, it is one type that is known to transpire. Scrooge's experience fits this category exceptionally well.

## Comparing Scrooge's Adventure to the Near-Death Experience and the Alien Abduction

Ring provides an exhaustive chart for the purpose of comparing the features of a typical near-death experience with that of a typical alien abduction. Using the fourteen elements included in his chart, the nature of Scrooge's "mixed motif" experience will be examined.

### Element One

**Precipitating Event**: From the chart, we learn that an NDE is most often precipitated by a "life-threatening crisis," while a CE-IV begins with a "sudden capture." While Scrooge was in no clear danger of a life-threatening crisis that was physical in nature, in a sense, he was presented with a life crisis of graveness: either to live fully awake in a spiritual sense, or to continue living in a state of spiritual deadness.

Like an experiencer of a CE-IV, Scrooge was suddenly captured; he had no choice in the matter. Although Marley, the "supernatural visitor," did warn him of the impending visitation, Scrooge's participation in it was mandatory. Try as he might to deny it, he could not avoid the encounter; Marley left him no room for avoidance.

Before the Ghost of Christmas Past entered, Dickens wrote that "light flashed up in the room upon the instant" (30). This is reminiscent of the "riveting light in the sky" that Ring tells us usually heralds the beginning of the alien encounter episode. The Spirit itself was truly alien in appearance:

> It was a strange figure—like a child: yet not so like a child as like
> an old man, viewed through some supernatural medium, which
> gave him the appearance of having receded from the view, and
> being diminished to a child's proportions (30).

Many modern-day accounts of aliens match this description in terms of the man-child quality of the creature as described by Dickens. To add to its eerie quality, we are told that it possessed a glittering belt, which flashed lights in such a way so that the Spirit:

> [F]luctuated in its distinctness: being now a thing with one arm,
> now with one leg, now with twenty legs, now a pair of legs with-
> out a head, now a head without a body (31).

This description of the mutable appearance of the Spirit is somewhat reminiscent of the "wondrously multicolored craft" so often described to Ring by those who have had alien encounters.

Dickens wrote that "It would have been in vain for Scrooge to plead" (32) with the Spirit about going with him. We are left with no doubt that Scrooge had no choice in the matter: "The grasp, though gentle as a woman's hand, was not to be resisted" (33). Therefore, it appears that the precipitating event was more typical of a CE-IV event than a NDE.

## Element Two

**Form of Separation:** Ring tells us that in an NDE, the person is "swept up into a light-filled realm," while in a CE-IV, the person is "taken away to an alien environment." Upon Marley's departure, Scrooge glimpsed an alien environment outside of his window, but he was not taken into it:

> The air was filled with phantoms, wandering hither and thither in restless haste, and moaning as they went. Every one of them wore chains like Marley's Ghost; some few (they might be guilty governments) were linked together; none were free. Many had been personally known to Scrooge in their lives. He had been quite familiar with one old ghost, in a white waistcoat, with a monstrous iron safe attached to its ankle, who cried piteously at being unable to assist a wretched woman with an infant, whom it saw below, upon a door-step. The misery with them all was, clearly, that they sought to interfere, for good, in human matters, and had lost the power forever (26, 28).

When the Ghost of Christmas Past did "abduct" Scrooge, he took him, instead, into a light-filled realm:

> As the words were spoken, they passed through the wall, and stood upon an open country road, with fields on either hand. The city had entirely vanished. Not a vestige of it was to be seen. The darkness and the mist had vanished with it, for it was a clear, cold, winter day, with snow upon the ground (33).

It is obvious from this passage that Scrooge was taken out of the darkness into an environment filled with light. This experience, then, seems more in alignment with an NDE than a CE-IV.

## Element Three

**Initial Response:** Ring states that for near-death experiencers, it is common to have a feeling of "peace" or "security" at the onset. For people going through a CE-IV, however, it is more likely that "fright" or "terror" will be the first response. There is no indication that Scrooge felt anything like peace or security at the beginning of his journey.

Despite his initial bravado with the appearance of Marley's phantom, it is clear he did experience fright and terror.

When Marley's face first appeared in Scrooge's door knocker, he experienced the reactivation of his kundalini life-force (see Chapter Five) as a "terrible sensation" (15). Once in his room, immediately after Marley reappeared in the tiles surrounding his fireplace, Scrooge felt "a strange, inexplicable dread" (17) when a bell in his room began to swing on its own. Dickens wrote of Scrooge that "his colour changed" (18) when Marley passed through a bolted door to enter the house.

Scrooge continued to attempt to deny the existence of the appari- tion by bantering sarcastically with Marley. Of this exchange, Dickens wrote the following:

> Scrooge was not much in the habit of cracking jokes, nor did he feel, in his heart, by any means waggish then. The truth is, that he tried to be smart, as a means of distracting his own attention, and keeping down his terror; for the spectre's voice disturbed the very marrow in his bones (20).

Still later, Dickens related that "Scrooge fell on his hands and knees, and clasped his hands before his face," he "trembled more and more," he "began to quake exceedingly," and that he "shivered, and wiped the perspiration from his brow." All of this is indicative of the terror involved with a CE-IV experience.

## Element Four

**Perception of Reality**: Ring states that during the CE-IV experience, the person is thrust into a "dreamlike, fantastic" world. During the Marley segment of the experience, especially, Scrooge was exposed to the bizarre elements (the description of the spirit, the appearance of the phantom world outside of his window) associated with an alien encounter. In a near-death experience, on the other hand, Ring says the person is in a "hyperreal" state, and is convinced that "the reality of the events witnessed is beyond doubt."

The morning following his Christmas Eve ordeal, there is no doubt that Scrooge was convinced of the reality of what had happened to him:

> 'There's the saucepan that the gruel was in,' cried Scrooge, starting off again, and going round the fireplace. 'There's the door, by which the Ghost of Jacob Marley entered. There's the corner where the Ghost of Christmas Present sat. There's the window where I saw the wandering Spirits. It's all right, it's all true, it all happened. Ha, ha, ha!' (112).

In the modern near-death experience, especially those associated with clinical death and resuscitation, Ring tells us the following about the heightened perception of reality in terms of the out of body experience, or OBE: "Nowhere is the sense of hyperreality of NDEs more evident than in the phase where the experiencer finds himself out of his body and somehow able to look upon it from this external perspective." At no time during *A Christmas Carol* did Scrooge have this sort of "hovering" sensation. He did, however, view himself repeatedly from an external perspective when guided by the Spirits of Christmas Past and Christmas Future. Dickens gave this following account of the first external episode, during Scrooge's childhood, as he sat alone in the desolate boarding school:

> At one of these [desks] a lonely boy was reading near a feeble fire; and Scrooge sat down upon a form, and wept to see his poor forgotten self as he used to be (35).

This form of external viewing appears to be Dickens' nineteenth-century manner of relating the out-of-body experience to his readers.

In terms of perception of reality, Scrooge had some initial "dream-like, fantastic" perceptions, and some again at the end of his encounter during his time with the Ghost of the Future. The predominance of the perceptions that he sustained during the adventure, however, were much more closely associated with the hyperreality reported by a person having a near-death experience, rather than those reported by a person deeply enmeshed in an alien encounter.

## Element Five

**Nature of Beings:** Ring relates that during near-death experiences, the encounters are with "beings of light" and with "spirits of deceased relatives or friends." In the CE-IV, the experiencer is exposed to "hideous alien creatures." It is apparent that Scrooge was exposed to both.

The first being Scrooge encountered was that of Jacob Marley, his deceased business partner and "friend" for most of his adult life. The Ghost of Christmas Past, the second being he encountered, was unmistakably one of light, which is obvious from the description provided by Dickens:

> But the strangest thing about it was, that from the crown of its head there sprung a bright clear jet of light, by which all this was visible; and which was doubtless the occasion of its using, in its duller moments, a great extinguisher for a cap, which it now held under its arm (31).

The third being encountered, The Ghost of Christmas Present, was also one of light. Even before Scrooge got out of his bed, he saw a "blaze of ruddy light," (56) which the spirit emitted from an adjacent room in the house. When Scrooge finally got the nerve up to find the source of the light, he saw the following:

> In easy state upon this couch, there sat a jolly Giant, glorious to see, who bore a glowing torch, in shape not unlike Plenty's horn, and held it up, high up, to shed its light on Scrooge, as he came peeping round the door. (57)

So far, all three of Scrooge's encounters are with beings closely matched with those that might be expected during a near-death experience.

The fourth being, the Ghost of Christmas Yet to Come, however, was much closer in description to the "hideous alien creature" one might expect during an alien encounter:

> It was shrouded in a deep black garment, which concealed its head, its face, its form, and left nothing of it visible save one outstretched

*hand. But for this it would have been difficult to detach its figure*
*from the night, and separate it from the darkness by which it was*
*surrounded (89).*

Compare that description to the following examples provided by
Kenneth Ring. These were taken from people participating in The
Omega Project who experienced close encounters of the fourth kind:

1. *"They were all black and had an ant-like appearance with large*
*black eyes."*

2. *"They were all black, and I cannot recall any features or cloth-*
*ing details."*

3. *"A tall, totally black, featureless being came through a doorway*
*at the other end of the room, walked to me and stood looking down*
*at me."*

Despite the fact that most of Scrooge's encounters were more typical of the near-death experience, his all-important confrontation with
the Ghost of the Future was definitely in congruence with that of a CE-
IV experience.

## Element Six

**Nature of Encounter:** Ring tells us that the nature of the near-death
experience is one of "compassionate self-examination," where "insights
of profound spiritual import" are learned. In the CE-IV, on the other
hand, the experiencer goes through a "clinical physical examination,"
and eventually develops an "awareness of obscure alien purposes."

In this sense, there is no doubt that what Scrooge underwent was
completely congruent with the near-death experience. At no point was
he subjected to the physical examination indicative of the alien
encounter. Marley left absolutely no doubt in Scrooge's mind the clearly intended purpose of the visitation:

*'I am here to-night to warn you, that you have yet a chance and hope of escaping my fate. A chance and hope of my procuring, Ebenezer'* (25).

The self-examination that Scrooge endured was not pleasant, but it was compassionate. During the experience, he was subjected to numerous painful realities that he had avoided throughout his adult life. In order to be reborn spiritually, it was necessary for Scrooge to go into his personal black hole, and finally deal with the repressed information he so desperately avoided through denial.

Compassionate confrontation implies learning to feel and identify with personal pain. It is compassionate because it is the only way to awaken. Only by doing so was Scrooge able to come out of the sleep of denial, transform his life, identify with the pain of others, and connect lovingly with them during his remaining time on earth.

## Element Seven

**Sense of Encounter:** In the CE-IV, a person is left with a feeling of "violation," while in the NDE, the person comes away from it with a sense of "total affirmation." While Scrooge most likely felt violated at the very onset of his encounter, in that he was compelled to go through it, there is little doubt that because of it, he felt totally affirmed for the duration of his life. As Dickens stated, Scrooge became as good a person as the world had known due to the experience. There is no better testimonial; after all, Scrooge's "own heart laughed, and that was quite enough for him" (121).

## Element Eight

**Motivation Regarding Encounter:** Many people who have near-death experiences report not wanting to leave the realm of the light. Ring and Moody (1978) both report that those forced to return to life often are angry because they want to stay in the pleasant place. They also report that some experience depression for a period of time upon their return.

According to Ring, those who have gone through alien encounters, on the other hand, are anxious "to be set free." The experience of the CE-IV is not at all pleasant; these people want to return to life on earth.

While watching the festivities taking place at his nephew Fred's party with the Ghost of Christmas Present, Scrooge "begged like a boy to be allowed to stay until the guests departed" (83). Despite this, plus the fact that he willingly accompanied that spirit, as well as the Ghost of Christmas Future, his main goal and purpose was to be set free. Scrooge did not want to die. He wanted to return and to alter his life; he wanted a chance to demonstrate reformation.

## Element Nine

**Determination of Return:** Ring informs us that for a near-death experiencer, the person returns: (a) by "personal choice," (b) by an "externally imposed injunction," or (c) there is "no indication of a condition necessary for return." For the alien encounter experiencer, the return of the person is "totally under the control of alien beings."

For Scrooge, the determination of his return was a true blend of both. It seems that the restoration to life was predicated upon his personal decision to conduct himself in a spiritual manner; this is indicative of the near-death experience. But the Ghost of the Future would not allow Scrooge's return until after he had satisfied all of the necessary criteria: connecting with his feelings, opening at the heart level, and finally and most importantly, praying for the first time. This feature is very much in line with a CE-IV experience.

Ring included anecdotal accounts of a fifty-one-year-old woman, who experienced serial abductions during her life. In both her childhood abduction scenario and her adult vignette, Ring tells us that "prior to leaving, she realizes when she gets to the door that she has to wait." In similar fashion, before Scrooge was allowed to leave, he had to "wait" until he prayed. Once he did, he was returned to the exact place where the abduction had begun with the Ghost of Christmas Past—his bed.

## Element Ten

**Emotions Upon Return**: Ring informs us that a person just returning from a near-death experience often does not want to come back to life after having been encircled in the glow of eternal light. The return can result in feelings of "disappointment, regret, sorrow," and "resentment." For a willing returner, however, he tells us "exhilaration" is apparent.

For a person just restored from a CE-IV experience, he says that "relief" is apparent. Also, the person can be "panicky," in a state of "confusion," "angry," or can manifest feelings of "hatred." There is no doubt that Scrooge was immensely relieved upon his return:

> *Yes! And the bedpost was his own. The bed was his own, the room was his own. Best and happiest of all, the Time before him was his own, to make amends in!* (111).

In homage to his relief, he repeated his vow to "live in the Past, the Present, and the Future," and praised "Heaven and the Christmas Time" (111), while down upon his knees.

In addition, there is clear evidence that Scrooge was in a state of confusion at the onset of his return. As noted earlier, he had a difficult time dressing himself and declared "I don't know what to do!" (112). He stated aloud that he didn't know what day it was, he didn't know how long he was gone, and finally said "I don't know anything" (112).

Despite these alien encounter symptoms, it is apparent that predominantly, Scrooge was filled with absolute exhilaration immediately after his return. This is denotative of a willing return from a near-death experience. His elation is illustrated in the following passage:

> *'I am as light as a feather, I am as happy as an angel, I am as merry as a schoolboy. I am as giddy as a drunken man. A merry Christmas to everybody! A happy New Year to all the world! Hallo here! Whoop! Hallo!'* (112).

Scrooge was so excited at his return that we learn from Dickens that he was " perfectly winded."

## Element Eleven

**Memory of Encounter**: Ring informs us that the memory of a CE-IV experience is "often impaired" in the experiencer. On the other hand, a person's memory of an NDE is "usually intact."

While there is no indication that Scrooge had lost any memory of what had occurred, there are examples to illustrate that he did know exactly what had happened. After Scrooge learned what day it was from the young boy he had called to from his window, Dickens wrote:

> 'It's Christmas Day,' said Scrooge to himself. 'I haven't missed it.
> The Spirits have done it all in one night. They can do anything
> they like. Of course they can' (113).

Earlier in this chapter, of course, we learned that Scrooge accurately recounted the details from the very beginning of his adventure, and concluded that "it's all true, it all happened" (112). All of this indicates that his journey was more typical of a near-death experience.

## Element Twelve

**Immediate Aftermath**: Ring reports that undergoing an alien abduction often leads to "post-traumatic stress symptoms." *The Diagnostic and Statistical Manual of Mental Disorders* (DSM-IV) states that a person who shows signs of post-traumatic stress:

> [H]as experienced an event that is outside the range of usual
> human experience and that would be markedly distressing to almost
> everyone."

Rape, war, riots, floods, earthquakes, airplane crashes, and car accidents are just some of the situations listed that can lead to the development of this disorder.

The DSM-IV lists these following symptoms as just a few of the possible ramifications of post-traumatic stress:

1. recurrent and intrusive distressing recollections… or dreams of the event
2. feeling of detachment or estrangement from others

3. irritability or outbursts of anger

4. hypervigilance

The manual states that in order to qualify for this diagnosis, the person must show symptoms for a period of at least one month. It is clear that while Scrooge certainly suffered a non-ordinary event, he developed no long-term post-traumatic symptomology associated with the experience.

Ring tells us that the immediate aftermath of the near-death experience can lead to "variable, strong emotions." Scrooge eventually settled down from the very powerful initial surge of emotional energy coursing through his body on that wonderful Christmas morning, when he alternated between "sobbing violently" (111) and laughing splendidly.

In spite of this eventual reduction, he still experienced a long-lasting range of emotions not known to him before the transformation. For example, later that same day, Scrooge felt "a pang across his heart" (116) when he saw the gentleman solicitor whom he had rudely rebuffed the day before. Still later, he felt fear before screwing up the courage to knock on Fred's door; he was well aware of the possible rejection he might encounter because of the way he had coldly refused his nephew's invitation.

In addition to being in touch with negative emotions, Scrooge was also able to experience very positive ones. Note what Dickens said about his Christmas Day trek around London:

> He went to church, and walked about the streets, and watched the people hurrying to and fro, and patted children on the head, and questioned beggars, and looked down into the kitchens of houses, and up to the windows, and found that everything could yield him pleasure. He had never dreamed that any walk—that anything— could give him so much happiness (116-117).

By now, we know that Scrooge's life ended happily, and that "His own heart laughed, and that was quite enough for him" (121). It is clear that what he experienced is indicative of a near-death experience.

## Element Thirteen

**Frequency**: We are informed by Ring that with CE-IVs, a person often has "recurrent episodes," while near-death experiences "usually only once." Dickens directly told us of Scrooge that after this one significant emotional event, "He had no further intercourse with Spirits" (121).

## Element Fourteen

**Occurrence**: Finally, Ring tells us that the NDE occurs "usually in adulthood," while the CE-IV takes place "often in early childhood." Quite obviously, Scrooge's manifestation is very much in alignment with that of a person who has had a near-death experience.

# Summary of Mixed Motif Findings

It is clear that a large portion of what Scrooge underwent and felt closely matches that of a person going through a near-death experience. During this one-time adult event, he encountered a deceased friend, and was swept into a light-filled, hyperreal realm by beings of light. He was put through a compassionate self-examination during the time his life flashed before him, and he developed insights of profound spiritual import. Ultimately, he had to make a personal choice in order to return. When he did, he was restored to life, and experienced tremendous initial exhilaration. His memory of the event was totally intact, and ultimately, he was left with a much wider range of emotions than he had ever known before. Finally, there is no evidence that he ever discussed the importance of this totally life-affirming event with anyone.

Despite this, it is apparent that some of what Scrooge experienced is very closely aligned with that of a person going through a close encounter of the fourth kind. While in no real danger of physical death, he did have feelings of fright and terror at the beginning and at the end of the journey. He was captured against his will by the Ghost of Christmas Past, who in some ways closely resembled an eerie alien creature. At least part of what he experienced had a dreamlike, fantastic quality; in addition, he caught glimpses of terrifying "alien" environments during the event. There is the sense that his release was subject to the direct control of the Ghost of the Future, another spirit who possessed definite alien qualities. And upon return to the very site of his abduction, Scrooge felt initial panic and confusion, along with great relief.

# After-Effects of Scrooge's Mixed Motif Experience

Similar in nature to those who have had NDEs or CE-IVs, Scrooge also experienced a lasting change in his psychophysical functioning, which includes overt changes in physical sensitivities, physiological and neurological functioning, psychoenergetic functioning, emotional functioning, and expanded mental awareness. Earlier, Ring said that his results suggested:

> [T]here may be something about these encounters that may actually reprogram an experiencer's physiological and nervous system so as to make that individual inwardly and environmentally more sensitive.

There is no doubt whatsoever that Scrooge's physical functioning was transformed because of his experience.

In addition, Ring stated that as a result of his analysis of the data from the "life changes inventory," it appears reporters of both the near-death experience and the alien encounter demonstrated more altruism, increased spirituality, had a greater appreciation for life, had more self-acceptance, showed more concern for others, and became less materialistic. Without exception, the changes that occurred in Scrooge because of his mixed motif experience perfectly match the outcomes of Ring's findings.

# Psychobiological Evolution

## Electrical Sensitivity

In *The Omega Project*, Ring conjectures as to what accounts for the psychophysical changes noted in some people who have experienced NDEs or CE-IVs. He informs us that a statistically significant number of those who report having gone through either of these experiences, especially women, often relate that they have become "electrically sensitive." According to Ring, these people "complain about such things as causing electric lights inexplicably to blow, having persisting problems with their computers, wristwatches failing to work properly, and so on." Because there were no electrical appliances or machinery during the era that Dickens wrote *A Christmas Carol*, there is no direct way to know if Scrooge had developed this sensitivity after his mixed-motif experience.

Ring goes on to say that for people with increased electrical sensitivity, "there appears to be a generalized sensitivity effect stemming from extraordinary encounters." He cites the following additional areas where these experiencers have noted differences:

1. more allergic
2. more psychic
3. healing gift
4. sensitivity to light
5. hearing acuity
6. mood fluctuation

He conjectures that these experiencers may have undergone what amounts to a permanent "psychobiological transformation," at least partially because of their new-found sensitivity to electromagnetic fields.

There are subtle hints in the final chapter of *A Christmas Carol* to suggest that Scrooge had increased functioning in at least some of the areas listed above. In terms of sensitivity to light, we are told that when Scrooge opened his window on Christmas morning, he became immediately aware of, among other things, "Golden sunlight" and the clear "Heavenly sky" (113). Concerning auditory acuity, Dickens wrote that despite Scrooge's excited state, he "was checked in his transports by the churches ringing out the lustiest peals he had ever heard" (113). Finally, we know that his emotional range widened considerably, demonstrated by the fact that he could now feel sorrow, joy, and what John Bradshaw (1992) calls "healthy shame" about past callous behaviors. This change suggests at least the possibility of increased lability of moods.

## Kundalini Syndrome

In his book, *Heading Toward Omega*, Ring (1985) intriguingly explored the connection between NDEs and kundalini experiences (see chapters four and five of this book for a full treatment of this concept) in search of possible causal effects for the observed psychobiological changes. He stated the following:

> *In full kundalini awakenings, what is experienced is significantly similar to what many NDErs report from their experiences. And more than that: The aftereffects of these deep kundalini awakenings seem to lead to individual transformations and personal world views essentially indistinguishable from those found in NDErs. That these obvious parallels exist does not, of course, prove that they stem from a common cause, but it does suggest that there may be a general biological process that underlies both of them—as well as transcendental experiences at large.*

From the information he collected in that book concerning shifts in values for people who had experienced this particular event, Ring concluded that "it seems perfectly plausible to argue that NDEs may well serve to open the heart chakra in these individuals to a variable degree." As we have learned, once the heart chakra has opened, a person is in position to undergo a permanent spiritual transformation.

In *The Omega Project*, Ring continued to study the kundalini syndrome, but this time for both near-death experiencers and alien encounter experiencers. His "Kundalini Scale," designed to help determine the occurrence of these phenomenon, yielded the following information:

> [T]here is a clear-cut and consistent kundalini effect across all nine items of the scale demonstrating that experiential respondents are roughly three times more likely to report these symptoms afterward than our controls, with more than one third of the former doing so, on the average. Furthermore, when we examined the overall kundalini scores for our four basics groups... we not only again found an enormous statistical difference between the experiential and control groups, but once more, our UFO respondents were very similar to our NDErs. Both groups display substantial evidence of kundalini activation following their encounters, which of course reinforces our earlier findings pointing to their essential functional equivalence.

Based on these findings, Ring concluded that along with increased electrical sensitivity:

> [T]he kundalini syndrome, too, must be regarded as a part of, and possibly underlying, the pattern of psychophysical changes brought about by UFOEs and NDEs.

As stated earlier, merely because of the historical time period in which *A Christmas Carol* was written, we have no direct evidence to indicate that Scrooge had become sensitive to electrical stimuli. On the other hand, there is ample evidence (see Chapters Four and Five) to support the belief that Scrooge unequivocally underwent a kundalini experience.

# Scrooge and Ring's Kundalini Scale

Looking at Ring's "Kundalini Scale," Scrooge's experience matches up very well with quite a few of the included scale statements. He would have to agree that he felt energy in his "hands more often than before" and "that his body would occasionally shake, vibrate or tremble." When he attempted to shave, Dickens told us that it "was not an easy task, for his hands continued to shake very much" (115).

He would have to agree that he felt "a deep ecstatic sensation, something like an orgasm, for no reason." In two consecutive paragraphs, this is evident. The first described Scrooge's thinly veiled sexual reaction to the sound of the "lustiest peals" of churches bells "that he had ever heard" (113). The other detailed his rapturous reaction to the brightness and coldness of the Christmas morning. Dickens ends both paragraphs by repeating the phrase: "Oh Glorious. Glorious" (113).

He would have to agree with the statement that he had the "sensation of extreme heat" flowing through his body "more often than before." For a man who had formerly "carried his own low temperature" (3), Dickens wrote that Scrooge was now "glowing with good intentions" (111). Any increase of warmth would most likely feel extreme to Scrooge, a man defined by coldness before the transformational awakening.

Finally, he most likely would agree with the scale statement that he would "occasionally experience sensations of tickling, itching, or tingling on or underneath my skin." For a man who formerly flashed only sarcastic humor before the change, he now freely smiled, chuckled, shouted, and began a "long line of brilliant laughs" (112); it can be conjectured that he was being tickled by something physical.

Ring concludes his search for the causes of the permanent psychobiological and spiritual transformations of people who have been through either a near-death experience or an alien encounter by saying:

> Our own data, at any rate, suggest that at the very least electrical
> sensitivity and kundalini activation are likely to be correlated

*effects associated with extraordinary encounters. Therefore, it seems reasonable at this juncture to suppose that they tend to arise togeth- er as part of the psychobiological alchemy of these experiences.*

He goes on to say that he feels that of the two, kundalini activation is basic to the psychobiological shifts he has observed.

## Summary and Conclusions

To summarize, because of the childhood abuse and abandonment Scrooge was subjected to, he snapped in order to physically survive. He paid a price by concomitantly developing the ability to go into extended states of dissociation. In these states, because of his fertile imagination and his love of fanciful fiction, his mind developed the ability to perceive alternate realities. The characters he projected onto the physical plane helped him to survive the extended isolation he was forced to endure.

As Scrooge grew, he developed a variety of adult defense mecha- nisms, the ego's fearful and inadequate attempt to deny the past and to defend against the threat of further pain. Instead, he compulsively repeated the abandonment and neglect he experienced in his childhood for a large part of his adult life on himself and on others. Fortunately, however, as he aged, his defense mechanisms naturally weakened.

On that fateful Christmas Eve, at the darkest time of the year, he was presented with a late mid-life crisis. Because of the charity solici- tors' visit, Marley, his dysfunctional "twin," reentered his consciousness. In addition, because of his nephew Fred's compassionate visit, his deceased loving sister, Fan, somehow also broke into his preconscious mind. The combination of their return to him, and the "psychological absorption" that he had developed during his childhood because of his abuse and trauma, caused him to shift into the realm of an "alternate reality" with the onset of the crisis.

Later that night, his combination, or mixed motif, NDE/CE-IV experience began in earnest. Like on an initiatory mythological adventure, typical of either experience, he went through the process of separation, ordeal, and return. Upon his return, the phenomenon caused a tremendous rise of kundalini energy to flow through his physical system. This led, of course, to his wondrous and permanent psychobiological transformation and spiritual awakening.

# Scrooge Resurrected

Ring presents an interesting, insightful, and positive interpretation of this situation:

> From my own personal point of view,...these UFOers and NDErs are actually the unwitting beneficiaries of a kind of compensatory gift in return for the wounds they have incurred in growing up. That is, through the exigencies of their difficult and in some cases even tormented childhoods, they also come to develop an extended range of human perception beyond normally recognized limits. Thus, they may experience what the rest of us with unexceptional childhoods may only wonder at.

While not many of us may be as "fortunate" as Scrooge, the reluctant adventurer, to transform exactly in the manner he did (in fact like many people do), each of us can still go on our own difficult "hero's journey."

Similar to Scrooge, all of us have the hurts and fears he so "successfully" held down for so long. We, too, in our own unique ways, can "push the envelope" of our binding personal perceptions in order to experience the world in more spiritually caring ways. How courageous it is to actively seek out the adventure, endure the necessary pain, and resurrect, before it is too late. Christ showed us the way; we need to follow it, right here and right now.

Ring reported that when he asked NDErs and CE-IVers what their adventures yielded in terms of answering the question: What is the meaning of life?, many loudly and clearly replied, "LOVE." He summarized their replies in the following way:

> Love is very important. It is the main reason for our existence as human beings in our physical bodies. We must understand love— and we must understand love in a holistic sense, altruistic love, etc. We can never fully experience love or give love unless we also know compassion. To understand compassion, we must know pain, and loss—not just our own pain and loss, but the ability to feel the pain and loss of others. Love is a complex and powerful force. We must become part of the consciousness of love, for it is an entity in itself. Yet it is part of us, and we are part of it. When we are separated from this force we are not total, we are not whole.

Like Scrooge, it is time for all of us to become whole.

## CHAPTER SEVEN

# Dickens' Prophecy for the Twentieth Century

In *A Christmas Carol*, Dickens issued an apocalyptic prophesy to society. It is one that grows in relevance as time passes. Its chilling message was one that was applicable to the nineteenth century world he lived in, and it is infinitely more appropriate for our world, especially as we move into the twenty-first century. If we do not heed his dire warning soon, collectively, we may be in for more catastrophic trouble than we may be able to endure.

At the end of his time with the Ghost of Christmas Present, well into the eleventh hour, Scrooge noticed "something strange" protruding from beneath the spirit's robe. He asked the Ghost if what he saw was "a foot or a claw." The Spirit responded that "It might be a claw." Then he presented to Scrooge what had been hidden: "two children; wretched, abject, frightful, hideous, miserable" (86).

Dickens then provided this detailed description of the children:

> They were a boy and a girl. Yellow, meagre, ragged, scowling, wolfish; but prostrate, too, in their humility. Where graceful youth should have filled their features out, and touched them with its freshest tints, a stale and shriveled hand, like that of age, had pinched, and twisted them, and pulled them into shreds. Where

135

*angels might have sat enthroned, devils lurked, and glared out men-*
*acing. No change, no degradation, no perversion of humanity, in*
*any grade, through all the mysteries of wonderful creation, has*
*monsters half so horrible and dread (86).*

When Scrooge asked the Spirit if they belonged to him, he shot back, "They are Man's" (88).

At this point, we are made aware of Dickens' dire warning concerning society's shameful, life-killing treatment of children. The Spirit stated:

*'This boy is Ignorance. This girl is Want. Beware of them both,*
*and all of their degree, but most of all beware this boy, for on his*
*brow I see that written which is Doom, unless the writing be erased.*
*'Deny it,' cried the Spirit, stretching out its hand toward the city.*
*'Slander those who tell it ye. Admit it for your factious purposes,*
*and make it worse. And bide the end' (88).*

It is possible to narrowly interpret this admonition to relate specifically to Scrooge's transformation, which indirectly resulted in the saving of Tiny Tim's endangered life. By his individual awakening, it can be reasoned, he heeded the Spirit's warning, thus saving this particular boy from the predicted "doom" of death.

To interpret the warning in this limited manner, however, is a monumental mistake. It causes us to miss the main motive that Dickens had in mind when he wrote his gravely serious caveat. With this warning of doom, he was prophesying the devastating destruction that children, especially aggressive boys, would angrily inflict upon the world. This rageful retribution would be exacted upon others after they had grown up and had gained in strength and power. It would be done in a subconscious and generalized response to the horrible neglect and abuse to which they were subjected as defenseless children.

By his inclusion of the phrase "and all of their degree," note that Dickens left absolutely no space for doubt that these violated children did not have to appear to be so obviously damaged as the young ones clinging desperately to the Spirit. In other words, the doom inflicted upon the world could be done at the hands of abused people who do not necessarily appear on the surface to be dysfunctionally impaired.

In the middle of this century, we have already witnessed mass doom brought about by two severely damaged boys who grew up to fulfill this ominous Dickensian prophecy. On the surface, neither of them obviously appeared to be capable of the desperate, barbaric human behavior they eventually perpetrated on society. In fact, both were admired and loved, even considered saviors by countless millions of people they had led in their respective countries. Despite these social accolades, they became the all-too-real manifestations of the horrible, dreadful monsters Dickens forewarned us nothing else in creation could possibly produce. There names were, of course, Joseph Stalin and Adolf Hitler.

In his book, *The Soviet Colossus*, Michael Kort (1985) wrote the following about Stalin's painful youth:

> *Born into poverty, he was the victim of a particularly brutal child-hood, enduring terrible beatings from his drunken father until the latter was killed in a brawl when Joseph was eleven. Despite this, young Joseph excelled in a local church primary school and won a scholarship to a seminary in Tiflis, the Georgian capital. Here he met more mistreatment at the hand of obscurant monks until he rebelled and was expelled in 1899.*

Kort went to say that Stalin eventually became known as a *"kinto,* an insulting Georgian term connoting a combination of street tough and petty thief." He concluded that the adult Stalin ultimately became a man without "many human sensibilities and restraints and was capable of extraordinary cruelty."

Although many of Hitler's biographers tend to exonerate his parents from culpability to varying degrees, there is no doubt that he, like Stalin, was also subjected to a significant amount of damaging childhood abuse. Unlike Stalin, he did not come from poverty. Author Alice Miller (1990) tells us that his elderly father was an extremely harsh authoritarian figure, who showed infinitely more interest in his beekeeping than in his children. Her research discovered that when he wanted his son to come to him, he never called him by name. He would whistle for him, in the manner that a person would whistle for a dog. When he did take time to interact with his obstinate son, invariably it took place only to verbally chastise him, to control his youthful behavior, or to inflict corporal punishment on him.

Young Hitler, who for a short time was a good student who displayed promising talent, wanted to become an artist. When the father absolutely demanded that he become, like himself, a civil servant, his son rebelled. Miller (1990) provided the following quote about Hitler's rebelliousness, given by his younger sister, Paula. The passage was originally from Stierlin's 1976 book, *Adolf Hitler: A Family Perspective*:

> *It was my brother Adolf who especially provoked my father to extreme harshness and who got his due measure of beatings every day. He was a rather nasty little fellow, and all his father's attempts to beat the impudence out of him and make him choose the career of civil servant were in vain.*

Stierlin also wrote of a time when Hitler contemplated running away from home to escape his father's unbending authority. Young Adolf was:

> *[P]lanning to float down the river on a homemade raft and thus flee from his violent father. Just for the very thought of trying to escape, he was nearly beaten to death.*

Even though his father died when Hitler was only fourteen, the neglect, control, and physical abuse inflicted on him by that time had left its damaging mark on him for the rest of his life.

Although some biographers claim that Klara Hitler was a very loving mother to her son, Miller disputes her parental effectiveness:

*[If] Adolf's mother had been a strong woman, she would not—in the child's mind—have allowed him to be exposed to these torments and to constant fear and dread. But because she herself was a total slave to her husband, she was not able to shield her child.*

Hitler's mother, significantly younger than her tyrannical husband, apparently was just as much a victim of his harsh control as were their children.

In response to the terrible physical abuse and neglect both Stalin and Hitler were subjected to as children, they eventually were driven by their damaged psyches to use their intelligent minds in obscenely twisted, bestial ways. First, through the use of rhetoric, empty promises, intimidation, and violent fear tactics, they consolidated their political power bases to gain control over millions of compliant people. Next, they built the two biggest war machines known to the world at that time, accumulating vast arsenals of destructive military weaponry. Finally, they unleased their unresolved childhood rage upon their own countries, the world in general, and on each other in titanic and unspeakably hideous ways. During their reigns of terror, Stalin and Hitler were directly responsible for the barbaric deaths of close to thirty million people.

Although it can be argued that the world will never allow megalomaniacs like Stalin and Hitler to rise to positions of great power ever again, there is cause for concern. Incredibly, despite the fact that both of these barbarians are long gone, their legacies continue to linger. There are hateful people today who honor their sick politics and miss their misanthropic leadership. As Bradshaw (1992) tells us, decades after their demise, Stalin and Hitler continue to make deep psychological connections with the exposed nerve endings of millions of people, especially young ones, who carry dissociated, unresolved childhood rage. These people, too, are frantically searching for visible scapegoats in order to vent their deeply harbored resentments toward the world.

Neo-Nazi groups have surfaced worldwide, especially in unified Germany. In that country, an estimated two thousand ethnic attacks attributed to various factions of these hate groups were reported in 1994 (*Hitler and Stalin*—CBS video). Since the fall of the Soviet Union in the late 1980s, people in Russia have demonstrated increasing nostalgia for Stalin. Many carry pictures of him in marches, yearning for the emergence of a new leader to mimic and restore his violent brand of rigid control and iron-fisted leadership style.

Dickens' prophecy of doom, written upon the brows of boys and unleashed upon society as they grew up, is no less apparent now than it was in the middle part of this century. The world stood by as the Pol Pot regime systematically murdered over one million people in Cambodia during the 1970s. Recently, warring factions in Bosnia have participated in unchecked "ethnic cleansing." Warlords in Africa continue to cause death by torture and mass starvation to millions of people in third-world countries like Somalia and Rwanda. Despite being slowed down by the Gulf War, Saddam Hussein still attempts to wield destructive power in the Middle East. The male-dominated leadership in China continues to ignore human rights for its vast citizenry. Under Chairman Mao's cultural revolution, a reported twenty million people died.

Like their predecessors Stalin and Hitler, the people responsible for these atrocities were no doubt abused, neglected, and traumatized during their childhoods. They, too, are projecting their unresolved rage onto the world. Alice Miller (1991) teaches us that every war that the world has have ever been subjected to has been instigated by aggressive people with significant power bases, intent upon inflicting their unresolved, subconscious childhood angers onto the world in futile attempts to diffuse this rage.

Even when abused "leaders" do not achieve the power to control huge numbers of people, they are still able to wield their domination in more limited, but equally destructive ways. Cult leaders such as Charles Manson, Jim Jones, and David Koresh testify to this truth.

Nuclear families across the world are headed by "little Hitlers," people who over years of uncontested control, systematically brainwash, abuse, and even kill their own spouses and children while administering physical, sexual, and emotional punishment.

Individuals who either aren't interested in or can't muster the power to control ready-made groups, often still perversely kill staggering numbers of people. Until they were caught, killers such as John Wayne Gacy, Ted Bundy, Wayne Williams, Jeffrey Dahmer, and David Berkowitz acted out in this manner for extended periods of time. In recent years, growing numbers of men have walked into post offices, restaurants, schools, trains, and other public places, and in quick outbursts of destructive violence, shot at and killed large numbers of people, including children. Every single one of these killers has a family background which, in some significant way, includes some or all of the following elements: neglect, abandonment, emotional abuse, physical abuse, or sexual abuse.

In the United States, despite our high standard of living and the misguided belief that we treat our children extremely well, child neglect and abuse is shockingly high. In her book *When the Bough Breaks*, Sylvia Ann Hewlett (1992) provides these shamefully revealing current statistics:

1. 20 percent of all children are growing up in poverty
2. 330,000 children are homeless
3. the rate of suicide among adolescents has tripled since 1960
4. 42 percent of fathers fail to see their children in the wake of divorce
5. 27 percent of teenagers drop out of high school

*Newsweek* (January 10, 1994) reported on a recent national study, which found that the number of American child abuse victims has increased an incredible forty percent during a recent six-year period. Experts in the field believe that more than two thousand children die of abuse per year (*St. Louis Post-Dispatch*). Other statistics indicate that one in four of our girls and one in six of our boys have been sexually abused before reaching adulthood. Hewlett tells us that compared to other nations, our "country does not even make it into the top ten on any significant indicator of child welfare." She also cited the results of an index used to measure the overall social health and well-being of America's young; it indicated a seriously alarming decline since 1970.

Increasingly, we are paying the price for neglecting, abandoning, and abusing our children. As a result, they are acting on their rage at younger and younger ages, and in increasingly violent ways. A 1994 survey by *Newsweek* showed that seventeen percent of our youth from ages ten through seventeen have either directly seen or know of someone who has been the victim of firearm violence. The survey also found that American children under age eighteen are almost two and one half times more likely to be killed by guns than they were less than a decade ago.

Gang organization has spread across our violence-worshipping, gun-saturated culture; every major American city reports gang-related deaths in a numbingly regular basis. Lost youth are joining gangs in a desperate search for family. In a February 1994 National Public Radio report by Ira Glass, one interviewed gang member stated he joined because the members swore they would die for him, and that he would die for them. He ended by saying that no one in his family ever showed that much love to him or cared that much about him.

Through our ego-driven neglect, abandonment, and abuse of children, and in spite of our enormous resources to rectify this situation, the United States has become a lethal breeding ground, producing millions of children identified by Dickens as "Ignorance" and "Want." In the process, we are dooming them, we are dooming ourselves, and we are dooming our collective future. Untold numbers of these lost children have already grown up: they have stopped caring, they are full of rage, and they are currently involved in criminal activities.

They are taking their anger out on each other and they are taking it out on society. Unless we stop denying the reality of this situation, wake up, and deal with it effectively, millions of others will continue to grow up in neglect, abandonment, and abuse. They, too, will deny their childhood pain, become more and more angry as they grow in strength and power, and manifest the same criminal behavior.

In *Banished Knowledge*, Alice Miller (1988) tells of a mid-1980s interview she participated in on National Public Radio. She stated the following concerning the connections among childhood abuse, denial, and criminal behavior:

> *Although my interviewer had difficulty accepting the mechanism of denial as an explanation for crime, she told me that statistics confirmed my statements. Those statistics showed that ninety percent of inmates in American prisons had been abused as children. I told her that I was convinced that it was not ninety but a full one hundred percent. It was simply that the remaining ten percent were not yet able to admit it: They were not merely repressing their feelings, but also denying the facts.*

Stettbacher (1991), like Dickens in the last century, recently wrote the following explanation and warning about neglected and abused children:

> *Criminality is a perversion of the need for respect. Perverted behavior toward society, others, and life in general is the result of this nonrespect. If parents fail to respect and satisfy their children's needs, their sons and daughters will later transfer their claim to other people and institutions. Using violence or manipulation they will attempt to force the world at large to respect and satisfy their, by now perverted, needs.*

By nature, children are totally vulnerable. When they are subjected to mistreatment by the very people they desperately depend on to provide them with the respect (unconditional love) that Stettbacher spoke of, they have no recourse but to powerlessly accept this fate. To survive the reality of this monumental loss, they must consciously deny it to themselves and others. Despite this denial, they are severely damaged by this loss. They then spend the rest of their lives blindly searching for ways to fill this void, or what Bradshaw (1988) calls the "holes in their souls." They spend the rest of their lives contending with the painful ramifications and subconscious after-shocks of this loss.

A variety of addictive substances are often used in an attempt to manage this ever-present pain. Alcohol and illegal drugs are ingested to escape into a mental state where the pain is temporarily anesthetized. Cigarettes are used to suppress a wide variety of unpleasant bodily sensations  in an attempt to micromanage them. Sex and gambling addictions take root to create excitement where chronic boredom rules. Food is either compulsively overeaten to quell psychic pain, or obsessively avoided to create the illusion of control. Workaholism occurs to completely occupy the mind, in an attempt to avoid feeling the angst of life. Each one of these pain-killing, life-avoiding addictions eventually exacts its own uniquely damaging price.

In a search for unconditional love, some people, especially females, often enter into a lifelong pattern of victimization. Through a combination of nature and nurture, women have not been nearly as aggressive as men in lashing out in rage at society. Instead, in a search for respect, they often compulsively and repetitively entangle themselves in highly dysfunctional relationships with men who do carry this rage. Their codependent enmeshment with them never leads to the love and respect they were deprived of as girls. Ultimately, they end up being abandoned, neglected, or abused in the same ways they were as children.

Other people, especially aggressive males, in a vain attempt to demand the respect and love they were denied while growing up, eventually turn to the use of the very same violence and control tactics over others that they were subjected to in their youths. It never works; there is no way to force respect from others, and it never successfully fills the painful void created in childhood. How paradoxical that Hitler and Stalin, who hated their violent fathers, ended up using even more brutal forms of violence than they did, killing millions upon millions of innocent people in their futile searches for security.

Dickens was absolutely correct when he wrote that our children's lives should be filled with grace. Instead, he told us, they have had them "pulled into shreds" by "a stale and shriveled hand." This is the hand of neglect and abandonment, that pushes our children away when they crave attention. This is the hand of abuse, clenched in hate, that physically violates our children in service to unresolved childhood anger. This is the hand of constriction, that squeezes the spiritual life-force energy out of our children, causing it to trickle rather than to flow unfettered. This is the hand of evil enthronement, that ensconces lurking, glaring, menacing devils in our children, where angels of light and love should flourish. This is, indeed, our collective hand of Doom.

We had all better wake up to this reality. It is time to turn ourselves and our children around. There is a lot of painful work that needs to be accomplished—right here, and right now.

## CHAPTER EIGHT

# Dickens' Plan for a Twenty-first Century Awakening

Over 150 years ago, Dickens warned us of the consequences we would pay for the neglect, abandonment, and abuse of our children. It is time we heed his warning, stop paying "factious" lip-service to this reality, and wake up, or in his words, "bide the end." Some say it is too late to change the world, that the problems we have are far too complicated, and have completely given up. It is NOT too late for us to wake up from denial, cynicism, and social impotence. If enough people stop denying this possibility, enter into the process necessary to permanently alter their lives and the ultimate fate of the world, a critical mass will be achieved. Miracles will really begin to occur.

Through his character Ebenezer Scrooge, Dickens provided the essential blueprint for this psychospiritual transformation. While most people may not be able to enter into the change situation the way Scrooge did, and while it may take considerably longer than one night's hard work, Dickens did provide all of the necessary elements required to evolve into spiritual beings. Out of the mid-nineteenth century comes the plan for us to quite literally transform the world as we approach the twenty-first century. It was always there; we just couldn't see it.

The first thing that absolutely must occur in order to begin this process is for us to stop running away from our individual problems. In the book *Power through Constructive Thinking*, Emmet Fox (1990) says the following:

> *This running away from one's problems is probably the most futile thing in the whole world, for the simple reason that all your problems are really in your own consciousness and, your consciousness being the essential You, it is not possible to run from it. It does not make the slightest difference how fast you run, or how far you get; you will have to stop running some time, and when you do stop, there you will find your problems, all lined up waiting for you. Having brought your consciousness—that is, yourself—along, you will naturally have brought your problems along too, unless and until you have solved them—in consciousness.*

Like most people, Scrooge futilely attempted to run from his problems for most of his life, and almost "succeeded." Fortunately, he did not allow himself to get away with it. We need to follow his example.

Scrooge's mind used his Christmas Eve interactions with the charitable solicitors and his nephew Fred as joint catalysts to surface long-repressed memories and unresolved feelings about two very important people in his life: his dysfunctional "twin," Marley, and his loving sister, Fan. Marley's serendipitous reintroduction into Scrooge's consciousness served later that night to bring to light the undeniable truth of his own desperately wretched state. Fred's consistent, loving demeanor caused his mother's memory to reenter Scrooge's preconscious mind; later that night, she viscerally emerged into his conscious mind, causing him to reexperience her unconditional love and courageous advocacy for him during his horrid childhood.

The synchronistic reentry of these polar opposite people into Scrooge's mind, and all that they represented, created the conditions necessary for him to experience a late mid-life emotional crisis. The associated stress, coupled with his particular background, triggered the onset of his unique "mixed motif" near-death experience and alien encounter. During his psychospiritual therapy process, which can also legitimately be described as his internal mythological hero's journey, he courageously:

1. faced the parental childhood abandonment memories that were repressed for so long
2. allowed himself to feel the intense pain associated with this parental abandonment
3. realized his dysfunctional treatment toward others and how he was perceived by those he abused
4. opened up, like Christ, at the heart level in loving compassion for the pain of others
5. came to terms with his own mortality by directly confronting death
6. came to terms with his fundamental aloneness in the world
7. prayed for the first time

As a result of this psychospiritual work, pent-up kundalini life-force energy, suppressed since infancy, returned to his physical system. The psychobiological transformation he underwent altered his life forever; upon his awakening, he joyfully and lovingly participated with all of mankind for the duration of his life.

# Dickens' Elements of Psychospiritual Awakening

## Face Long-Repressed Childhood Abandonment, Neglect, and Abuse

Everything that Scrooge eventually experienced was predicated upon his initial ability to bring vital subconscious information into the light of consciousness. Emmet Fox wrote that "In the Bible, the heart usually stands for what we call the subconscious mind, and it is our subconscious mentality that we have to redeem and purify." He is telling us that in order to open up at the heart, it is imperative to excavate and deal with the information buried deeply in the subconscious.

As has been clearly shown, the subconscious mind contains all of the unresolved pain from childhood. In an attempt to cope, the subconscious develops its own powerful methods and defense mechanisms to suppress this pain. These solutions, however, never eradicate the pain. In *Thou Shalt Not Be Aware*, Miller (1990) states:

> *Children only seem to forget what has been done to them, for they have a photographic memory in the unconscious, and it has been demonstrated that under certain conditions this memory can be reactivated. If these conditions are not present, however, if the crucial traumas are forgotten and childhood remains highly idealized, then there is often the danger that as adults these people will torment others or themselves the same way they were once tormented— without their even remembering the past.*

It is our job to seek out the conditions to bring these painful subconscious memories to the surface. This is the first step that must be taken in order to avoid continued torment of others or ourselves. It is time to stop denying the existence of these memories. It is time to stop protecting our parents by hiding behind the attitude that it is morally wrong and dishonorable for us to besmirch them by "blaming" them for our problems. It is time to stop denying the connection between that past pain and our present problems. The linkage is undeniable. The more it is denied, the more it affects our lives in dysfunctional ways.

We should never uncover these painful truths with the intent to hurt or change parents. Hurting them with this information or attempting to change them now does absolutely nothing to change the dysfunctional pitch of our lives. Furthermore, it does not matter if what they did was done intentionally or unintentionally. Parents rarely set out to intentionally hurt their children. Simply, we take this courageous step to clearly understand that what they did or didn't do, for whatever reason, has had a continuing dysfunctional effect upon us, and that our lives are being adversely affected to this day, all these years later.

It is our sole responsibility to face the truth about our pasts as the necessary first step needed to freely get on with our lives. We do this to bring this submerged pain to light, to liberate ourselves from its unconscious control. We do this to take direct control of it. We do this to free ourselves so that we can be in the best possible position to begin our vital psychospiritual awakening. We do this so that we can consciously choose not to pass this pain on to our children as part of a vicious unconscious cycle termed the "multigenerational transmission of dysfunction." We do this to stop passing the buck.

## Feel the Pain Associated with Parental Neglect, Abandonment, and Abuse

Once we have allowed ourselves to bring these painful childhood memories to the surface, it is imperative to grieve them. Many, many people get stuck here. It is not enough to develop just a cerebral understanding; it is important to directly reconnect with the full range of human emotions associated with this pain. It is not weak to allow yourself to feel and express your feelings. Rather, it is an extraordinarily powerful thing to do. We need to realize that grief work allows us to truly let go of the past. When we deny we were hurt, we only guarantee ourselves the continued existence of the painful past upon our present lives. When we accept it and grieve it, we finally let go of it.

As a group, men generally have had trouble expressing emotions, especially those they consider weak, or feminine. When will men finally allow themselves to realize that God gave them tear ducts, too, and that it is perfectly acceptable to cry and to grieve for the hurt little boys within them? Scrooge finally sobbed and cried for the abandoned, totally isolated boy within him. When will men realize that parental deprivation of vital childhood needs, whether to a boy or girl child, causes deep hurt, and that denying this painful reality and projecting toughness to mask its current existence in their lives accomplishes nothing constructive?

Joseph Stalin tried to deny and mask his pain. Kort (1989) tells us that his real family name was Dzhugashvili. The meaning of Stalin, the surname he eventually gave himself, translates to "man of steel." Undoubtedly, he gave himself this social identity in response to the severe beatings he repeatedly took as a child from his alcoholic, violent father. He took this stalwart name to "steel" himself from further pain, to prove his toughness to the world. How different the world might be today if he had been able to directly feel and grieve his horrid childhood pain. Without a doubt, he would not have turned into the violent monster he ultimately became.

Through Scrooge, Dickens let us know that it is essential for us to bring this painful unconscious information into consciousness and to emotionally grieve it. Once Scrooge finally did this, he was cleared and in position to move forward in his psychospiritual recovery. He did not waste time castigating his father for abandoning and psychically wounding him. He simply recognized the truth of it, grieved it, and let go of it. By doing this work, he did what Fox stated is essential for all of us to accomplish:

> [T]o purify and re-educate the subconscious from the errors which have accumulated there in the course of time. If we do this work faithfully, we shall sooner or later arrive at the point where we really have a pure heart in the full Bible sense, and then we shall see God.

## Realize and Attempt to Make Amends for Our Damaging Treatment of Others and Ourselves

Dickens included scene after scene in *A Christmas Carol* to clearly indicate that Scrooge's adult defense mechanisms, which arose in response to the unresolved pain from his damaged childhood, ultimately served only to hurt himself and others in the present. Scrooge realized that he lost the love of his life, Belle, because of them. In addition, he saw how he was hurting the entire Cratchit family, Tiny Tim in particular. He recognized how he had completely shunned his sister's only son, Fred, and Fred's wife. He came to understand that he had totally neglected his responsibilities toward those anonymous people less fortunate than himself.

Through these scenes, Dickens is clearly indicating that we all need to take a fearless moral inventory of our behavior toward others. He wants us to fully realize the connection between our dysfunctional childhoods and the defense mechanisms we use in the present, applied in a futile and ineffective effort to protect ourselves from further rejection and hurts. He wants us to realize that these fear-driven mechanisms of the ego only serve to guarantee the continuation of our submerged pain and to cut us off from any possible meaningful connections with our "fellow travelers" on the planet.

By having Scrooge demonstrate the courage to risk rejection in an effort to make amends with the charitable solicitor he encountered on Christmas morning, and with Fred and his wife later that same day, Dickens is indicating that we all need to take these kinds of risks in the effort to connect meaningfully with others. Although these attempts do not always work out, at least we can say that we tried. No one can make other people let go of their defense mechanisms until they are ready.

Marianne Williamson tells us that *The Course in Miracles* also teaches this important truth. She states that if we do not react negatively to rejections, we engage in win-win behavior. By doing so, we help ourselves on our own spiritual paths of enlightenment, and we provide the rejecters with the valuable learning experience that retaliation is not necessary. By doing so, we lovingly help to put them in position to eventually realize that defense mechanisms are unnecessary. It puts them in position to drop them and to open up at the heart level when they are ready.

Dickens also showed us that we need to treat ourselves better after we come to this realization. Scrooge clearly came to realize that in response to his childhood abandonment experience, he kept inflicting the same conditions upon himself that he was forced to endure in his childhood. As we know, despite his vast monetary wealth, he ate little, he isolated himself from others, and he kept his environment cold and dark. After his transformation, however, he immediately set about the task of connecting with others, dealing with food in much healthier ways, and bringing light and warmth into his personal environments. And he learned to laugh.

Dickens is telling us that we should stop punishing ourselves and learn to take care of our personal needs. We need to take the time to enjoy the company of others. We must learn to find quiet time just for us. We must work to drop our addictive behaviors. We need to exercise and/or take part in physical activities. We need to fill our personal environments with a variety of things that nurture the development of our souls and bring beauty into our lives. We need to eat healthy, quality foods. We need to laugh. In short, we need to treat ourselves well, just as we need to treat others well.

## Open Up with Compassion at the Heart Level

Nothing Scrooge did was more important than to open up compassionately at the heart level. Dickens is telling us that this element is vital on the path to spiritual awakening. This was achieved after Scrooge stopped denying the reality of his own childhood wounds. Because of that, he was no longer able to continue denying the childhood wounds of Tiny Tim, and the fact that he was contributing to them.

Once this compassionate realization of shared suffering occurred, Scrooge died to his ego-driven self and achieved what Joseph Campbell (Flowers, 1988) called spiritual rebirth at the level of the heart, which he also referred to as virgin birth. It was with clear intention that Dickens had Scrooge achieve this spiritual birth precisely on the day of Jesus's physical birth. And it was with full intention that Dickens connected the painful death of Scrooge's ego-driven self with Christ's excruciating death by crucifixion on the cross, which intersects at the level of the heart. Both sufferings were necessary before resurrection was possible.

Like Christ's resurrection, Scrooge's rebirth ultimately resulted in his performing "good deeds springing from the wound, to sow the world with life immortal" (100). His heart opened wide and he found Christ within him.

Dickens is telling us that to achieve Christ-consciousness, we all need to compassionately identify with the suffering and wounds of others. He is clearly telling us that this is not possible until we have deeply connected with our own suffering and wounds. The denial of our own pain always leads to the denial of the pain of others. Conversely, allowing ourselves to feel our pain opens the path for us to empathize compassionately with the pain of others.

Jesus was criticized for spending his life in the company of many people considered to be social "undesirables." He did not waste time judging them, criticizing them, or condemning them for their various life circumstances, or for their past or present dysfunctional behaviors. According to Stephen Mitchell (1991), He was able to recognize that:

> [W]e were all born between urine and feces, and even in the most degraded among us, the innocence we once came from is still somewhere alive. Beneath all our pain and delusions and unsatisfied desires, it shines with its pristine light, as it did in the beginning.

Jesus did not fixate on their fear-driven egos; instead, He focused on the latent good buried deeply within them. His compassion gave them the opportunity to also realize the love of which they were capable. We all need to follow His lead.

## Come to Terms with Personal Mortality

Despite the fact that Scrooge initially "longed to do it" (100), he could not bring himself to look directly at his own corpse. When the Ghost of the Future once more directed him to look, he stated "I have not the power, Spirit. I have not the power" (101). Even after being taken to his grave, and made to read his own name carved in the stone, he still maintained his denial. Finally, after the Spirit kept up his relentless pressure, Scrooge broke down and came to terms with his own mortality.

By these scenes, Dickens is telling us that, like Scrooge, we must also confront our own mortality. He is letting us know in no uncertain terms that in order to live, we must urgently confront the absolute certainty and reality of our own deaths. In the play *Our Town*, Thornton Wilder sums up what happens to people who do not wake up to the reality of death. Simon Stimson angrily says the following to the dead Emily, after her disappointing visit from life, back to her grave:

> *'Yes, now you know. Now you know! That's what it was like to be alive. To move about in a cloud of ignorance; to go up and down trampling on the feelings of those...of those about you. To spend and waste time as though you had a million years. To be always at the mercy of one self-centered passion, or another. Now you know—that's the happy existence you wanted to go back to. Ignorance and blindness'* (Miller, James E., Duenas-Gonzalez, Roseann, Millet, Nancy C., 1982).

In *Awareness*, Anthony deMello (1990) suggests the following exercise to achieve this essential realization:

> *I've often said to people that the way to really live is to die. The passport to living is to imagine yourself in your grave. Imagine that you're lying in your coffin. Any posture you like. In India we put them in cross-legged. Sometimes they're carried that way to the burning ground. Sometimes, though, they're lying flat. So imagine you're lying flat and you're dead. Now look at your problems from that viewpoint. Changes everything, doesn't it?*

In his mixed motif experience, Scrooge was able to do this. It was excruciating, difficult work. He tried to deny it, but he did it. We all need to follow his example. Time is wasting. As deMello says, "Death is resurrection."

## Realize Fundamental Aloneness in the World

Scrooge desperately clutched at the Ghost of the Future as he pleaded to have his fate reversed. Dickens wrote:

> *In his agony he caught the spectral hand. It sought to free itself, but he was strong in his entreaty, and detained it. The Spirit, stronger yet, repulsed him (110).*

No matter how intensely Scrooge attempted to hold on, it was not to be. The Spirit forced him into aloneness.

Dickens is telling us that we need to face the fact that psychologically and emotionally, we are fundamentally alone in the world. No matter how hard we try to cling either to our defense mechanisms or to other people in the delusion that they can save us from our fates, it does not work—they can't. Our parents can't save us, our siblings can't save us, our spouses can't save us, our children can't save us, our friends can't save us. Only we can save ourselves. This part of the journey into spiritual transformation makes us come to the stark realization that, ultimately, we must learn to stand on our own two feet.

By coming to terms with aloneness, it guarantees that we will never be lonely again. Once again, deMello (1990) captures the sense of what we need to achieve:

> *What I really enjoy is not you; it's something that's greater than both you and me. It is something that I discovered, a kind of symphony, a kind of orchestra that plays one melody in your presence, but when you depart, the orchestra doesn't stop. When I meet someone else, it plays another melody, which is also very delightful. And when I'm alone, it continues to play. There's a great repertoire and it never ceases to play.*

When we come to aloneness, we are finally connected to the great symphony of the universe. We can hear the sound of God everywhere.

## Begin to Pray

Scrooge was not totally transformed until after he prayed. When he finally prayed, his fate was immediately reversed, and he returned to the world of reality, psychobiologically altered from that point forward. He no longer merely survived, living dysfunctionally out of his lower three animal chakras. He had become a spiritualized being, his body entirely infused with precious life-force energy.

Dickens is letting us know that through prayer, all things are possible. Prayer is the free-will choice to turn to what Emmet Fox calls the Indwelling Christ. This turning inward acknowledges the existence of this powerful Presence. It is done with the realization that by ourselves, we cannot totally overcome our fear-driven egos. By letting go—and letting God direct our lives—we call forth the power of love into our lives. It awaits to be called into action.

In *The Thunder of Silence* (1993), mystic Joel S. Goldsmith captures the essential nature of effective prayer. No matter what magnitude the problem in life we are facing, he suggests this type of prayer, immediately followed by silent meditation:

> *'Not my will but Thine be done in me. Thou art the all-knowing, infinite wisdom and intelligence of the universe, and I surrender myself—I surrender my hopes and desires, my fears, my aims and ambitions—into Thy hand.'*

He concludes be saying that if we petition in this manner, "we make our prayer an emptiness of self." With this action, we begin the spiritual process of replacing the false self with the true Self.

By working on developing these seven Dickensian elements, it is possible to transform our lives. When each one of us finally decides to undertake this glorious task, the world will change. Children will no longer have Ignorance and Want stamped upon their foreheads. We will no longer be at the brink of doom. Marianne Williamson (1992) states that:

> We can all contribute to a global rebirth to the extent that we allow ourselves to be awakened from our own personal dream of separation and guilt, to release our own past and accept a new life in the present.

It is time that we begin to properly honor Scrooge for accomplishing this heroic goal. It is time for us to wake up from our own dysfunctional dreams and see the light.

PART TWO

# A Christmas Carol

## CHARLES DICKENS

# A Christmas Carol

## CONTENTS

# A CHRISTMAS CAROL.

---

## STAVE ONE.

### MARLEY'S GHOST.

MARLEY was dead: to begin with. There is no doubt whatever about that. The register of his burial was signed by the clergyman, the clerk, the undertaker, and the chief mourner. Scrooge signed it. And Scrooge's name was good upon Change, for anything he chose to put his hand to.

Old Marley was as dead as a door-nail.

Mind! I don't mean to say that I know, of my own knowledge, what there is particularly dead about a door-nail. I might have been inclined, myself, to regard a coffin-nail as the deadest piece of ironmongery in the trade. But the wisdom of our ancestors is in the simile; and my unhallowed hands shall not disturb it, or the Country's done for. You will therefore permit me to repeat, emphatically, that Marley was as dead as a door-nail.

Scrooge knew he was dead? Of course he did. How could it be otherwise? Scrooge and he were partners for

I don't know how many years. Scrooge was his sole executor, his sole administrator, his sole assign, his sole residuary legatee, his sole friend, and sole mourner. And even Scrooge was not so dreadfully cut up by the sad event, but that he was an excellent man of business on the very day of the funeral, and solemnised it with an undoubted bargain.

The mention of Marley's funeral brings me back to the point I started from. There is no doubt that Marley was dead. This must be distinctly understood, or nothing wonderful can come of the story I am going to relate. If we were not perfectly convinced that Hamlet's Father died before the play began, there would be nothing more remarkable in his taking a stroll at night, in an easterly wind, upon his own ramparts, than there would be in any other middle-aged gentleman rashly turning out after dark in a breezy spot—say Saint Paul's Churchyard for instance— literally to astonish his son's weak mind.

Scrooge never painted out Old Marley's name. There it stood, years afterwards, above the warehouse door: Scrooge and Marley. The firm was known as Scrooge and Marley. Sometimes people new to the business called Scrooge Scrooge, and sometimes Marley, but he answered to both names. It was all the same to him.

Oh! But he was a tight-fisted hand at the grindstone, Scrooge! a squeezing, wrenching, grasping, scraping, clutching, covetous, old sinner! Hard and sharp as flint, from which no steel had ever struck out generous fire; secret, and self-contained, and solitary as an oyster. The cold within him froze his old features, nipped his pointed nose, shrivelled his cheek, stiffened his gait; made his eyes red, his thin lips blue; and spoke out shrewdly in his grating voice. A frosty rime was on his head, and on his eyebrows, and his wiry chin. He carried his own low temperature always about with him; he iced his office in the dogdays; and didn't thaw it one degree at Christmas.

External heat and cold had little influence on Scrooge. No warmth could warm, no wintry weather chill him. No wind that blew was bitterer than he, no falling snow was more intent upon its purpose, no pelting rain less open to entreaty. Foul weather didn't know where to have him. The heaviest rain, and snow, and hail, and sleet, could boast of the advantage over him in only one respect. They often "came down" handsomely, and Scrooge never did.

Nobody ever stopped him in the street to say, with gladsome looks, "My dear Scrooge, how are you? When will you come to see me?" No beggars implored him to bestow a trifle, no children asked him what it was o'clock, no man or woman ever once in all his life inquired the way to such and such a place, of Scrooge. Even the blind men's dogs appeared to know him; and when they saw him coming on, would tug their owners into doorways and up courts; and then would wag their tails as though they said, "No eye at all is better than an evil eye, dark master!"

But what did Scrooge care! It was the very thing he liked. To edge his way along the crowded paths of life, warning all human sympathy to keep its distance, was what the knowing ones call "nuts" to Scrooge.

Once upon a time—of all the good days in the year, on Christmas Eve—old Scrooge sat busy in his counting-house. It was cold, bleak, biting weather: foggy withal: and he could hear the people in the court outside, go wheezing up and down, beating their hands upon their breasts, and stamping their feet upon the pavement stones to warm them. The city clocks had only just gone three, but it was quite dark already—it had not been light all day—and candles were flaring in the windows of the neighbouring offices, like ruddy smears upon the palpable brown air. The fog came pouring in at every chink and keyhole, and was so dense without, that although the court was of the narrowest, the houses opposite were mere phantoms. To see the dingy cloud come drooping down, obscuring everything, one might have thought that Nature lived hard by, and was brewing on a large scale.

The door of Scrooge's counting-house was open that he might keep his eye upon his clerk, who in a dismal little cell beyond, a sort of tank, was copying letters. Scrooge had a very small fire, but the clerk's fire was so very much smaller that it looked like one coal. But he couldn't replenish it, for Scrooge kept the coal-box in his own room; and so surely as the clerk came in with the shovel, the master predicted that it would be necessary for them to part. Wherefore the clerk put on his white comforter, and tried to warm himself at the candle; in which effort, not being a man of a strong imagination, he failed.

"A merry Christmas, uncle! God save you!" cried a cheerful voice. It was the voice of Scrooge's nephew, who came upon him so quickly that this was the first intimation he had of his approach.

"Bah!" said Scrooge, "Humbug!"

He had so heated himself with rapid walking in the fog and frost, this nephew of Scrooge's, that he was all in a glow; his face was ruddy and handsome; his eyes sparkled, and his breath smoked again.

"Christmas a humbug, uncle!" said Scrooge's nephew. "You mean that, I am sure?"

"I do," said Scrooge. "Merry Christmas! What right have you to be merry? What reason have you to be merry? You're poor enough."

"Come, then," returned the nephew gaily. "What right have you to be dismal? What reason have you to be morose? You're rich enough."

Scrooge having no better answer ready on the spur of the moment, said "Bah!" again; and followed it up with "Humbug."

"Don't be cross, uncle!" said the nephew.

"What else can I be," returned the uncle, "when I live in such a world of fools as this? Merry Christmas! Out upon merry Christmas! What's Christmas time to you but a time for paying bills without money; a time for finding yourself a year older, but not an hour richer; a time for balancing your books and having every item in 'em through a round dozen of months presented dead against you? If I could work my will," said Scrooge indignantly, "every idiot who goes about with 'Merry Christmas' on his lips, should be boiled with his own pudding, and buried with a stake of holly through his heart. He should!"

"Uncle!" pleaded the nephew.

"Nephew!" returned the uncle sternly, "keep Christmas in your own way, and let me keep it in mine."

"Keep it!" repeated Scrooge's nephew. "But you don't keep it."

"Let me leave it alone, then," said Scrooge. "Much good may it do you! Much good it has ever done you!"

"There are many things from which I might have derived good, by which I have not profited, I dare say," returned the nephew. "Christmas among the rest. But I am sure I have always thought of Christmas time, when it has come round—apart from the veneration due to its sacred name and origin, if anything belonging to it can be apart from that—as a good time; a kind, forgiving, charitable, pleasant time: the only time I know of, in the long calendar of the year, when men and women seem by one consent to open their shut-up hearts freely, and to think of people below them as if they really were fellow-passengers to the grave, and not another race of creatures bound on other journeys. And therefore, uncle, though it has never put a scrap of gold or silver in my pocket, I believe that it has done me good, and will do me good; and I say, God bless it!"

The clerk in the Tank involuntarily applauded. Becoming immediately sensible of the impropriety, he poked the fire, and extinguished the last frail spark for ever.

"Let me hear another sound from you," said Scrooge, "and you'll keep your Christmas by losing your situation! You're quite a powerful speaker, sir," he added, turning to his nephew. "I wonder you go into Parliament."

"Don't be angry, uncle. Come! Dine with us tomorrow."

Scrooge said that he would see him—yes, indeed he did. He went the whole length of the expression, and said that he would see him in that extremity first.

"But why?" cried Scrooge's nephew. "Why?"

"Why did you get married?" said Scrooge.

"Because I fell in love."

"Because you fell in love!" growled Scrooge, as if that were the only one thing in the world more ridiculous than a merry Christmas. "Good afternoon!"

"Nay, uncle, but you never came to see me before that happened. Why give it as a reason for not coming now?"

"Good afternoon," said Scrooge.

"I want nothing from you; I ask nothing of you; why cannot we be friends?"

"Good afternoon," said Scrooge.

"I am sorry, with all my heart, to find you so resolute. We have never had any quarrel, to which I have been a party. But I have made the trial in homage to Christmas, and I'll keep my Christmas humour to the last. So A Merry Christmas, uncle!"

"Good afternoon," said Scrooge.

"And a Happy New Year!"

"Good afternoon," said Scrooge.

His nephew left the room without an angry word, notwithstanding. He stopped at the outer door to bestow the greetings of the season on the clerk, who cold as he was, was warmer than Scrooge; for he returned them cordially.

"There's another fellow," muttered Scrooge; who overheard him: "my clerk, with fifteen shillings a week, and a wife and family, talking about a merry Christmas. I'll retire to Bedlam."

This lunatic, in letting Scrooge's nephew out, had let two other people in. They were portly gentlemen, pleasant to behold, and now stood, with their hats off, in Scrooge's office. They had books and papers in their hands, and bowed to him.

"Scrooge and Marley's, I believe," said one of the gentlemen, referring to his list. "Have I the pleasure of addressing Mr. Scrooge, or Mr. Marley?"

"Mr. Marley has been dead these seven years," Scrooge replied. "He died seven years ago, this very night."

"We have no doubt his liberality is well represented by his surviving partner," said the gentleman, presenting his credentials.

It certainly was; for they had been two kindred spirits. At the ominous word "liberality," Scrooge frowned, and shook his head, and handed the credentials back.

"At this festive season of the year, Mr. Scrooge," said the gentleman, taking up a pen, "it is more than usually desirable that we should make some slight provision for the Poor and Destitute, who suffer greatly at the present time. Many thousands are in want of common necessaries; hundreds of thousands are in want of common comforts, sir."

"Are there no prisons?" asked Scrooge.

"Plenty of prisons," said the gentleman, laying down the pen again.

"And the Union workhouses?" demanded Scrooge. "Are they still in operation?"

"They are. Still," returned the gentleman, "I wish I could say they were not."

"The Treadmill and the Poor Law are in full vigour, then?" said Scrooge.

"Both very busy, sir."

"Oh! I was afraid, from what you said at first, that something had occurred to stop them in their useful course," said Scrooge. "I'm very glad to hear it."

"Under the impression that they scarcely furnish Christian cheer of mind or body to the multitude," returned the gentleman, "a few of us are endeavouring to raise a fund to buy the Poor some meat and drink, and means of warmth. We choose this time, because it is a time, of all others, when Want is keenly felt, and Abundance rejoices. What shall I put you down for?"

"Nothing!" Scrooge replied.

"You wish to be anonymous?"

"I wish to be left alone," said Scrooge. "Since you ask me what I wish, gentlemen, that is my answer. I don't make merry myself at Christmas and I can't afford to make idle people merry. I help to support the establishments I have mentioned—they cost enough; and those who are badly off must go there."

"Many can't go there; and many would rather die."

"If they would rather die," said Scrooge, "they had better do it, and decrease the surplus population. Besides—excuse me—I know that."

"But you might know it," observed the gentleman.

"It's not my business," Scrooge returned. "It's enough for a man to understand his own business, and not to interfere with other people's. Mine occupies me constantly. Good afternoon, gentlemen!"

Seeing clearly that it would be useless to pursue their

point, the gentlemen withdrew. Scrooge returned to his labours with an improved opinion of himself, and in a more facetious temper than was usual with him.

Meanwhile the fog and darkness thickened so, that people ran about with flaring links, proffering their services to go before horses in carriages, and conduct them on their way. The ancient tower of a church, whose gruff old bell was always peeping slily down at Scrooge out of a Gothic window in the wall, became invisible, and struck the hours and quarters in the clouds, with tremulous vibrations afterwards as if its teeth were chattering in its frozen head up there. The cold became intense. In the main street at the corner of the court, some labourers were repairing the gas-pipes, and had lighted a great fire in a brazier, round which a party of ragged men and boys were gathered: warming their hands and winking their eyes before the blaze in rapture. The water-plug being left in solitude, its overflowing sullenly congealed, and turned to misanthropic ice. The brightness of the shops where holly sprigs and berries crackled in the lamp heat of the windows, made pale faces ruddy as they passed. Poulterers' and grocers' trades became a splendid joke; a glorious pageant, with which it was next to impossible to believe that such dull principles as bargain and sale had anything to do. The Lord Mayor, in the stronghold of the mighty Mansion House, gave orders to his fifty cooks and butlers to keep Christmas as a Lord Mayor's household should; and even the little tailor, whom he had fined five shillings on the previous Monday for being drunk and bloodthirsty in the streets, stirred up to-morrow's pudding in his garret, while his lean wife and the baby sallied out to buy the beef.

Foggier yet, and colder! Piercing, searching, biting cold. If the good Saint Dunstan had but nipped the Evil Spirit's nose with a touch of such weather as that, instead of using his familiar weapons, then indeed he would have roared to lusty purpose. The owner of one scant young nose, gnawed and mumbled by the hungry cold as bones are gnawed by dogs, stooped down at Scrooge's keyhole to regale him with a Christmas carol: but at the first sound of—

"God bless you, merry gentleman! May nothing you dismay!"

Scrooge seized the ruler with such energy of action, that the singer fled in terror, leaving the keyhole to the fog and even more congenial frost.

At length the hour of shutting up the counting-house arrived. With an ill-will Scrooge dismounted from his stool, and tacitly admitted the fact to the expectant clerk in the Tank, who instantly snuffed his candle out, and put on his hat.

"You'll want all day to-morrow, I suppose?" said Scrooge.

"If quite convenient, sir."

"It's not convenient," said Scrooge, "and it's not fair. If I was to stop half-a-crown for it, you'd think yourself ill-used, I'll be bound?"

The clerk smiled faintly.

"And yet," said Scrooge, "you think me ill-used, when I pay a day's wages for no work."

The clerk observed that it was only once a year.

"A poor excuse for picking a man's pocket every twenty-fifth of December!" said Scrooge, buttoning his great-coat to the chin. "But I suppose you must have the whole day. Be here all the earlier next morning."

The clerk promised that he would; and Scrooge walked out with a growl. The office was closed in a twinkling, and the clerk, with the long ends of his white comforter dangling below his waist (for he boasted no great-coat), went down a slide on Cornhill, at the end of a lane of boys, twenty times, in honour of its being Christmas Eve, and then ran home to Camden Town as hard as he could pelt, to play at blindman's-buff.

Scrooge took his melancholy dinner in his usual melancholy tavern; and having read all the newspapers, and beguiled the rest of the evening with his banker's-book, went home to bed. He lived in chambers which had once belonged to his deceased partner. They were a gloomy suite of rooms, in a lowering pile of building up a yard, where it had so little business to be, that one could scarcely help fancying it must have run there when it was a young house, playing at hide-and-seek with other houses, and forgotten the way out again. It was old enough now, and dreary enough, for nobody lived in it but Scrooge, the other rooms being all let out as offices. The yard was so dark that even Scrooge, who knew its every stone, was fain to grope with his hands. The fog and frost so hung about the black old gateway of the house, that it seemed as if the Genius of the Weather sat in mournful meditation on the threshold.

Now, it is a fact, that there was nothing at all particular about the knocker on the door, except that it was very large. It is also a fact, that Scrooge had seen it, night and morning, during his whole residence in that place; also that Scrooge had as little of what is called fancy about him as any man in the city of London, even including—which is a bold word—the corporation, aldermen, and livery. Let it also be borne in mind that Scrooge had not bestowed one thought on Marley, since his last mention of his seven years' dead partner that afternoon. And then let any man explain to me, if he can, how it happened that Scrooge, having his key in the lock of the door, saw in the knocker, without its undergoing any intermediate process of change—not a knocker, but Marley's face.

Marley's face. It was not in impenetrable shadow as the other objects in the yard were, but had a dismal light about it, like a bad lobster in a dark cellar. It was not angry or ferocious, but looked at Scrooge as Marley used to look: with ghostly spectacles turned up on its ghostly forehead. The hair was curiously stirred, as if by breath or hot air; and, though the eyes were wide open, they were perfectly motionless. That, and its livid colour, made it horrible; but its horror seemed to be in spite of the face and beyond its control, rather than a part or its own expression.

As Scrooge looked fixedly at this phenomenon, it was a knocker again.

To say that he was not startled, or that his blood was not conscious of a terrible sensation to which it had been a stranger from infancy, would be untrue. But he put his hand upon the key he had relinquished, turned it sturdily, walked in, and lighted his candle.

He did pause, with a moment's irresolution, before he shut the door; and he did look cautiously behind it first, as if he half-expected to be terrified with the sight of Marley's pigtail sticking out into the hall. But there was nothing on the back of the door, except the screws and nuts that held the knocker on, so he said "Pooh, pooh!" and closed it with a bang.

The sound resounded through the house like thunder. Every room above, and every cask in the wine-merchant's cellars below, appeared to have a separate peal of echoes of its own. Scrooge was not a man to be frightened by echoes. He fastened the door, and walked across the hall, and up the stairs; slowly too: trimming his candle as he went.

You may talk vaguely about driving a coach-and-six up a good old flight of stairs, or through a bad young Act of Parliament; but I mean to say you might have got a hearse up that staircase, and taken it broadwise, with the splinter-bar towards the wall and the door towards the balustrades: and done it easy. There was plenty of width for that, and room to spare; which is perhaps the reason why Scrooge thought he saw a locomotive hearse going on before him in the gloom. Half a dozen gas-lamps out of the street wouldn't have lighted the entry too well, so you may suppose that it was pretty dark with Scrooge's dip.

Up Scrooge went, not caring a button for that. Darkness is cheap, and Scrooge liked it. But before he shut his heavy door, he walked through his rooms to see that all was right. He had just enough recollection of the face to desire to do that.

Sitting-room, bedroom, lumber-room. All as they should be. Nobody under the table, nobody under the sofa; a small fire in the grate; spoon and basin ready; and the little saucepan of gruel (Scrooge had a cold in his head) upon the hob. Nobody under the bed; nobody in the closet; nobody in his dressing-gown, which was hanging up in a suspicious attitude against the wall. Lumber-room as usual. Old fire-guards, old shoes, two fish-baskets, washing-stand on three legs, and a poker.

Quite satisfied, he closed his door, and locked him-self in; double-locked himself in, which was not his cus-tom. Thus secured against surprise, he took off his cra-vat; put on his dressing-gown and slippers, and his nightcap; and sat down before the fire to take his gruel.

It was a very low fire indeed; nothing on such a bit-ter night. He was obliged to sit close to it, and brood

over it, before he could extract the least sensation of
warmth from such a handful of fuel. The fireplace was
an old one, built by some Dutch merchant long ago, and
paved all round with quaint Dutch tiles, designed to
illustrate the Scriptures. There were Cains and Abels,
Pharaohs' daughters; Queens of Sheba, Angelic messen-
gers descending through the air on clouds like feather-
beds, Abrahams, Belshazzars, Apostles putting off to sea
in butter-boats, hundreds of figures to attract his
thoughts—and yet that face of Marley, seven years dead,
came like the ancient Prophet's rod, and swallowed up
the whole. If each smooth tile had been a blank at first,
with power to shape some picture on its surface from the
disjointed fragments of his thoughts, there would have
been a copy of old Marley's head on every one.

"Humbug!" said Scrooge; and walked across the room.

After several turns, he sat down again. As he threw
his head back in the chair, his glance happened to rest
upon a bell, a disused bell, that hung in the room, and
communicated for some purpose now forgotten with a
chamber in the highest story of the building. It was with
great astonishment, and with a strange, inexplicable
dread, that as he looked, he saw this bell begin to swing.
It swung so softly in the outset that it scarcely made a
sound; but soon it rang out loudly, and so did every bell
in the house.

This might have lasted half a minute, or a minute,
but it seemed an hour. The bells ceased as they had

begun, together. They were succeeded by a clanking noise, deep down below; as if some person were dragging a heavy chain over the casks in the wine merchant's cellar. Scrooge then remembered to have heard that ghosts in haunted houses were described as dragging chains.

The cellar-door flew open with a booming sound, and then he heard the noise much louder, on the floors below; then coming up the stairs; then coming straight towards his door.

"It's humbug still!" said Scrooge. "I won't believe it."

His colour changed though, when, without a pause, it came on through the heavy door, and passed into the room before his eyes. Upon its coming in, the dying flame leaped up, as though it cried, "I know him; Marley's Ghost!" and fell again.

The same face: the very same. Marley in his pigtail, usual waistcoat, tights and boots; the tassels on the latter bristling, like his pigtail, and his coat-skirts, and the hair upon his head. The chain he drew was clasped about his middle. It was long, and wound about him like a tail; and it was made (for Scrooge observed it closely) of cash-boxes, keys, padlocks, ledgers, deeds, and heavy purses wrought in steel. His body was transparent; so that Scrooge, observing him, and looking through his waistcoat, could see the two buttons on his coat behind.

Scrooge had often heard it said that Marley had no bowels, but he had never believed it until now.

*Marley's Ghost*

*Mr. Fezziwig's Ball*

*Scrooge's Third Visitor*

*The Last of the Spirits*

No, nor did he believe it even now. Though he looked the phantom through and through, and saw it standing before him; though he felt the chilling influence of its death-cold eyes; and marked the very texture of the folded kerchief bound about its head and chin, which wrapper he had not observed before; he was still incredulous, and fought against his senses.

"How now!" said Scrooge, caustic and cold as ever. "What do you want with me?"

"Much!"—Marley's voice, no doubt about it.

"Who are you?"

"Ask me who I was."

"Who were you then?" said Scrooge, raising his voice. "You're particular, for a shade." He was going to say "to a shade," but substituted this, as more appropriate.

"In life I was your partner, Jacob Marley."

"Can you—can you sit down?" asked Scrooge, looking doubtfully at him.

"I can."

"Do it, then."

Scrooge asked the question, because he didn't know whether a ghost so transparent might find himself in a condition to take a chair; and felt that in the event of its being impossible, it might involve the necessity of an embarrassing explanation. But the ghost sat down on the opposite side of the fireplace, as if he were quite used to it.

"You believe in me," observed the Ghost.

"I," said Scrooge.

"What evidence would you have of my reality beyond that of your senses?"

"I know," said Scrooge.

"Why do you doubt your senses?"

"Because," said Scrooge, "a little thing affects them. A slight disorder of the stomach makes them cheats. You may be an undigested bit of beef, a blot of mustard, a crumb of cheese, a fragment of an underdone potato. There's more of gravy than of grave about you, whatever you are!"

Scrooge was not much in the habit of cracking jokes, nor did he feel, in his heart, by any means waggish then. The truth is, that he tried to be smart, as a means of distracting his own attention, and keeping down his terror; for the spectre's voice disturbed the very marrow in his bones.

To sit, staring at those fixed glazed eyes, in silence for a moment, would play, Scrooge felt, the very deuce with him. There was something very awful, too, in the spectre's being provided with an infernal atmosphere of its own. Scrooge could not feel it himself, but this was clearly the case; for though the Ghost sat perfectly motionless, its hair, and skirts, and tassels, were still agitated as by the hot vapour from an oven.

"You see this toothpick?" said Scrooge, returning quickly to the charge, for the reason just assigned; and wishing, though it were only for a second, to divert the vision's stony gaze from himself.

"I do," replied the Ghost.

"You are not looking at it," said Scrooge.

"But I see it," said the Ghost, "notwithstanding."

"Well!" returned Scrooge, "I have but to swallow this, and be for the rest of my days persecuted by a legion of goblins, all of my own creation. Humbug, I tell you; humbug!"

At this the spirit raised a frightful cry, and shook its chain with such a dismal and appalling noise, that Scrooge held on tight to his chair, to save himself from falling in a swoon. But how much greater was his horror, when the phantom taking off the bandage round its head, as if it were too warm to wear indoors, its lower jaw dropped down upon its breast!

Scrooge fell upon his knees, and clasped his hands before his face.

"Mercy!" he said. "Dreadful apparition, why do you trouble me?"

"Man of the worldly mind!" replied the Ghost, "do you believe in me or not?"

"I do," said Scrooge. "I must. But why do spirits walk the earth, and why do they come to me?"

"It is required of every man," the Ghost returned, "that the spirit within him should walk abroad among his fellowmen, and travel far and wide; and if that spirit goes not forth in life, it is condemned to do so after death. It is doomed to wander through the world—oh, woe is me!—and witness what it cannot share, but might have shared on earth, and turned to happiness!"

Again the spectre raised a cry, and shook its chain and wrung its shadowy hands.

"You are fettered," said Scrooge, trembling. "Tell me why?"

"I wear the chain I forged in life," replied the Ghost. "I made it link by link, and yard by yard; I girded it on of my own free will, and of my own free will I wore it. Is its pattern strange to you?"

Scrooge trembled more and more.

"Or would you know," pursued the Ghost, "the weight and length of the strong coil you bear yourself? It was full as heavy and as long as this, seven Christmas Eves ago. You have laboured on it, since. It is a ponderous chain!"

Scrooge glanced about him on the floor, in the expectation of finding himself surrounded by some fifty or sixty fathoms of iron cable: but he could see nothing.

"Jacob," he said, imploringly. "Old Jacob Marley, tell me more. Speak comfort to me, Jacob!"

"I have none to give," the Ghost replied. "It comes from other regions, Ebenezer Scrooge, and is conveyed by other ministers, to other kinds of men. Nor can I tell you what I would. A very little more, is all permitted to me. I cannot rest, I cannot stay, I cannot linger anywhere. My spirit never walked beyond our counting-house—mark me!—in life my spirit never roved beyond the narrow limits of our money-changing hole; and weary journeys lie before me!"

It was a habit with Scrooge, whenever he became thoughtful, to put his hands in his breeches pockets. Pondering on what the Ghost had said, he did so now, but without lifting up his eyes, or getting off his knees.

"You must have been very slow about it, Jacob," Scrooge observed, in a business-like manner, though with humility and deference.

"Slow!" the Ghost repeated.

"Seven years dead," mused Scrooge. "And travelling all the time!"

"The whole time," said the Ghost. "No rest, no peace. Incessant torture of remorse."

"You travel fast?" said Scrooge.

"On the wings of the wind," replied the Ghost.

"You might have got over a great quantity of ground in seven years," said Scrooge.

The Ghost, on hearing this, set up another cry, and clanked its chain so hideously in the dead silence of the night, that the Ward would have been justified in indicting it for a nuisance.

"Oh! captive, bound, and double-ironed," cried the phantom, "not to know, that ages of incessant labour, by immortal creatures, for this earth must pass into eternity before the good of which it is susceptible is all developed. Not to know that any Christian spirit working kindly in its little sphere, whatever it may be, will find its mortal life too short for its vast means of usefulness. Not to know that no space of regret can make amends for one life's opportunity misused! Yet such was I! Oh! such was I!"

"But you were always a good man of business, Jacob," faltered Scrooge, who now began to apply this to himself.

"Business!" cried the Ghost, wringing its hands again. "Mankind was my business. The common welfare was my business; charity, mercy, forbearance, and benevolence, were, all, my business. The dealings of my trade were but a drop of water in the comprehensive ocean of my business!"

It held up its chain at arm's length, as if that were the cause of all its unavailing grief, and flung it heavily upon the ground again.

"At this time of the rolling year," the spectre said, "I suffer most. Why did I walk through crowds of fellow-beings with my eyes turned down, and never raise them to that blessed Star which led the Wise Men to a poor abode! Were there no poor homes to which its light would have conducted me!"

Scrooge was very much dismayed to hear the spectre going on at this rate, and began to quake exceedingly.

"Hear me!" cried the Ghost. "My time is nearly gone."

"I will," said Scrooge. "But don't be hard upon me! Don't be flowery, Jacob! Pray!"

"How it is that I appear before you in a shape that you can see, I may not tell. I have sat invisible beside you many and many a day."

It was not an agreeable idea. Scrooge shivered, and wiped the perspiration from his brow.

"That is no light part of my penance," pursued the Ghost. "I am here to-night to warn you, that you have yet a chance and hope of escaping my fate. A chance and hope of my procuring, Ebenezer."

"You were always a good friend to me," said Scrooge. "Thank'ee!"

"You will be haunted," resumed the Ghost, "by Three Spirits."

Scrooge's countenance fell almost as low as the Ghost's had done.

"Is that the chance and hope you mentioned, Jacob?" he demanded, in a faltering voice.

"It is."

"I—I think I'd rather not," said Scrooge.

"Without their visits," said the Ghost, "you cannot hope to shun the path I tread. Expect the first tomor-row, when the bell tolls One."

"Couldn't I take 'em all at once, and have it over, Jacob?" hinted Scrooge.

"Expect the second on the next night at the same hour. The third upon the next night when the last stroke of Twelve has ceased to vibrate. Look to see me no more; and look that, for your own sake, you remem-ber what has passed between us!"

When it had said these words, the spectre took its wrapper from the table, and bound it round its head, as before. Scrooge knew this, by the smart sound its teeth made, when the jaws were brought together by the bandage. He ventured to raise his eyes again, and found his supernatural visitor confronting him in an erect attitude, with its chain wound over and about its arm.

The apparition walked backward from him; and at every step it took, the window raised itself a little, so that when the spectre reached it, it was wide open.

It beckoned Scrooge to approach, which he did. When they were within two paces of each other, Marley's Ghost held up its hand, warning him to come no nearer. Scrooge stopped.

Not so much in obedience, as in surprise and fear: for on the raising of the hand, he became sensible of confused noises in the air; incoherent sounds of lamentation and regret; wailings inexpressibly sorrowful and self-accusatory. The spectre, after listening for a moment, joined in the mournful dirge; and floated out upon the bleak, dark night.

Scrooge followed to the window: desperate in his curiosity. He looked out.

The air was filled with phantoms, wandering hither and thither in restless haste, and moaning as they went. Every one of them wore chains like Marley's Ghost; some few (they might be guilty governments) were linked together; none were free. Many had been personally known to Scrooge in their lives. He had been quite familiar with one old ghost, in a white waistcoat, with a

monstrous iron safe attached to its ankle, who cried piteously at being unable to assist a wretched woman with an infant, whom it saw below, upon a door-step. The misery with them all was, clearly, that they sought to interfere, for good, in human matters, and had lost the power forever.

Whether these creatures faded into mist, or mist enshrouded them, he could not tell. But they and their spirit voices faded together; and the night became as it had been when he walked home.

Scrooge closed the window, and examined the door by which the Ghost had entered. It was double-locked, as he had locked it with his own hands, and the bolts were undisturbed. He tried to say "Humbug!" but stopped at the first syllable. And being, from the emotion he had undergone, or the fatigues of the day, or his glimpse of the Invisible World, or the dull conversation of the Ghost, or the lateness of the hour, much in need of repose; went straight to bed, without undressing, and fell asleep upon the instant.

## STAVE TWO.

———⬥———

### THE FIRST OF THE THREE SPIRITS.

WHEN Scrooge awoke, it was so dark, that looking out of bed, he could scarcely distinguish the transparent window from the opaque walls of his chamber. He was endeavouring to pierce the darkness with his ferret eyes, when the chimes of a neighbouring church struck the four quarters. So he listened for the hour.

To his great astonishment the heavy bell went on from six to seven, and from seven to eight, and regularly up to twelve; then stopped. Twelve. It was past two when he went to bed. The clock was wrong. An icicle must have got into the works. Twelve.

He touched the spring of his repeater, to correct this most preposterous clock. Its rapid little pulse beat twelve: and stopped.

"Why, it isn't possible," said Scrooge, "that I can have slept through a whole day and far into another night. It isn't possible that anything has happened to the sun, and this is twelve at noon."

The idea being an alarming one, he scrambled out of bed, and groped his way to the window. He was obliged to rub the frost off with the sleeve of his dressing-gown before he could see anything; and could see very little then. All he could make out was, that it was still very foggy and extremely cold, and that there was no noise of people running to and with a deep, dull, hollow, melancholy One. Light flashed up in the room upon the instant, and the curtains of his bed were drawn.

The curtains of his bed were drawn aside, I tell you, by a hand. Not the curtains at his feet, nor the curtains at his back, but those to which his face was addressed. The curtains of his bed were drawn aside; and Scrooge, starting up into a half-recumbent attitude, found himself face to face with the unearthly visitor who drew them: as close to it as I am now to you, and I am standing in the spirit at your elbow.

It was a strange figure—like a child: yet not so like a child as like an old man, viewed through some supernatural medium, which gave him the appearance of having receded from the view, and being diminished to a child's proportions. Its hair, which hung about its neck and down its back, was white as if with age; and yet the face had not a wrinkle in it, and the tenderest bloom was on the skin. The arms were very long and muscular; the hands the same, as if its hold were of uncommon strength. Its legs and feet, most delicately formed, were, like those upper members, bare. It wore a tunic of the purest white, and round its waist was bound a lustrous belt, the sheen of which was beautiful. It held a branch of fresh green holly in its hand; and, in singular contra-diction of that wintry emblem, had its dress trimmed with summer flowers. But the strangest thing about it was, that from the crown of its head there sprung a bright clear jet of light, by which all this was visible; and which was doubtless the occasion of its using, in its duller moments, a great extinguisher for a cap, which it now held under its arm.

Even this, though, when Scrooge looked at it with increasing steadiness, was not its strangest quality. For as its belt sparkled and glittered now in one part and now in another, and what was light one instant, at another time was dark, so the figure itself fluctuated in its distinctness: being now a thing with one arm, now with one leg, now with twenty legs, now a pair of legs without a head, now a head without a body: of which dissolving parts, no outline would be visible in the dense gloom wherein they melted away. And in the very wonder of this, it would be itself again; distinct and clear as ever.

"Are you the Spirit, sir, whose coming was foretold to me?" asked Scrooge.

"I am."

The voice was soft and gentle. Singularly low, as if instead of being so close beside him, it were at a distance.

"Who, and what are you?" Scrooge demanded.

"I am the Ghost of Christmas Past."

"Long Past?" inquired Scrooge: observant of its dwarfish stature.

"No. Your past."

Perhaps, Scrooge could not have told anybody why, if anybody could have asked him; but he had a special desire to see the Spirit in his cap; and begged him to be covered.

"What!" exclaimed the Ghost, "would you so soon put out, with worldly hands, the light I give? Is it not enough that you are one of those whose passions made this cap, and force me through whole trains of years to wear it low upon my brow?"

Scrooge reverently disclaimed all intention to offend or any knowledge of having wilfully bonneted the Spirit at any period of his life. He then made bold to inquire what business brought him there.

"Your welfare," said the Ghost.

Scrooge expressed himself much obliged, but could not help thinking that a night of unbroken rest would have been more conducive to that end. The Spirit must have heard him thinking, for it said immediately:

"Your reclamation, then. Take heed."

It put out its strong hand as it spoke, and clasped him gently by the arm.

"Rise, and walk with me."

It would have been in vain for Scrooge to plead that the weather and the hour were not adapted to pedestrian purposes; that bed was warm, and the thermometer a long way below freezing; that he was clad but lightly in his slippers, dressing-gown, and nightcap; and that he had a cold upon him at that time. The grasp, though gentle as a woman's hand, was not to be resisted. He rose: but finding that the Spirit made towards the window, clasped his robe in supplication.

"I am mortal," Scrooge remonstrated, "and liable to fall."

"Bear but a touch of my hand there," said the Spirit, laying it upon his heart, "and you shall be upheld in more than this."

As the words were spoken, they passed through the wall, and stood upon an open country road, with fields on either hand. The city had entirely vanished. Not a vestige of it was to be seen. The darkness and the mist had vanished with it, for it was a clear, cold, winter day, with snow upon the ground.

"Good Heaven!" said Scrooge, clasping his hands together, as he looked about him. "I was bred in this place. I was a boy here."

The Spirit gazed upon him mildly. Its gentle touch, though it had been light and instantaneous, appeared still present to the old man's sense of feeling. He was conscious of a thousand odours floating in the air, each one connected with a thousand thoughts, and hopes, and joys, and cares long, long, forgotten.

"Your lip is trembling," said the Ghost. "And what is that upon your cheek?"

Scrooge muttered, with an unusual catching in his voice, that it was a pimple; and begged the Ghost to lead him where he would.

"You recollect the way?" inquired the Spirit.

"Remember it!" cried Scrooge with fervour. "I could walk it blindfold!"

"Strange to have forgotten it for so many years," observed the Ghost. "Let us go on."

They walked along the road, Scrooge recognising every gate, and post, and tree; until a little market-town appeared in the distance, with its bridge, its church, and winding river. Some shaggy ponies now were seen trotting towards them with boys upon their backs, who called to other boys in country gigs and carts, driven by farmers. All these boys were in great spirits, and shouted to each other, until the broad fields were so full of merry music, that the crisp air laughed to hear it.

"These are but shadows of the things that have been," said the Ghost. "They have no consciousness of us."

The jocund travellers came on; and as they came, Scrooge knew and named them every one. Why was he rejoiced beyond all bounds to see them? Why did his cold eye glisten, and his heart leap up as they went past?Why was he filled with gladness when he heard them give each other Merry Christmas, as they parted at cross-roads and bye-ways, for their several homes? What was merry Christmas to Scrooge? Out upon merry Christmas. What good had it ever done to him?

"The school is not quite deserted," said the Ghost. "A solitary child, neglected by his friends, is left there still."

Scrooge said he knew it. And he sobbed.

They left the high-road, by a well-remembered lane, and soon approached a mansion of dull red brick, with a little weathercock-surmounted cupola, on the roof, and a bell hanging in it. It was a large house, but one of broken fortunes; for the spacious offices were little used, their walls were damp and mossy, their windows broken, and their gates decayed. Fowls clucked and strutted in the stables; and the coach-houses and sheds were over-run with grass. Nor was it more retentive of its ancient state, within; for entering the dreary hall, and glancing through the open doors of many rooms, they found them poorly furnished, cold, and vast. There was an earthy savour in the air, a chilly bareness in the place, which associated itself somehow with too much getting up by candle-light, and not too much to eat.

They went, the Ghost and Scrooge, across the hall, to a door at the back of the house. It opened before them, and disclosed a long, bare, melancholy room, made barer still by lines of plain deal forms and desks. At one of these a lonely boy was reading near a feeble fire; and Scrooge sat down upon a form, and wept to see his poor forgotten self as he used to be.

Not a latent echo in the house, not a squeak and scuffle from the mice behind the panelling, not a drip from the half-thawed water-spout in the dull yard behind, not a sigh among the leafless boughs of one despondent poplar, not the idle swinging of an empty store-house door, no, not a clicking in the fire, but fell upon the heart of Scrooge with a softening influence, and gave a freer passage to his tears.

The Spirit touched him on the arm, and pointed to his younger self, intent upon his reading. Suddenly a man, in foreign garments: wonderfully real and distinct to look at: stood outside the window, with an axe stuck in his belt, and leading by the bridle an ass laden with wood.

"Why, it's Ali Baba," Scrooge exclaimed in ecstasy. "It's dear old honest Ali Baba. Yes, yes, I know. One Christmas time, when yonder solitary child was left here all alone, he did come, for the first time, just like that. Poor boy. And Valentine," said Scrooge, "and his wild brother, Orson; there they go. And what's his name, who was put down in his drawers, asleep, at the Gate of Damascus; you see him. And the Sultan's Groom turned upside down by the Genii; there he is upon his head. Serve him right. I'm glad of it. What business had he to be married to the Princess?"

To hear Scrooge expending all the earnestness of his nature on such subjects, in a most extraordinary voice between laughing and crying; and to see his heightened and excited face; would have been a surprise to his business friends in the city, indeed.

"There's the Parrot," cried Scrooge. "Green body and yellow tail, with a thing like a lettuce growing out of the top of his head; there he is. Poor Robin Crusoe, he called him, when he came home again after sailing round the island. Poor Robin Crusoe, where have you been, Robin Crusoe. The man thought he was dreaming, but he wasn't. It was the Parrot, you know. There goes Friday, running for his life to the little creek. Halloa. Hoop. Hallo."

Then, with a rapidity of transition very foreign to his usual character, he said, in pity for his former self, "Poor boy," and cried again.

"I wish," Scrooge muttered, putting his hand in his pocket, and looking about him, after drying his eyes with his cuff: "but it's too late now."

"What is the matter?" asked the Spirit.

"Nothing," said Scrooge. "Nothing. There was a boy singing a Christmas Carol at my door last night. I should like to have given him something: that's all."

The Ghost smiled thoughtfully, and waved its hand: saying as it did so, "Let us see another Christmas."

Scrooge's former self grew larger at the words, and the room became a little darker and more dirty. The panels shrunk, the windows cracked; fragments of plaster fell out of the ceiling, and the naked laths were shown instead; but how all this was brought about, Scrooge knew no more than you do. He only knew that it was quite correct; that everything had happened so;

that there he was, alone again, when all the other boys had gone home for the jolly holidays.

He was not reading now, but walking up and down despairingly. Scrooge looked at the Ghost, and with a mournful shaking of his head, glanced anxiously towards the door.

It opened; and a little girl, much younger than the boy, came darting in, and putting her arms about his neck, and often kissing him, addressed him as her "Dear, dear brother."

"I have come to bring you home, dear brother," said the child, clapping her tiny hands, and bending down to laugh. "To bring you home, home, home."

"Home, little Fan?" returned the boy.

"Yes," said the child, brimful of glee. "Home, for good and all. Home, for ever and ever. Father is so much kinder than he used to be, that home's like Heaven. He spoke so gently to me one dear night when I was going to bed, that I was not afraid to ask him once more if you might come home; and he said Yes, you should; and sent me in a coach to bring you. And you're to be a man." said the child, opening her eyes, "and are never to come back here; but first, we're to be together all the Christmas long, and have the merriest time in all the world."

"You are quite a woman, little Fan!" exclaimed the boy.

She clapped her hands and laughed, and tried to touch his head; but being too little, laughed again, and stood on tiptoe to embrace him. Then she began to drag him, in her childish eagerness, towards the door; and he, nothing loth to go, accompanied her.

A terrible voice in the hall cried. "Bring down Master Scrooge's box, there!" and in the hall appeared the schoolmaster himself, who glared on Master Scrooge with a ferocious condescension, and threw him into a dreadful state of mind by shaking hands with him. He then conveyed him and his sister into the veriest old well of a shivering best-parlour that ever was seen, where the maps upon the wall, and the celestial and ter-restrial globes in the windows, were waxy with cold. Here he produced a decanter of curiously light wine, and a block of curiously heavy cake, and administered instalments of those dainties to the young people: at the same time, sending out a meagre servant to offer a glass of something to the postboy, who answered that he thanked the gentleman, but if it was the same tap as he had tasted before, he had rather not. Master Scrooge's trunk being by this time tied on to the top of the chaise, the children bade the schoolmaster good-bye right will-ingly; and getting into it, drove gaily down the garden-sweep: the quick wheels dashing the hoar-frost and snow from off the dark leaves of the evergreens like spray.

"Always a delicate creature, whom a breath might have withered," said the Ghost. "But she had a large heart."

"So she had," cried Scrooge. "You're right. I will not gainsay it, Spirit. God forbid."

"She died a woman," said the Ghost, "and had, as I think, children."

"One child," Scrooge returned.

"True," said the Ghost. "Your nephew."

Scrooge seemed uneasy in his mind; and answered briefly, "Yes."

Although they had but that moment left the school behind them, they were now in the busy thoroughfares of a city, where shadowy passengers passed and repassed; where shadowy carts and coaches battle for the way, and all the strife and tumult of a real city were. It was made plain enough, by the dressing of the shops, that here too it was Christmas time again; but it was evening, and the streets were lighted up.

The Ghost stopped at a certain warehouse door, and asked Scrooge if he knew it.

"Know it," said Scrooge. "Was I apprenticed here."

They went in. At sight of an old gentleman in a Welsh wig, sitting behind such a high desk, that if he had been two inches taller he must have knocked his head against the ceiling, Scrooge cried in great excitement:

"Why, it's old Fezziwig. Bless his heart; it's Fezziwig alive again."

Old Fezziwig laid down his pen, and looked up at the clock, which pointed to the hour of seven. He rubbed his hands; adjusted his capacious waistcoat; laughed all over himself, from his shows to his organ of benevolence; and called out in a comfortable, oily, rich, fat,

THE FIRST OF THE THREE SPIRITS

jovial voice:

"Yo ho, there, Ebenezer. Dick."

Scrooge's former self, now grown a young man, came briskly in, accompanied by his fellow-prentice.

"Dick Wilkins, to be sure." said Scrooge to the Ghost. "Bless me, yes. There he is. He was very much attached to me, was Dick. Poor Dick. Dear, dear."

"Yo ho, my boys," said Fezziwig. "No more work to-night. Christmas Eve, Dick. Christmas, Ebenezer. Let's have the shutters up," cried old Fezziwig, with a sharp clap of his hands," before a man can say Jack Robinson."

You wouldn't believe how those two fellows went at it. They charged into the street with the shutters—one, two, three—had them up in their places—four, five, six—barred them and pinned them—seven, eight, nine—and came back before you could have got to twelve, panting like race-horses.

"Hilli-ho!" cried old Fezziwig, skipping down from the high desk, with wonderful agility. "Clear away, my lads, and let's have lots of room here. Hilli-ho, Dick. Chirrup, Ebenezer."

Clear away. There was nothing they wouldn't have cleared away, or couldn't have cleared away, with old Fezziwig looking on. It was done in a minute. Every movable was packed off, as if it were dismissed from public life for evermore; the floor was swept and watered, the lamps were trimmed, fuel was heaped upon the fire; and the warehouse was as snug, and warm, and dry, and bright a ball-room, as you would desire to see upon a winter's night.

In came a fiddler with a music-book, and went up to the lofty desk, and made an orchestra of it, and tuned like fifty stomach-aches. In came Mrs. Fezziwig, one vast substantial smile. In came the three Miss Fezziwigs, beaming and lovable. In came the six young followers whose hearts they broke. In came all the young men and women employed in the business. In came the house-maid, with her cousin, the baker. In came the cook, with her brother's particular friend, the milkman. In came the boy from over the way, who was suspected of not having board enough from his master; trying to hide himself behind the girl from next door but one, who was proved to have had her ears pulled by her mistress. In they all came, one after another; some shyly, some boldly, some gracefully, some awkwardly, some pushing, some pulling; in they all came, anyhow and everyhow. Away they all went, twenty couple at once; hands half round and back again the other way; down the middle and up again; round and round in various stages of affectionate grouping; old top couple always turning up in the wrong place; new top couple starting off again, as soon as they got there; all top couples at last, and not a bottom one to help them. When this result was brought about, old Fezziwig, clapping his hands to stop the dance, cried out, "Well done." and the fiddler plunged his hot face into a pot of porter, especially provided for that purpose. But scorning rest, upon his reappearance, he instantly began again, though there were no dancers yet, as if the other fiddler had been carried home, exhausted, on a shutter, and he were a bran-new man resolved to beat him out of sight, or perish.

There were more dances, and there were forfeits, and more dances, and there was cake, and there was negus, and there was a great piece of Cold Roast, and there was a great piece of Cold Boiled, and there were mince-pies, and plenty of beer. But the great effect of the evening came after the Roast and Boiled, when the fiddler (an artful dog, mind. The sort of man who knew his business better than you or I could have told it him.) struck up "Sir Roger de Coverley." Then old Fezziwig stood out to dance with Mrs. Fezziwig. Top couple, too; with a good stiff piece of work cut out for them; three or four and twenty pair of partners; people who were not to be trifled with; people who would dance, and had no notion of walking.

But if they had been twice as many—ah, four times— old Fezziwig would have been a match for them, and so would Mrs. Fezziwig. As to her, she was worthy to be his partner in every sense of the term. If that's not high praise, tell me higher, and I'll use it. A positive light appeared to issue from Fezziwig's calves. They shone in every part of the dance like moons. You couldn't have predicted, at any given time, what would have become of them next. And when old Fezziwig and Mrs. Fezziwig had gone all through the dance; advance and retire, both hands to your partner, bow and curtsey, corkscrew, thread-the-needle, and back again to your place; Fezziwig cut—cut so deftly, that he appeared to wink with his legs, and came upon his feet again without a stagger.

When the clock struck eleven, this domestic ball broke up. Mr. and Mrs. Fezziwig took their stations, one on either side of the door, and shaking hands with every person individually as he or she went out, wished him or her a Merry Christmas. When everybody had retired but the two prentices, they did the same to them; and thus the cheerful voices died away, and the lads were left to their beds; which were under a counter in the back-shop.

During the whole of this time, Scrooge had acted like a man out of his wits. His heart and soul were in the scene, and with his former self. He corroborated everything, remembered everything, enjoyed everything, and underwent the strangest agitation. It was not until now, when the bright faces of his former self and Dick were turned from them, that he remembered the Ghost, and became conscious that it was looking full upon him, while the light upon its head burnt very clear.

"A small matter," said the Ghost, "to make these silly folks so full of gratitude."

"Small," echoed Scrooge.

The Spirit signed to him to listen to the two apprentices, who were pouring out their hearts in praise of Fezziwig: and when he had done so, said,

"Why. Is it not. He has spent but a few pounds of your mortal money: three or four perhaps. Is that so much that he deserves this praise?"

"It isn't that," said Scrooge, heated by the remark, and speaking unconsciously like his former, not his latter, self. "It isn't that, Spirit. He has the power to render us happy or unhappy; to make our service light or burdensome; a pleasure or a toil. Say that his power lies in words and looks; in things so slight and insignificant that it is impossible to add and count them up: what then? The happiness he gives, is quite as great as if it cost a fortune."

He felt the Spirit's glance, and stopped.

"What is the matter?" asked the Ghost.

"Nothing in particular," said Scrooge.

"Something, I think," the Ghost insisted.

"No," said Scrooge, "No. I should like to be able to say a word or two to my clerk just now. That's all."

His former self turned down the lamps as he gave utterance to the wish; and Scrooge and the Ghost again stood side by side in the open air.

"My time grows short," observed the Spirit. "Quick."

This was not addressed to Scrooge, or to any one whom he could see, but it produced an immediate effect. For again Scrooge saw himself. He was older now, a man in the prime of life. His face had not the harsh and rigid lines of later years but it had begun to wear the signs of care and avarice. There was an eager, greedy, restless

motion in the eye, which showed the passion that had
taken root, and where the shadow of the growing tree
would fall.

He was not alone, but sat by the side of a fair young
girl in a mourning-dress: in whose eyes there were tears,
which sparkled in the light that shone out of the Ghost
of Christmas Past.

"It matters little," she said, softly. "To you, very little. Another idol has displaced me; and if it can cheer
and comfort you in time to come, as I would have tried
to do, I have no just cause to grieve."

"What Idol has displaced you?" he rejoined.

"A golden one."

"This is the even-handed dealing of the world," he
said. "There is nothing on which it is so hard as poverty; and there is nothing it professes to condemn with
such severity as the pursuit of wealth."

"You fear the world too much," she answered, gently.
"All your other hopes have merged into the hope of
being beyond the chance of its sordid reproach. I have
seen your nobler aspirations fall off one by one, until
the master-passion, Gain, engrosses you. Have I not?"

"What then?" he retorted. "Even if I have grown so
much wiser, what then? I am not changed towards you."

She shook her head.

"Am I?"

"Our contract is an old one. It was made when we
were both poor and content to be so, until, in good

season, we could improve our worldly fortune by our patient industry. You are changed. When it was made, you were another man."

"I was a boy," he said impatiently.

"Your own feeling tells you that you were not what you are," she returned. "I am. That which promised happiness when we were one in heart, is fraught with misery now that we are two. How often and how keenly I have thought of this, I will not say. It is enough that I have thought of it, and can release you."

"Have I ever sought release?"

"In words? No. Never."

"In what, then?"

"In a changed nature; in an altered spirit; in another atmosphere of life; another Hope as its great end. In everything that made my love of any worth or value in your sight. If this had never been between us," said the girl, looking mildly, but with steadiness, upon him; "tell me, would you seek me out and try to win me now? Ah, no."

He seemed to yield to the justice of this supposition, in spite of himself. But he said with a struggle, "You think not."

"I would gladly think otherwise if I could," she answered, "Heaven knows. When I have learned a Truth like this, I know how strong and irresistible it must be. But if you were free to-day, to-morrow, yesterday, can even I believe that you would choose a dowerless girl—

you who, in your very confidence with her, weigh everything by Gain: or, choosing her, if for a moment you
were false enough to your one guiding principle to do so,
do I not know that your repentance and regret would
surely follow? I do; and I release you. With a full heart,
for the love of him you once were."

He was about to speak; but with her head turned
from him, she resumed.

"You may—the memory of what is past half makes me
hope you will—have pain in this. A very, very brief time,
and you will dismiss the recollection of it, gladly, as an
unprofitable dream, from which it happened well that you
awoke. May you be happy in the life you have chosen."

She left him, and they parted.

"Spirit," said Scrooge," show me no more. Conduct
me home. Why do you delight to torture me?"

"One shadow more," exclaimed the Ghost.

"No more," cried Scrooge. "No more, I don't wish to
see it. Show me no more."

But the relentless Ghost pinioned him in both his
arms, and forced him to observe what happened next.

They were in another scene and place; a room, not
very large or handsome, but full of comfort. Near to the
winter fire sat a beautiful young girl, so like that last
that Scrooge believed it was the same, until he saw her,
now a comely matron, sitting opposite her daughter. The
noise in this room was perfectly tumultuous, for there
were more children there, than Scrooge in his agitated

state of mind could count; and, unlike the celebrated
herd in the poem, they were not forty children conducting themselves like one, but every child was conducting
itself like forty. The consequences were uproarious
beyond belief; but no one seemed to care; on the con-
trary, the mother and daughter laughed heartily, and
enjoyed it very much; and the latter, soon beginning to
mingle in the sports, got pillaged by the young brigands
most ruthlessly. What would I not have given to one of
them. Though I never could have been so rude, no, no. I
wouldn't for the wealth of all the world have crushed
that braided hair, and torn it down; and for the precious
little shoe, I wouldn't have plucked it off, God bless my
soul, to save my life. As to measuring her waist in sport,
as they did, bold young brood, I couldn't have done it; I
should have expected my arm to have grown round it for
a punishment, and never come straight again. And yet I
should have dearly liked, I own, to have touched her
lips; to have questioned her, that she might have opened
them; to have looked upon the lashes of her downcast
eyes, and never raised a blush; to have let loose waves of
hair, an inch of which would be a keepsake beyond price:
in short, I should have liked, I do confess, to have had
the lightest licence of a child, and yet to have been man
enough to know its value.

But now a knocking at the door was heard, and such
a rush immediately ensued that she with laughing face
and plundered dress was borne towards it the centre of a

flushed and boisterous group, just in time to greet the father, who came home attended by a man laden with Christmas toys and presents. Then the shouting and the struggling, and the onslaught that was made on the defenceless porter! The scaling him with chairs for lad- ders to dive into his pockets, despoil him of brown- paper parcels, hold on tight by his cravat, hug him round his neck, pommel his back, and kick his legs in irrepressible affection. The shouts of wonder and delight with which the development of every package was received. The terrible announcement that the baby had been taken in the act of putting a doll's frying-pan into his mouth, and was more than suspected of having swal- lowed a fictitious turkey, glued on a wooden platter. The immense relief of finding this a false alarm. The joy, and gratitude, and ecstasy. They are all indescrib- able alike. It is enough that by degrees the children and their emotions got out of the parlour, and by one stair at a time, up to the top of the house; where they went to bed, and so subsided.

And now Scrooge looked on more attentively than ever, when the master of the house, having his daughter leaning fondly on him, sat down with her and her moth- er at his own fireside; and when he thought that such another creature, quite as graceful and as full of promise, might have called him father, and been a spring-time in the haggard winter of his life, his sight grew very dim indeed.

"Belle," said the husband, turning to his wife with a smile, "I saw an old friend of yours this afternoon."

"Who was it?"

"Guess."

"How can I. Tut, I know," she added in the same breath, laughing as he laughed. "Mr. Scrooge."

"Mr. Scrooge it was. I passed his office window; and as it was not shut up, and he had a candle inside, I could scarcely help seeing him. His partner lies upon the point of death, I hear; and there he sat alone. Quite alone in the world, I do believe."

"Spirit," said Scrooge in a broken voice, "remove me from this place."

"I told you these were shadows of the things that have been," said the Ghost. "That they are what they are, do not blame me."

"Remove me!" Scrooge exclaimed. "I cannot bear it."

He turned upon the Ghost, and seeing that it looked upon him with a face, in which in some strange way there were fragments of all the faces it had shown him, wrestled with it.

"Leave me. Take me back. Haunt me no longer."

In the struggle, if that can be called a struggle in which the Ghost with no visible resistance on its own part was undisturbed by any effort of its adversary, Scrooge observed that its light was burning high and bright; and dimly connecting that with its influence

over him, he seized the extinguisher-cap, and by a sudden action pressed it down upon its head.

The Spirit dropped beneath it, so that the extinguisher covered its whole form; but though Scrooge
pressed it down with all his force, he could not hide the
light, which streamed from under it, in an unbroken
flood upon the ground.

He was conscious of being exhausted, and overcome by an irresistible drowsiness; and, further, of being in his own bedroom. He gave the cap a parting squeeze, in which his hand relaxed; and had barely time to reel to bed, before he sank into a heavy sleep.

# STAVE THREE.

———❦———

## THE SECOND OF THE THREE SPIRITS.

AWAKING in the middle of a prodigiously tough snore, and sitting up in bed to get his thoughts together, Scrooge had no occasion to be told that the bell was again upon the stroke of One. He felt that he was restored to consciousness in the right nick of time, for the especial purpose of holding a conference with the second messenger despatched to him through Jacob Marley's intervention. But, finding that he turned uncomfortably cold when he began to wonder which of his curtains this new spectre would draw back, he put them every one aside with his own hands, and lying down again, established a sharp look-out all round the bed. For, he wished to challenge the Spirit on the moment of its appearance, and did not wish to be taken by surprise, and made nervous.

Gentlemen of the free-and-easy sort, who plume themselves on being acquainted with a move or two, and being usually equal to the time-of-day, express the wide range of their capacity for adventure by observing that they are good for anything from pitch-and-toss to manslaughter; between which opposite extremes, no doubt, there lies a tolerably wide and comprehensive range of subjects. Without venturing for Scrooge quite as hardily as this, I mind calling on you to believe that he was ready for a good broad field of strange appearances, and that nothing between a baby and rhinoceros would have astonished him very much.

Now, being prepared for almost anything, he was not by any means prepared for nothing; and, consequently, when the Bell struck One, and no shape appeared, he was taken with a violent fit of trembling. Five minutes, ten minutes, a quarter of an hour went by, yet nothing came. All this time, he lay upon his bed, the very core and centre of a blaze of ruddy light, which streamed upon it when the clock proclaimed the hour; and which, being only light, was more alarming than a dozen ghosts, as he was powerless to make out what it meant, or would be at; and was sometimes apprehensive that he might be at that very moment an interesting case of spontaneous combustion, without having the consolation of knowing it. At last, however, he began to think—as you or I would have thought at first; for it is always the person not in the predicament who knows what ought to have been done in it, and would unquestionably have done it too—at last, I say, he began to think that the source and secret of this ghostly light might be in the adjoining room, from whence, on further tracing it, it seemed to shine. This idea taking full possession of his mind, he got up softly and shuffled in his slippers to the door.

The moment Scrooge's hand was on the lock, a strange voice called him by his name, and bade him enter. He obeyed.

It was his own room. There was no doubt about that. But it had undergone a surprising transformation. The walls and ceiling were so hung with living green, that it looked a perfect grove; from every part of which, bright gleaming berries glistened. The crisp leaves of holly, mistletoe, and ivy reflected back the light, as if so many little mirrors had been scattered there; and such a mighty blaze went roaring up the chimney, as that dull petrification of a hearth had never known in Scrooge's time, or Marley's, or for many and many a winter season gone. Heaped up on the floor, to form a kind of throne, were turkeys, geese, game, poultry, brawn, great joints of meat, sucking-pigs, long wreaths of sausages, mince-pies, plum-puddings, barrels of oysters, red-hot chestnuts, cherry-cheeked apples, juicy oranges, luscious pears, immense twelfth-cakes, and seething bowls of punch, that made the chamber dim with their delicious steam. In easy state upon this couch, there sat a jolly Giant, glorious to see, who bore a glowing torch, in shape not unlike Plenty's horn, and held it up, high up, to shed its light on Scrooge, as he came peeping round the door.

"Come in," exclaimed the Ghost. "Come in, and know me better, man."

Scrooge entered timidly, and hung his head before this Spirit. He was not the dogged Scrooge he had been; and though the Spirit's eyes were clear and kind, he did not like to meet them.

"I am the Ghost of Christmas Present," said the Spirit. "Look upon me."

Scrooge reverently did so. It was clothed in one simple green robe, or mantle, bordered with white fur. This garment hung so loosely on the figure, that its capacious breast was bare, as if disdaining to be warded or concealed by any artifice. Its feet, observable beneath the ample folds of the garment, were also bare; and on its head it wore no other covering than a holly wreath, set here and there with shining icicles. Its dark brown curls were long and free; free as its genial face, its sparkling eye, its open hand, its cheery voice, its unconstrained demeanour, and its joyful air. Girded round its middle was an antique scabbard; but no sword was in it, and the ancient sheath was eaten up with rust.

"You have never seen the like of me before," exclaimed the Spirit.

"Never," Scrooge made answer to it.

"Have never walked forth with the younger members of my family; meaning (for I am very young) my elder brothers born in these later years?" pursued the Phantom.

"I think I have," said Scrooge. "I am afraid I have not. Have you had many brothers, Spirit?"

"More than eighteen hundred," said the Ghost.

"A tremendous family to provide for," muttered Scrooge.

The Ghost of Christmas Present rose.

"Spirit," said Scrooge submissively, "conduct me where you will. I went forth last night on compulsion, and I learnt a lesson which is working now. To-night, if you have aught to teach me, let me profit by it."

"Touch my robe."

Scrooge did as he was told, and held it fast.

Holly, mistletoe, red berries, ivy, turkeys, geese, game, poultry, brawn, meat, pigs, sausages, oysters, pies, puddings, fruit, and punch, all vanished instantly. So did the room, the fire, the ruddy glow, the hour of night, and they stood in the city streets on Christmas morning, where (for the weather was severe) the people made a rough, but brisk and not unpleasant kind of music, in scraping the snow from the pavement in front of their dwellings, and from the tops of their houses, whence it was mad delight to the boys to see it come plumping down into the road below, and splitting into artificial little snow-storms.

The house fronts looked black enough, and the windows blacker, contrasting with the smooth white sheet of snow upon the roofs, and with the dirtier snow upon the ground; which last deposit had been ploughed up in deep furrows by the heavy wheels of carts and wagons; furrows that crossed and recrossed each other hundreds of times where the great streets branched off; and made intricate channels, hard to trace in the thick yellow mud and icy water. The sky was gloomy, and the shortest streets were choked up with a dingy mist, half thawed, half frozen, whose heavier particles descended in shower of sooty atoms, as if all the chimneys in Great Britain had, by one consent, caught fire, and were blazing away to their dear hearts' content. There was nothing very cheerful in the climate or the town, and yet was there an air of cheerfulness abroad that the clearest summer air and brightest summer sun might have endeavoured to diffuse in vain.

For, the people who were shovelling away on the housetops were jovial and full of glee; calling out to one another from the parapets, and now and then exchanging a facetious snowball—better-natured missile far than many a wordy jest—laughing heartily if it went right and not less heartily if it went wrong. The poulterers' shops were still half open, and the fruiterers' were radiant in their glory. There were great, round, pot-bellied baskets of chestnuts, shaped like the waistcoats of jolly old gentlemen, lolling at the doors, and tumbling out into the street in their apoplectic opulence. There were ruddy, brown-faced, broad-girthed Spanish Friars, and winking from their shelves in wanton slyness at the girls as they went by, and glanced demurely at the hung-up mistletoe. There were pears and apples, clustered high in blooming pyramids; there were bunches of grapes, made, in the shopkeepers' benevolence to dangle from conspicuous hooks, that people's mouths might water gratis as they passed; there were piles of filberts, mossy and brown, recalling, in their fragrance, ancient walks among the woods, and pleasant shufflings ankle deep through withered leaves; there were Norfolk Biffins, squab and swarthy, setting off the yellow of the oranges and lemons, and, in the great compactness of their juicy persons, urgently entreating and beseeching to be carried home in paper bags and eaten after dinner. The very gold and silver fish, set forth among these choice fruits in a bowl, though members of a dull and stagnant-blooded race, appeared to know that there was something going on; and, to a fish, went gasping round and round their little world in slow and passionless excitement.

The Grocers'! oh the Grocers', nearly closed, with perhaps two shutters down, or one; but through those gaps such glimpses. It was not alone that the scales descending on the counter made a merry sound, or that the twine and roller parted company so briskly, or that the canisters were rattled up and down like juggling tricks, or even that the blended scents of tea and coffee were so grateful to the nose, or even that the raisins were so plentiful and rare, the almonds so extremely white, the sticks of cinnamon so long and straight, the other spices so delicious, the candied fruits so caked and spotted with molten sugar as to make the coldest lookers-on feel faint and subsequently bilious. Nor was it that the figs were moist and pulpy, or that the French plums blushed in modest tartness from their highly-decorated boxes, or that everything was good to eat and in its Christmas dress; but the customers were all so hurried and so eager in the hopeful promise of the day, that they tumbled up against each other at the door, crashing their wicker baskets wildly, and left their purchases upon the counter, and came running back to fetch them, and committed hundreds of the like mistakes, in the best humour possible; while the Grocer and his people were so frank and fresh that the polished hearts with which they fastened their aprons behind might have been their own, worn outside for general inspection, and for Christmas daws to peck at if they chose.

But soon the steeples called good people all, to church and chapel, and away they came, flocking through the streets in their best clothes, and with their gayest faces. And at the same time there emerged from scores of bye-streets, lanes, and nameless turnings, innumerable people, carrying their dinners to the bakers' shops. The sight of these poor revellers appeared to interest the Spirit very much, for he stood with Scrooge beside him in a baker's doorway, and taking off the covers as their bearers passed, sprinkled incense on their dinners from his torch. And it was a very uncommon kind of torch, for once or twice when there were angry words between some dinner-carriers who had jostled each other, he shed a few drops of water on them from it, and their good humour was restored directly. For they said, it was a shame to quarrel upon Christmas Day. And so it was. God love it, so it was.

In time the bells ceased, and the bakers were shut up; and yet there was a genial shadowing forth of all these dinners and the progress of their cooking, in the thawed blotch of wet above each baker's oven; where the pavement smoked as if its stones were cooking, too.

"Is there a peculiar flavour in what you sprinkle from your torch?" asked Scrooge.

"There is. My own."

"Would it apply to any kind of dinner on this day?" asked Scrooge.

"To any kindly given. To a poor one most."

"Why to a poor one most?" asked Scrooge.

"Because it needs it most."

"Spirit," said Scrooge, after a moment's thought, "I wonder you, of all the beings in the many worlds about us, should desire to cramp these people's opportunities of innocent enjoyment."

"I?" cried the Spirit.

"You would deprive them of their means of dining every seventh day, often the only day on which they can be said to dine at all," said Scrooge. "Wouldn't you?"

"I?" cried the Spirit.

"You seek to close these places on the Seventh Day." said Scrooge. "And it comes to the same thing."

"I seek?" exclaimed the Spirit.

"Forgive me if I am wrong. It has been done in your name, or at least in that of your family," said Scrooge.

"There are some upon this earth of yours," returned the Spirit, "who lay claim to know us, and who do their deeds of passion, pride, ill-will, hatred, envy, bigotry, and selfishness in our name, who are as strange to us and all out kith and kin, as if they had never lived. Remember that, and charge their doings on themselves, not us."

Scrooge promised that he would; and they went on, invisible, as they had been before, into the suburbs of the town. It was a remarkable quality of the Ghost (which Scrooge had observed at the baker's), that notwithstanding his gigantic size, he could accommodate himself to any place with ease; and that he stood beneath a low roof quite as gracefully and like a supernatural creature, as it was possible he could have done in any lofty hall.

And perhaps it was the pleasure the good Spirit had in showing off this power of his, or else it was his own kind, generous, hearty nature, and his sympathy with all poor men, that led him straight to Scrooge's clerk's; for there he went, and took Scrooge with him, holding to his robe; and on the threshold of the door the Spirit smiled, and stopped to bless Bob Cratchit's dwelling with the sprinkling of his torch. Think of that. Bob had but fifteen "Bob" a-week himself; he pocketed on Saturdays but fifteen copies of his Christian name; and yet the Ghost of Christmas Present blessed his four-roomed house.

Then up rose Mrs. Cratchit, Cratchit's wife, dressed out but poorly in a twice-turned gown, but brave in ribbons, which are cheap and make a goodly show for sixpence; and she laid the cloth, assisted by Belinda Cratchit, second of her daughters, also brave in ribbons; while Master Peter Cratchit plunged a fork into the saucepan of potatoes, and getting the corners of his monstrous shirt collar (Bob's private property, conferred upon his son and heir in honour of the day) into his mouth, rejoiced to find himself so gallantly attired, and yearned to show his linen in the fashionable Parks. And now two smaller Cratchits, boy and girl, came tearing in, screaming that outside the baker's they had smelt the goose, and known it for their own; and basking in luxurious thoughts of sage and onion, these young Cratchits danced about the table, and exalted Master Peter Cratchit to the skies, while he (not proud, although his collars nearly choked him) blew the fire, until the slow potatoes bubbling up, knocked loudly at the saucepan-lid to be let out and peeled.

"What has ever got your precious father then?" said Mrs. Cratchit. "And your brother, Tiny Tim. And Martha warn't as late last Christmas Day by half-an-hour."

"Here's Martha, mother," said a girl, appearing as she spoke.

"Here's Martha, mother." cried the two young Cratchits. "Hurrah. There's such a goose, Martha."

"Why, bless your heart alive, my dear, how late you are," said Mrs. Cratchit, kissing her a dozen times, and taking off her shawl and bonnet for her with officious zeal.

"We'd a deal of work to finish up last night," replied the girl, "and had to clear away this morning, mother."

"Well. Never mind so long as you are come," said Mrs. Cratchit. "Sit ye down before the fire, my dear, and have a warm, Lord bless ye."

"No, no. There's father coming," cried the two young Cratchits, who were everywhere at once. "Hide, Martha, hide."

So Martha hid herself, and in came little Bob, the father, with at least three feet of comforter exclusive of the fringe, hanging down before him; and his threadbare clothes darned up and brushed, to look seasonable; and Tiny Tim upon his shoulder. Alas for Tiny Tim, he bore a little crutch, and had his limbs supported by an iron frame.

"Why, where's our Martha?" cried Bob Cratchit, looking round.

"Not coming," said Mrs. Cratchit.

"Not coming?" said Bob, with a sudden declension in his high spirits; for he had been Tim's blood horse all the way from church, and had come home rampant. "Not coming upon Christmas Day."

Martha didn't like to see him disappointed, if it were only in joke; so she came out prematurely from behind the closet door, and ran into his arms, while the two young Cratchits hustled Tiny Tim, and bore him off into the wash-house, that he might hear the pudding singing in the copper.

"And how did little Tim behave?" asked Mrs. Cratchit, when she had rallied Bob on his credulity, and Bob had hugged his daughter to his heart's content.

"As good as gold," said Bob, "and better. Somehow he gets thoughtful, sitting by himself so much, and thinks the strangest things you ever heard. He told me, coming home, that he hoped the people saw him in the church, because he was a cripple, and it might be pleasant to them to remember upon Christmas Day, who made lame beggars walk, and blind men see."

Bob's voice was tremulous when he told them this, and trembled more when he said that Tiny Tim was growing strong and hearty.

His active little crutch was heard upon the floor, and back came Tiny Tim before another word was spoken, escorted by his brother and sister to his stool before the fire; and while Bob, turning up his cuffs—as if, poor fellow, they were capable of being made more shabby—compounded some hot mixture in a jug with gin and lemons, and stirred it round and round and put it on the hob to simmer; Master Peter, and the two ubiquitous young Cratchits went to fetch the goose, with which they soon returned in high procession.

Such a bustle ensued that you might have thought a goose the rarest of all birds; a feathered phenomenon, to which a black swan was a matter of course—and in truth it was something very like it in that house. Mrs. Cratchit made the gravy (ready beforehand in a little saucepan) hissing hot; Master Peter mashed the potatoes with incredible vigour; Miss Belinda sweetened up the apple-sauce; Martha dusted the hot plates; Bob took Tiny Tim beside him in a tiny corner at the table; the two young Cratchits set chairs for everybody, not forgetting themselves, and mounting guard upon their posts, crammed spoons into their mouths, lest they should shriek for goose before their turn came to be helped. At last the dishes were set on, and grace was said. It was succeeded by a breathless pause, as Mrs. Cratchit, looking slowly all along the carving-knife, prepared to plunge it in the breast; but when she did, and when the long expected gush of stuffing issued forth, one murmur of delight arose all round the board, and even Tiny Tim, excited by the two young Cratchits, beat on the table with the handle of his knife, and feebly cried Hurrah.

There never was such a goose. Bob said he didn't believe there ever was such a goose cooked. Its tenderness and flavour, size and cheapness, were the themes of universal admiration. Eked out by apple-sauce and mashed potatoes, it was a sufficient dinner for the whole family; indeed, as Mrs. Cratchit said with great delight (surveying one small atom of a bone upon the dish), they hadn't ate it all at last. Yet every one had had enough, and the youngest Cratchits in particular, were steeped in sage and onion to the eyebrows. But now, the plates being changed by Miss Belinda, Mrs. Cratchit left the room alone—too nervous to bear witnesses—to take the pudding up and bring it in.

Suppose it should not be done enough. Suppose it should break in turning out. Suppose somebody should have got over the wall of the back-yard, and stolen it, while they were merry with the goose—a supposition at which the two young Cratchits became livid. All sorts of horrors were supposed.

Hallo. A great deal of steam. The pudding was out of the copper. A smell like a washing-day. That was the cloth. A smell like an eating-house and a pastrycook's next door to each other, with a laundress's next door to that. That was the pudding. In half a minute Mrs. Cratchit entered—flushed, but smiling proudly—with the pudding, like a speckled cannon-ball, so hard and firm, blazing in half of half-a-quartern of ignited brandy, and bedight with Christmas holly stuck into the top.

Oh, a wonderful pudding. Bob Cratchit said, and calmly too, that he regarded it as the greatest success achieved by Mrs. Cratchit since their marriage. Mrs. Cratchit said that now the weight was off her mind, she would confess she had had her doubts about the quantity of flour. Everybody had something to say about it, but nobody said or thought it was at all a small pudding for a large family. It would have been flat heresy to do so. Any Cratchit would have blushed to hint at such a thing.

At last the dinner was all done, the cloth was cleared, the hearth swept, and the fire made up. The compound in the jug being tasted, and considered perfect, apples and oranges were put upon the table, and a shovel-full of chestnuts on the fire. Then all the Cratchit family drew round the hearth, in what Bob Cratchit called a circle, meaning half a one; and at Bob Cratchit's elbow stood the family display of glass. Two tumblers, and a custard-cup without a handle.

These held the hot stuff from the jug, however, as well as golden goblets would have done; and Bob served it out with beaming looks, while the chestnuts on the fire sputtered and cracked noisily. Then Bob proposed:

"A Merry Christmas to us all, my dears. God bless us."

Which all the family re-echoed.

"God bless us every one," said Tiny Tim, the last of all.

He sat very close to his father's side upon his little stool. Bob held his withered little hand in his, as if he loved the child, and wished to keep him by his side, and dreaded that he might be taken from him.

"Spirit," said Scrooge, with an interest he had never felt before, "tell me if Tiny Tim will live."

"I see a vacant seat," replied the Ghost, "in the poor chimney-corner, and a crutch without an owner, carefully preserved. If these shadows remain unaltered by the Future, the child will die."

"No, no," said Scrooge. "Oh, no, kind Spirit, say he will be spared."

"If these shadows remain unaltered by the Future, none other of my race," returned the Ghost, "will find him here. What then? If he be like to die, he had better do it, and decrease the surplus population."

Scrooge hung his head to hear his own words quoted by the Spirit, and was overcome with penitence and grief.

"Man," said the Ghost, "if man you be in heart, not adamant, forbear that wicked cant until you have dis-covered What the surplus is, and Where it is. Will you decide what men shall live, what men shall die? It may be, that in the sight of Heaven, you are more worthless and less fit to live than millions like this poor man's child. Oh God, to hear the Insect on the leaf pronounc-ing on the too much life among his hungry brothers in the dust."

Scrooge bent before the Ghost's rebuke, and trem-bling cast his eyes upon the ground. But he raised them speedily, on hearing his own name.

"Mr. Scrooge," said Bob; "I'll give you Mr. Scrooge, the Founder of the Feast."

"The Founder of the Feast indeed," cried Mrs. Cratchit, reddening. "I wish I had him here. I'd give him a piece of my mind to feast upon, and I hope he'd have a good appetite for it."

"My dear," said Bob, "the children. Christmas Day."

"It should be Christmas Day, I am sure," said she, "on which one drinks the health of such an odious, stingy, hard, unfeeling man as Mr. Scrooge. You know he is, Robert. Nobody knows it better than you do, poor fellow."

"My dear," was Bob's mild answer, "Christmas Day."

"I'll drink his health for your sake and the Day's," said Mrs. Cratchit, "not for his. Long life to him. A merry Christmas and a happy new year. He'll be very merry and very happy, I have no doubt."

The children drank the toast after her. It was the first of their proceedings which had no heartiness. Tiny Tim drank it last of all, but he didn't care twopence for it. Scrooge was the Ogre of the family. The mention of his name cast a dark shadow on the party, which was not dispelled for full five minutes.

After it had passed away, they were ten times merrier than before, from the mere relief of Scrooge the Baleful being done with. Bob Cratchit told them how he had a situation in his eye for Master Peter, which would bring in, if obtained, full five-and-sixpence weekly. The two young Cratchits laughed tremendously at the idea of Peter's being a man of business; and Peter himself looked thoughtfully at the fire from between his collars, as if he were deliberating what particular investments he should favour when he came into the receipt of that bewildering income. Martha, who was a poor apprentice at a milliner's, then told them what kind of work she had to do, and how many hours she worked at a stretch, and how she meant to lie abed to-morrow morning for a good long rest; to-morrow being a holiday she passed at home. Also how she had seen a countess and a lord some days before, and how the lord was much about as tall as Peter; at which Peter pulled up his collars so high that you couldn't have seen his head if you had been there. All this time the chestnuts and the jug went round and round; and by-and-bye they had a song, about a lost child travelling in the snow, from Tiny Tim, who had a plaintive little voice, and sang it very well indeed.

There was nothing of high mark in this. They were not a handsome family; they were not well dressed; their shoes were far from being water-proof; their clothes were scanty; and Peter might have known, and very likely did, the inside of a pawnbroker's. But, they were happy, grateful, pleased with one another, and content-ed with the time; and when they faded, and looked hap-pier yet in the bright sprinklings of the Spirit's torch at parting, Scrooge had his eye upon them, and especially on Tiny Tim, until the last.

By this time it was getting dark, and snowing pretty heavily; and as Scrooge and the Spirit went along the streets, the brightness of the roaring fires in kitchens, parlours, and all sorts of rooms, was wonderful. Here, the flickering of the blaze showed preparations for a cosy din-ner, with hot plates baking through and through before the fire, and deep red curtains, ready to be drawn to shut out cold and darkness. There all the children of the house were running out into the snow to meet their married sisters, brothers, cousins, uncles, aunts, and be the first to greet them. Here, again, were shadows on the window-blind of guests assembling; and there a group of handsome girls, all hooded and fur-booted, and all chattering at once, tripped lightly off to some near neighbour's house; where, woe upon the single man who saw them enter—artful witches, well they knew it—in a glow.

But, if you had judged from the numbers of people on their way to friendly gatherings, you might have thought that no one was at home to give them welcome when they got there, instead of every house expecting company, and piling up its fires half-chimney high. Blessings on it, how the Ghost exulted. How it bared its breadth of breast, and opened its capacious palm, and floated on, outpouring, with a generous hand, its bright and harmless mirth on everything within its reach. The very lamplighter, who ran on before, dotting the dusky street with specks of light, and who was dressed to spend the evening somewhere, laughed out loudly as the Spirit passed, though little kenned the lamplighter that he had any company but Christmas.

And now, without a word of warning from the Ghost, they stood upon a bleak and desert moor, where monstrous masses of rude stone were cast about, as though it were the burial-place of giants; and water spread itself wheresoever it listed, or would have done so, but for the frost that held it prisoner; and nothing grew but moss and furze, and coarse rank grass. Down in the west the setting sun had left a streak of fiery red, which glared upon the desolation for an instant, like a sullen eye, and frowning lower, lower, lower yet, was lost in the thick gloom of darkest night.

"What place is this?" asked Scrooge.

"A place where Miners live, who labour in the bowels of the earth," returned the Spirit. "But they know me. See."

A light shone from the window of a hut, and swiftly they advanced towards it. Passing through the wall of mud and stone, they found a cheerful company assembled round a glowing fire. An old, old man and woman, with their children and their children's children, and another generation beyond that, all decked out gaily in their holiday attire. The old man, in a voice that seldom rose above the howling of the wind upon the barren waste, was singing them a Christmas song—it had been a very old song when he was a boy—and from time to time they all joined in the chorus. So surely as they raised their voices, the old man got quite blithe and loud; and so surely as they stopped, his vigour sank again.

The Spirit did not tarry here, but bade Scrooge hold his robe, and passing on above the moor, sped—whither. Not to sea. To sea. To Scrooge's horror, looking back, he saw the last of the land, a frightful range of rocks,

behind them; and his ears were deafened by the thun-
dering of water, as it rolled and roared, and raged among
the dreadful caverns it had worn, and fiercely tried to
undermine the earth.

Built upon a dismal reef of sunken rocks, some league
or so from shore, on which the waters chafed and
dashed, the wild year through, there stood a solitary
lighthouse. Great heaps of sea-weed clung to its base,
and storm-birds—born of the wind one might suppose,
as sea-weed of the water—rose and fell about it, like the
waves they skimmed.

But even here, two men who watched the light had
made a fire, that through the loophole in the thick
stone wall shed out a ray of brightness on the awful sea.
Joining their horny hands over the rough table at which
they sat, they wished each other Merry Christmas in
their can of grog; and one of them: the elder, too, with
his face all damaged and scarred with hard weather, as
the figure-head of an old ship might be: struck up a stur-
dy song that was like a Gale in itself.

Again the Ghost sped on, above the black and heav-
ing sea—on, on—until, being far away, as he told
Scrooge, from any shore, they lighted on a ship. They
stood beside the helmsman at the wheel, the look-out in
the bow, the officers who had the watch; dark, ghostly
figures in their several stations; but every man among
them hummed a Christmas tune, or had a Christmas
thought, or spoke below his breath to his companion of

some bygone Christmas Day, with homeward hopes belonging to it. And every man on board, waking or sleeping, good or bad, had had a kinder word for another on that day than on any day in the year; and had shared to some extent in its festivities; and had remembered those he cared for at a distance, and had known that they delighted to remember him.

It was a great surprise to Scrooge, while listening to the moaning of the wind, and thinking what a solemn thing it was to move on through the lonely darkness over an unknown abyss, whose depths were secrets as profound as Death: it was a great surprise to Scrooge, while thus engaged, to hear a hearty laugh. It was a much greater surprise to Scrooge to recognise it as his own nephew's and to find himself in a bright, dry, gleaming room, with the Spirit standing smiling by his side, and looking at that same nephew with approving affability.

"Ha, ha," laughed Scrooge's nephew. "Ha, ha, ha."

If you should happen, by any unlikely chance, to know a man more blest in a laugh than Scrooge's nephew, all I can say is, I should like to know him too. Introduce him to me, and I'll cultivate his acquaintance.

It is a fair, even-handed, noble adjustment of things, that while there is infection in disease and sorrow, there is nothing in the world so irresistibly contagious as laughter and good-humour. When Scrooge's nephew laughed in this way: holding his sides, rolling his head, and twisting his face into the most extravagant contortions: Scrooge's niece, by marriage, laughed as heartily as he. And their assembled friends being not a bit behindhand, roared out lustily.

"Ha, ha. Ha, ha, ha, ha."

"He said that Christmas was a humbug, as I live," cried Scrooge's nephew. "He believed it too."

"More shame for him, Fred," said Scrooge's niece, indignantly. Bless those women; they never do anything by halves. They are always in earnest.

She was very pretty: exceedingly pretty. With a dimpled, surprised-looking, capital face; a ripe little mouth, that seemed made to be kissed—as no doubt it was; all kinds of good little dots about her chin, that melted into one another when she laughed; and the sunniest pair of eyes you ever saw in any little creature's head. Altogether she was what you would have called provoking, you know; but satisfactory.

"He's a comical old fellow," said Scrooge's nephew, "that's the truth: and not so pleasant as he might be. However, his offences carry their own punishment, and I have nothing to say against him."

"I'm sure he is very rich, Fred," hinted Scrooge's niece. "At least you always tell me so."

"What of that, my dear?" said Scrooge's nephew. "His wealth is of no use to him. He doesn't do any good with it. He make himself comfortable with it. He hasn't the satisfaction of thinking—ha, ha, ha—that he is ever going to benefit us with it."

"I have no patience with him," observed Scrooge's niece. Scrooge's niece's sisters, and all the other ladies, expressed the same opinion.

"Oh, I have," said Scrooge's nephew. "I am sorry for him; I couldn't be angry with him if I tried. Who suffers by his ill whims? Himself, always. Here, he takes it into his head to dislike us, and he won't come and dine with us. What's the consequence? He don't lose much of a dinner."

"Indeed, I think he loses a very good dinner," interrupted Scrooge's niece. Everybody else said the same, and they must be allowed to have been competent judges, because they had just had dinner; and, with the dessert upon the table, were clustered round the fire, by lamplight.

"Well. I'm very glad to hear it," said Scrooge's nephew, "because I haven't great faith in these young housekeepers. What do you say, Topper?"

Topper had clearly got his eye upon one of Scrooge's niece's sisters, for he answered that a bachelor was a wretched outcast, who had no right to express an opinion on the subject. Whereat Scrooge's niece's sister— the plump one with the lace tucker: not the one with the roses—blushed.

"Do go on, Fred," said Scrooge's niece, clapping her hands. "He never finishes what he begins to say. He is such a ridiculous fellow."

Scrooge's nephew revelled in another laugh, and as it was impossible to keep the infection off; though the plump sister tried hard to do it with aromatic vinegar; his example was unanimously followed.

"I was only going to say," said Scrooge's nephew, "that the consequence of his taking a dislike to us, and not making merry with us, is, as I think, that he loses some pleasant moments, which could do him no harm. I am sure he loses pleasanter companions than he can find in his own thoughts, either in his mouldy old office, or his dusty chambers. I mean to give him the same chance every year, whether he likes it or not, for I pity him. He may rail at Christmas till he dies, but he can't help thinking better of it—I defy him—if he finds me going there, in good temper, year after year, and saying Uncle Scrooge, how are you? If it only puts him in the vein to leave his poor clerk fifty pounds, that's something; and I think I shook him yesterday."

It was their turn to laugh now at the notion of his shaking Scrooge. But being thoroughly good-natured, and not much caring what they laughed at, so that they laughed at any rate, he encouraged them in their merriment, and passed the bottle joyously.

After tea they had some music. For they were a musical family, and knew what they were about, when they sung a Glee or Catch, I can assure you: especially Topper, who could growl away in the bass like a good one, and never swell the large veins in his forehead, or get red in the face over it. Scrooge's niece played well upon the harp; and played among other tunes a simple little air (a mere nothing: you might learn to whistle it in two minutes), which had been familiar to the child who fetched Scrooge from the boarding-school, as he had been reminded by the Ghost of Christmas Past. When this strain of music sounded, all the things that Ghost had shown him, came upon his mind; he softened more and more; and thought that if he could have listened to it often, years ago, he might have cultivated the kindnesses of life for his own happiness with his own hands, without resorting to the sexton's spade that buried Jacob Marley.

But they didn't devote the whole evening to music. After a while they played at forfeits; for it is good to be children sometimes, and never better than at Christmas, when its mighty Founder was a child himself. Stop. There was first a game at blind-man's buff. Of course there was. And I no more believe Topper was really blind than I believe he had eyes in his boots. My opinion is, that it was a done thing between him and Scrooge's nephew; and that the Ghost of Christmas Present knew it. The way he went after that plump sister in the lace tucker, was an outrage on the credulity of human nature. Knocking down the fire-irons, tumbling over the chairs, bumping against the piano, smothering himself among the curtains, wherever she went, there went he. He always knew where the plump sister was.

He wouldn't catch anybody else. If you had fallen up
against him (as some of them did), on purpose, he would
have made a feint of endeavouring to seize you, which
would have been an affront to your understanding, and
would instantly have sidled off in the direction of the
plump sister. She often cried out that it wasn't fair; and
it really was not. But when at last, he caught her; when,
in spite of all her silken rustlings, and her rapid flutter-
ings past him, he got her into a corner whence there was
no escape; then his conduct was the most execrable. For
his pretending not to know her; his pretending that it
was necessary to touch her head-dress, and further to
assure himself of her identity by pressing a certain ring
upon her finger, and a certain chain about her neck; was
vile, monstrous. No doubt she told him her opinion of
it, when, another blind-man being in office, they were
so very confidential together, behind the curtains.

Scrooge's niece was not one of the blind-man's buff
party, but was made comfortable with a large chair and a
footstool, in a snug corner, where the Ghost and Scrooge
were close behind her. But she joined in the forfeits, and
loved her love to admiration with all the letters of the
alphabet. Likewise at the game of How, When, and
Where, she was very great, and to the secret joy of
Scrooge's nephew, beat her sisters hollow: though they
were sharp girls too, as I could have told you. There
might have been twenty people there, young and old, but
they all played, and so did Scrooge, for, wholly forgetting

the interest he had in what was going on, that his voice made no sound in their ears, he sometimes came out with his guess quite loud, and very often guessed quite right, too; for the sharpest needle, best Whitechapel, warranted not to cut in the eye, was not sharper than Scrooge; blunt as he took it in his head to be.

The Ghost was greatly pleased to find him in this mood, and looked upon him with such favour, that he begged like a boy to be allowed to stay until the guests departed. But this the Spirit said could not be done.

"Here is a new game," said Scrooge. "One half hour, Spirit, only one."

It was a Game called Yes and No, where Scrooge's nephew had to think of something, and the rest must find out what; he only answering to their questions yes or no, as the case was. The brisk fire of questioning to which he was exposed, elicited from him that he was thinking of an animal, a live animal, rather a disagreeable animal, a savage animal, an animal that growled and grunted sometimes, and talked sometimes, and lived in London, and walked about the streets, and wasn't made a show of, and wasn't led by anybody, and didn't live in a menagerie, and was never killed in a market, and was not a horse, or an ass, or a cow, or a bull, or a tiger, or a dog, or a pig, or a cat, or a bear. At every fresh question that was put to him, this nephew burst into a fresh roar of laughter; and was so inexpressibly tickled, that he was obliged to get up off the sofa and stamp. At last the plump sister, falling into a similar state, cried out:

"I have found it out. I know what it is, Fred. I know what it is."

"What is it?" cried Fred.

"It's your Uncle Scrooge."

Which it certainly was. Admiration was the universal sentiment, though some objected that the reply to "Is it a bear?" ought to have been "Yes;" inasmuch as an answer in the negative was sufficient to have diverted their thoughts from Mr. Scrooge, supposing they had ever had any tendency that way.

"He has given us plenty of merriment, I am sure," said Fred, "and it would be ungrateful not to drink to his health. Here is a glass of mulled wine ready to our hand at the moment; and I say, 'Uncle Scrooge.'"

"Well. Uncle Scrooge!" they cried.

"A Merry Christmas and a Happy New Year to the old man, whatever he is," said Scrooge's nephew. "He wouldn't take it from me, but may he have it, nevertheless. Uncle Scrooge."

Uncle Scrooge had imperceptibly become so gay and light of heart, that he would have pledged the unconscious company in return, and thanked them in an inaudible speech, if the Ghost had given him time. But the whole scene passed off in the breath of the last word spoken by his nephew; and he and the Spirit were again upon their travels.

Much they saw, and far they went, and many homes they visited, but always with a happy end. The Spirit stood beside sick beds, and they were cheerful; on foreign lands, and they were close at home; by struggling men, and they were patient in their greater hope; by poverty, and it was rich. In almshouse, hospital, and jail, in misery's every refuge, where vain man in his little brief authority had not made fast the door and barred the Spirit out, he left his blessing, and taught Scrooge his precepts.

It was a long night, if it were only a night; but Scrooge had his doubts of this, because the Christmas Holidays appeared to be condensed into the space of time they passed together. It was strange, too, that while Scrooge remained unaltered in his outward form, the Ghost grew older, clearly older. Scrooge had observed this change, but never spoke of it, until they left a children's Twelfth Night party, when, looking at the Spirit as they stood together in an open place, he noticed that its hair was grey.

"Are spirits' lives so short?" asked Scrooge.

"My life upon this globe, is very brief," replied the Ghost. "It ends to-night."

"To-night?" cried Scrooge.

"To-night at midnight. Hark. The time is drawing near."

The chimes were ringing the three quarters past eleven at that moment.

"Forgive me if I am not justified in what I ask," said Scrooge, looking intently at the Spirit's robe, "but I see something strange, and not belonging to yourself, protruding from your skirts. Is it a foot or a claw?"

"It might be a claw, for the flesh there is upon it," was the Spirit's sorrowful reply. "Look here."

From the foldings of its robe, it brought two children; wretched, abject, frightful, hideous, miserable. They knelt down at its feet, and clung upon the outside of its garment.

"Oh, Man, look here. Look, look, down here," exclaimed the Ghost.

They were a boy and a girl. Yellow, meagre, ragged, scowling, wolfish; but prostrate, too, in their humility. Where graceful youth should have filled their features out, and touched them with its freshest tints, a stale and shrivelled hand, like that of age, had pinched, and twisted them, and pulled them into shreds. Where angels might have sat enthroned, devils lurked, and glared out menacing. No change, no degradation, no perversion of humanity, in any grade, through all the mysteries of wonderful creation, has monsters half so horrible and dread.

Scrooge started back, appalled. Having them shown to him in this way, he tried to say they were fine children, but the words choked themselves, rather than be parties to a lie of such enormous magnitude.

"Spirit, are they yours?" Scrooge could say no more.

"They are Man's," said the Spirit, looking down upon them. "And they cling to me, appealing from their fathers. This boy is Ignorance. This girl is Want. Beware them both, and all of their degree, but most of all beware this boy, for on his brow I see that written which is Doom, unless the writing be erased. Deny it," cried the Spirit, stretching out its hand towards the city. "Slander those who tell it ye. Admit it for your factious purposes, and make it worse. And bide the end."

"Have they no refuge or resource?" cried Scrooge.

"Are there no prisons?" said the Spirit, turning on him for the last time with his own words. "Are there no workhouses?" The bell struck twelve.

Scrooge looked about him for the Ghost, and saw it not. As the last stroke ceased to vibrate, he remembered the prediction of old Jacob Marley, and lifting up his eyes, beheld a solemn Phantom, draped and hooded, coming, like a mist along the ground, towards him.

# STAVE FOUR.

————

## THE LAST OF THE SPIRITS.

THE PHANTOM slowly, gravely, silently approached. When it came, Scrooge bent down upon his knee; for in the very air through which this Spirit moved it seemed to scatter gloom and mystery.

It was shrouded in a deep black garment, which concealed its head, its face, its form, and left nothing of it visible save one outstretched hand. But for this it would have been difficult to detach its figure from the night, and separate it from the darkness by which it was surrounded.

He felt that it was tall and stately when it came beside him, and that its mysterious presence filled him with a solemn dread. He knew no more, for the Spirit neither spoke nor moved.

"I am in the presence of the Ghost of Christmas Yet To Come," said Scrooge.

The Spirit answered not, but pointed onward with its hand.

"You are about to show me shadows of the things that have not happened, but will happen in the time before us," Scrooge pursued. "Is that so, Spirit?"

The upper portion of the garment was contracted for an instant in its folds, as if the Spirit had inclined its head. That was the only answer he received.

Although well used to ghostly company by this time, Scrooge feared the silent shape so much that his legs trembled beneath him, and he found that he could hardly stand when he prepared to follow it. The Spirit pauses a moment, as observing his condition, and giving him time to recover.

But Scrooge was all the worse for this. It thrilled him with a vague uncertain horror, to know that behind the dusky shroud, there were ghostly eyes intently fixed upon him, while he, though he stretched his own to the utmost, could see nothing but a spectral hand and one great heap of black.

"Ghost of the Future," he exclaimed, "I fear you more than any spectre I have seen. But as I know your purpose is to do me good, and as I hope to live to be another man from what I was, I am prepared to bear you company, and do it with a thankful heart. Will you not speak to me?"

It gave him no reply. The hand was pointed straight before them.

"Lead on." said Scrooge. "Lead on. The night is waning fast, and it is precious time to me, I know. Lead on, Spirit."

The Phantom moved away as it had come towards him. Scrooge followed in the shadow of its dress, which bore him up, he thought, and carried him along.

They scarcely seemed to enter the city; for the city rather seemed to spring up about them, and encompass them of its own act. But there they were, in the heart of it; on Change, amongst the merchants; who hurried up and down, and chinked the money in their pockets, and conversed in groups, and looked at their watches, and trifled thoughtfully with their great gold seals; and so forth, as Scrooge had seen them often.

The Spirit stopped beside one little knot of business men. Observing that the hand was pointed to them, Scrooge advanced to listen to their talk.

"No," said a great fat man with a monstrous chin, "I don't know much about it, either way. I only know he's dead."

"When did he die?" inquired another.

"Last night, I believe."

"Why, what was the matter with him?" asked a third, taking a vast quantity of snuff out of a very large snuff-box. "I thought he'd never die."

"God knows," said the first, with a yawn.

"What has he done with his money?" asked a red-faced gentleman with a pendulous excrescence on the end of his nose, that shook like the gills of a turkey-cock.

"I haven't heard," said the man with the large chin, yawning again. "Left it to his company, perhaps. He hasn't left it to me. That's all I know."

This pleasantry was received with a general laugh.

"It's likely to be a very cheap funeral," said the same speaker, "for upon my life I don't know of anybody to go to it. Suppose we make up a party and volunteer."

"I don't mind going if a lunch is provided," observed the gentleman with the excrescence on his nose. "But I must be fed, if I make one."

Another laugh.

"Well, I am the most disinterested among you, after all," said the first speaker, "for I never wear black gloves, and I never eat lunch. But I'll offer to go, if anybody else will. When I come to think of it, I'm not at all sure that I wasn't his most particular friend; for we used to stop and speak whenever we met. Bye, bye."

Speakers and listeners strolled away, and mixed with other groups. Scrooge knew the men, and looked towards the Spirit for an explanation.

The Phantom glided on into a street. Its finger pointed to two persons meeting. Scrooge listened again, thinking that the explanation might lie here.

He knew these men, also, perfectly. They were men of business: very wealthy, and of great importance. He had made a point always of standing well in their esteem: in a business point of view, that is; strictly in a business point of view.

"How are you?" said one.

"How are you?" returned the other.

"Well," said the first. "Old Scratch has got his own at last, hey."

"So I am told," returned the second. "Cold, isn't it."

"Seasonable for Christmas time. You're not a skater, I suppose."

"No. No. Something else to think of. Good morning."

Not another word. That was their meeting, their conversation, and their parting.

Scrooge was at first inclined to be surprised that the Spirit should attach importance to conversations apparently so trivial; but feeling assured that they must have some hidden purpose, he set himself to consider what it was likely to be. They could scarcely be supposed to have any bearing on the death of Jacob, his old partner, for that was Past, and this Ghost's province was the Future. Nor could he think of any one immediately connected with himself, to whom he could apply them. But nothing doubting that to whomsoever they applied they had some latent moral for his own improvement, he resolved to treasure up every word he heard, and everything he saw; and especially to observe the shadow of himself when it appeared. For he had an expectation that the conduct of his future self would give him the clue he missed, and would render the solution of these riddles easy.

He looked about in that very place for his own image; but another man stood in his accustomed corner, and though the clock pointed to his usual time of day for being there, he saw no likeness of himself among the multitudes that poured in through the Porch. It gave him little surprise, however; for he had been revolving in his mind a change of life, and thought and hoped he saw his new-born resolutions carried out in this.

Quiet and dark, beside him stood the Phantom, with its outstretched hand. When he roused himself from his thoughtful quest, he fancied from the turn of the hand, and its situation in reference to himself, that the Unseen Eyes were looking at him keenly. It made him shudder, and feel very cold.

They left the busy scene, and went into an obscure part of the town, where Scrooge had never penetrated before, although he recognised its situation, and its bad repute. The ways were foul and narrow; the shops and houses wretched; the people half-naked, drunken, slip-shod, ugly. Alleys and archways, like so many cesspools, disgorged their offences of smell, and dirt, and life, upon the straggling streets; and the whole quarter reeked with crime, with filth, and misery.

Far in this den of infamous resort, there was a low-browed, beetling shop, below a pent-house roof, where iron, old rags, bottles, bones, and greasy offal, were bought. Upon the floor within, were piled up heaps of rusty keys, nails, chains, hinges, files, scales, weights, and refuse iron of all kinds. Secrets that few would like to scrutinise were bred and hidden in mountains of unseemly rags, masses of corrupted fat, and sepulchres of bones. Sitting in among the wares he dealt in, by a charcoal stove, made of old bricks, was a grey-haired rascal, nearly seventy years of age; who had screened himself from the cold air without, by a frousy curtaining of miscellaneous tatters, hung upon a line; and smoked his pipe in all the luxury of calm retirement.

Scrooge and the Phantom came into the presence of this man, just as a woman with a heavy bundle slunk into the shop. But she had scarcely entered, when another woman, similarly laden, came in too; and she was closely followed by a man in faded black, who was no less startled by the sight of them, than they had been upon the recognition of each other. After a short period of blank astonishment, in which the old man with the pipe had joined them, they all three burst into a laugh.

"Let the charwoman alone to be the first," cried she who had entered first. "Let the laundress alone to be the second; and let the undertaker's man alone to be the third. Look here, old Joe, here's a chance. If we haven't all three met here without meaning it."

"You couldn't have met in a better place," said old Joe, removing his pipe from his mouth. "Come into the parlour. You were made free of it long ago, you know; and the other two an't strangers. Stop till I shut the door of the shop. Ah. How it skreeks. There ain't such a rusty bit of metal in the place as its own hinges, I believe; and I'm sure there's no such old bones here, as mine. Ha, ha. We're all suitable to our calling, we're well matched. Come into the parlour. Come into the parlour."

The parlour was the space behind the screen of rags. The old man raked the fire together with an old stair-rod, and having trimmed his smoky lamp (for it was night), with the stem of his pipe, put it in his mouth again.

While he did this, the woman who had already spoken threw her bundle on the floor, and sat down in a flaunting manner on a stool; crossing her elbows on her knees, and looking with a bold defiance at the other two.

"What odds then? What odds, Mrs. Dilber?" said the woman. "Every person has a right to take care of themselves. He always did."

"That's true, indeed," said the laundress. "No man more so."

"Why then, stand staring as if you was afraid, woman; who's the wiser? We're not going to pick holes in each other's coats, I suppose."

"No, indeed," said Mrs. Dilber and the man together. "We should hope not."

"Very well, then," cried the woman. "That's enough. Who's the worse for the loss of a few things like these? Not a dead man, I suppose."

"No, indeed," said Mrs. Dilber, laughing.

"If he wanted to keep them after he was dead, a wicked old screw," pursued the woman, "why wasn't he natural in his lifetime? If he had been, he'd have had somebody to look after him when he was struck with Death, instead of lying gasping out his last there, alone by himself."

"It's the truest word that ever was spoke," said Mrs. Dilber. "It's a judgment on him."

"I wish it was a little heavier judgment," replied the woman; "and it should have been, you may depend upon it, if I could have laid my hands on anything else. Open that bundle, old Joe, and let me know the value of it. Speak out plain. I'm not afraid to be the first, nor afraid for them to see it. We know pretty well that we were helping ourselves, before we met here, I believe. It's no sin. Open the bundle, Joe."

But the gallantry of her friends would not allow of this; and the man in faded black, mounting the breach first, produced his plunder. It was not extensive. A seal or two, a pencil-case, a pair of sleeve-buttons, and a brooch of no great value, were all. They were severally examined and appraised by old Joe, who chalked the sums he was disposed to give for each, upon the wall, and added them up into a total when he found there was nothing more to come.

"That's your account," said Joe, "and I wouldn't give another sixpence, if I was to be boiled for not doing it. Who's next?"

Mrs. Dilber was next. Sheets and towels, a little wearing apparel, two old-fashioned silver teaspoons, a pair of sugar-tongs, and a few boots. Her account was stated on the wall in the same manner.

"I always give too much to ladies. It's a weakness of mine, and that's the way I ruin myself," said old Joe.

"That's your account. If you asked me for another penny, and made it an open question, I'd repent of being so liberal and knock off half-a-crown."

"And now undo my bundle, Joe," said the first woman.

Joe went down on his knees for the greater convenience of opening it, and having unfastened a great many knots, dragged out a large and heavy roll of some dark stuff.

"What do you call this?" said Joe. "Bed-curtains."

"Ah," returned the woman, laughing and leaning forward on her crossed arms. "Bed-curtains."

"You mean to say you took them down, rings and all, with him lying there?" said Joe.

"Yes I do," replied the woman. "Why not?"

"You were born to make your fortune," said Joe," and you'll certainly do it."

"I certainly shan't hold my hand, when I can get anything in it by reaching it out, for the sake of such a man as he was, I promise you, Joe," returned the woman coolly. "Drop that oil upon the blankets, now."

"His blankets," asked Joe.

"Whose else's do you think." replied the woman. "He isn't likely to take cold without them, I dare say."

"I hope he didn't die of any thing catching. Eh." said old Joe, stopping in his work, and looking up.

"Don't you be afraid of that," returned the woman. "I an't so fond of his company that I'd loiter about him for such things, if he did. Ah, you may look through that shirt till your eyes ache; but you won't find a hole in it, nor a threadbare place. It's the best he had, and a fine one, too. They'd have wasted it, if it hadn't been for me."

"What do you call wasting of it?" asked old Joe.

"Putting it on him to be buried in, to be sure," replied the woman with a laugh. "Somebody was fool enough to do it, but I took it off again. If calico an't good enough for such a purpose, it isn't good enough for anything. It's quite as becoming to the body. He can't look uglier than he did in that one."

Scrooge listened to this dialogue in horror. As they sat grouped about their spoil, in the scanty light afforded by the old man's lamp, he viewed them with a detestation and disgust, which could hardly have been greater, though they demons, marketing the corpse itself.

"Ha, ha," laughed the same woman, when old Joe, producing a flannel bag with money in it, told out their several gains upon the ground. "This is the end of it, you see. He frightened every one away from him when he was alive, to profit us when he was dead. Ha, ha, ha."

"Spirit," said Scrooge, shuddering from head to foot. "I see, I see. The case of this unhappy man might be my own. My life tends that way, now. Merciful Heaven, what is this?"

He recoiled in terror, for the scene had changed, and now he almost touched a bed: a bare, uncurtained bed: on which, beneath a ragged sheet, there lay a something covered up, which, though it was dumb, announced itself in awful language.

The room was very dark, too dark to be observed with any accuracy, though Scrooge glanced round it in obedience to a secret impulse, anxious to know what kind of room it was. A pale light, rising in the outer air, fell straight upon the bed; and on it, plundered and bereft, unwatched, unwept, uncared for, was the body of this man.

Scrooge glanced towards the Phantom. Its steady hand was pointed to the head. The cover was so carelessly adjusted that the slightest raising of it, the motion of a finger upon Scrooge's part, would have disclosed the face. He thought of it, felt how easy it would be to do, and longed to do it; but had no more power to withdraw the veil than to dismiss the spectre at his side.

Oh cold, cold, rigid, dreadful Death, set up thine altar here, and dress it with such terrors as thou hast at thy command: for this is thy dominion. But of the loved, revered, and honoured head, thou canst not turn one hair to thy dread purposes, or make one feature odious. It is not that the hand is heavy and will fall down when released; it is not that the heart and pulse are still; but that the hand was open, generous, and true; the heart brave, warm, and tender; and the pulse a man's. Strike, Shadow, strike. And see his good deeds springing from the wound, to sow the world with life immortal.

No voice pronounced these words in Scrooge's ears, and yet he heard them when he looked upon the bed. He thought, if this man could be raised up now, what would be his foremost thoughts? Avarice, hard-dealing, griping cares? They have brought him to a rich end, truly.

He lay, in the dark empty house, with not a man, a woman, or a child, to say that he was kind to me in this or that, and for the memory of one kind word I will be kind to him. A cat was tearing at the door, and there was a sound of gnawing rats beneath the hearth-stone. What they wanted in the room of death, and why they were so restless and disturbed, Scrooge did not dare to think.

"Spirit," he said, "this is a fearful place. In leaving it, I shall not leave its lesson, trust me. Let us go."

Still the Ghost pointed with an unmoved finger to the head.

"I understand you," Scrooge returned, "and I would do it, if I could. But I have not the power, Spirit. I have not the power."

Again it seemed to look upon him.

"If there is any person in the town, who feels emotion caused by this man's death," said Scrooge quite agonised, "show that person to me, Spirit, I beseech you."

The Phantom spread its dark robe before him for a moment, like a wing; and withdrawing it, revealed a room by daylight, where a mother and her children were.

She was expecting some one, and with anxious eager-ness; for she walked up and down the room; started at every sound; looked out from the window; glanced at the clock; tried, but in vain, to work with her needle; and could hardly bear the voices of the children in their play.

At length the long-expected knock was heard. She hurried to the door, and met her husband; a man whose face was careworn and depressed, though he was young. There was a remarkable expression in it now; a kind of serious delight of which he felt ashamed, and which he struggled to repress.

He sat down to the dinner that had been boarding for him by the fire; and when she asked him faintly what news (which was not until after a long silence), he appeared embarrassed how to answer.

"Is it good," she said, "or bad?"—to help him.

"Bad," he answered.

"We are quite ruined."

"No. There is hope yet, Caroline."

"If he relents," she said, amazed, "there is. Nothing is past hope, if such a miracle has happened."

"He is past relenting," said her husband. "He is dead."

She was a mild and patient creature if her face spoke truth; but she was thankful in her soul to hear it, and she said so, with clasped hands. She prayed forgiveness the next moment, and was sorry; but the first was the emotion of her heart.

"What the half-drunken woman whom I told you of last night, said to me, when I tried to see him and obtain a week's delay; and what I thought was a mere excuse to avoid me; turns out to have been quite true. He was not only very ill, but dying, then."

"To whom will our debt be transferred?"

"I know. But before that time we shall be ready with the money; and even though we were not, it would be a bad fortune indeed to find so merciless a creditor in his successor. We may sleep to-night with light hearts, Caroline."

Yes. Soften it as they would, their hearts were lighter. The children's faces, hushed and clustered round to hear what they so little understood, were brighter; and it was a happier house for this man's death. The only emotion that the Ghost could show him, caused by the event, was one of pleasure.

"Let me see some tenderness connected with a death," said Scrooge, "or that dark chamber, Spirit, which we left just now, will be for ever present to me."

The Ghost conducted him through several streets familiar to his feet; and as they went along, Scrooge looked here and there to find himself, but nowhere was he to be seen. They entered poor Bob Cratchit's house; the dwelling he had visited before; and found the mother and the children seated round the fire.

Quiet. Very quiet. The noisy little Cratchits were as still as statues in one corner, and sat looking up at Peter, who had a book before him. The mother and her daughters were engaged in sewing. But surely they were very quiet.

"And he took a child, and set him in the midst of them."

Where had Scrooge heard those words? He had not dreamed them. The boy must have read them out, as he and the Spirit crossed the threshold. Why did he not go on?

The mother laid her work upon the table, and put her hand up to her face.

"The colour hurts my eyes," she said.

The colour. Ah, poor Tiny Tim.

"They're better now again," said Cratchit's wife. "It makes them weak by candle-light; and I wouldn't show weak eyes to your father when he comes home, for the world. It must be near his time."

"Past it rather," Peter answered, shutting up his book. "But I think he has walked a little slower than he used, these few last evenings, mother."

They were very quiet again. At last she said, and in a steady, cheerful voice, that only faltered once:

"I have known him walk with—I have known him walk with Tiny Tim upon his shoulder, very fast indeed."

"And so have I," cried Peter. "Often."

"And so have I," exclaimed another. So had all.

"But he was very light to carry," she resumed, intent upon her work, "and his father loved him so, that it was no trouble: no trouble. And there is your father at the door."

She hurried out to meet him; and little Bob in his comforter—he had need of it, poor fellow—came in. His tea was ready for him on the hob, and they all tried who should help him to it most. Then the two young Cratchits got upon his knees and laid, each child a little cheek, against his face, as if they said, "Don't mind it, father. Don't be grieved."

Bob was very cheerful with them, and spoke pleasantly to all the family. He looked at the work upon the table, and praised the industry and speed of Mrs. Cratchit and the girls. They would be done long before Sunday, he said.

"Sunday. You went to-day, then, Robert," said his wife.

"Yes, my dear," returned Bob. "I wish you could have gone. It would have done you good to see how green a place it is. But you'll see it often. I promised him that I would walk there on a Sunday. My little, little child," cried Bob. "My little child."

He broke down all at once. He couldn't help it. If he could have helped it, he and his child would have been farther apart perhaps than they were.

He left the room, and went up-stairs into the room above, which was lighted cheerfully, and hung with Christmas. There was a chair set close beside the child, and there were signs of some one having been there, lately. Poor Bob sat down in it, and when he had thought a little and composed himself, he kissed the little face. He was reconciled to what had happened, and went down again quite happy.

They drew about the fire, and talked; the girls and mother working still. Bob told them of the extraordinary kindness of Mr. Scrooge's nephew, whom he had scarcely seen but once, and who, meeting him in the street that day, and seeing that he looked a little, just a little down you know," said Bob, inquired what had happened to distress him. "On which," said Bob, "for he is the pleasantest-spoken gentleman you ever heard, I told him. 'I am heartily sorry for it, Mr. Cratchit,' he said, 'and heartily sorry for your good wife.' By the bye, how he ever knew that, I don't know."

"Knew what, my dear?"

"Why, that you were a good wife," replied Bob.

"Everybody knows that," said Peter.

"Very well observed, my boy," cried Bob. "I hope they do. 'Heartily sorry,' he said, 'for your good wife. If I can be of service to you in any way,' he said, giving me his card, 'that's where I live. Pray come to me.' Now, it wasn't," cried Bob, "for the sake of anything he might be able to do for us, so much as for his kind way, that this was quite delightful. It really seemed as if he had known our Tiny Tim, and felt with us."

"I'm sure he's a good soul." said Mrs. Cratchit.

"You would be surer of it, my dear," returned Bob, "if you saw and spoke to him. I shouldn't be at all surprised, mark what I say—if he got Peter a better situation."

"Only hear that, Peter," said Mrs. Cratchit.

"And then," cried one of the girls, "Peter will be keeping company with some one, and setting up for himself."

"Get along with you," retorted Peter, grinning.

"It's just as likely as not," said Bob, "one of these days; though there's plenty of time for that, my dear. But however and when ever we part from one another, I am sure we shall none of us forget poor Tiny Tim—shall we—or this first parting that there was among us."

"Never, father," cried they all.

"And I know," said Bob, "I know, my dears, that when we recollect how patient and how mild he was; although he was a little, little child; we shall not quarrel easily among ourselves, and forget poor Tiny Tim in doing it."

"No, never, father," they all cried again.

"I am very happy," said little Bob, "I am very happy."

Mrs. Cratchit kissed him, his daughters kissed him, the two young Cratchits kissed him, and Peter and himself shook hands. Spirit of Tiny Tim, thy childish essence was from God.

"Spectre," said Scrooge, "something informs me that our parting moment is at hand. I know it, but I know not how. Tell me what man that was whom we saw lying dead."

The Ghost of Christmas Yet To Come conveyed him, as before—though at a different time, he thought: indeed, there seemed no order in these latter visions, save that they were in the Future—into the resorts of business men, but showed him not himself. Indeed, the

Spirit did not stay for anything, but went straight on, as to the end just now desired, until besought by Scrooge to tarry for a moment.

"This courts," said Scrooge, "through which we hurry now, is where my place of occupation is, and has been for a length of time. I see the house. Let me behold what I shall be, in days to come."

The Spirit stopped; the hand was pointed elsewhere.

"The house is yonder," Scrooge exclaimed. "Why do you point away?"

The inexorable finger underwent no change.

Scrooge hastened to the window of his office, and looked in. It was an office still, but not his. The furniture was not the same, and the figure in the chair was not himself. The Phantom pointed as before.

He joined it once again, and wondering why and whither he had gone, accompanied it until they reached an iron gate. He paused to look round before entering.

A churchyard. Here, then, the wretched man whose name he had now to learn, lay underneath the ground. It was a worthy place. Walled in by houses; overrun by grass and weeds, the growth of vegetation's death, not life; choked up with too much burying; fat with repleted appetite. A worthy place.

The Spirit stood among the graves, and pointed down to One. He advanced towards it trembling. The Phantom was exactly as it had been, but he dreaded that he saw new meaning in its solemn shape.

"Before I draw nearer to that stone to which you point," said Scrooge, "answer me one question. Are these the shadows of the things that Will be, or are they shadows of things that May be, only?"

Still the Ghost pointed downward to the grave by which it stood.

"Men's courses will foreshadow certain ends, to which, if persevered in, they must lead," said Scrooge. "But if the courses be departed from, the ends will change. Say it is thus with what you show me."

The Spirit was immovable as ever.

Scrooge crept towards it, trembling as he went; and following the finger, read upon the stone of the neglected grave his own name, Ebenezer Scrooge.

"Am I that man who lay upon the bed?" he cried, upon his knees.

The finger pointed from the grave to him, and back again.

"No, Spirit. Oh no, no."

The finger still was there.

"Spirit," he cried, tight clutching at its robe, "hear me. I am not the man I was. I will not be the man I must have been but for this intercourse. Why show me this, if I am past all hope?"

For the first time the hand appeared to shake.

"Good Spirit," he pursued, as down upon the ground he fell before it: "Your nature intercedes for me, and pities me. Assure me that I yet may change these shadows you have shown me, by an altered life."

The kind hand trembled.

"I will honour Christmas in my heart, and try to keep it all the year. I will live in the Past, the Present, and the Future. The Spirits of all Three shall strive within me. I will not shut out the lessons that they teach. Oh, tell me I may sponge away the writing on this stone."

In his agony, he caught the spectral hand. It sought to free itself, but he was strong in his entreaty, and detained it. The Spirit, stronger yet, repulsed him.

Holding up his hands in a last prayer to have his fate reversed, he saw an alteration in the Phantom's hood and dress. It shrunk, collapsed, and dwindled down into a bedpost.

# STAVE FIVE.

---

## THE END OF IT.

YES! and the bedpost was his own. The bed was his own, the room was his own. Best and happiest of all, the Time before him was his own, to make amends in!

"I will live in the Past, the Present, and the Future," Scrooge repeated, as he scrambled out of bed. "The Spirits of all Three shall strive within me. Oh Jacob Marley, Heaven, and the Christmas Time be praised for this. I say it on my knees, old Jacob, on my knees."

He was so fluttered and so glowing with his good intentions, that his broken voice would scarcely answer to his call. He had been sobbing violently in his conflict with the Spirit, and his face was wet with tears.

"They are not torn down," cried Scrooge, folding one of his bed-curtains in his arms, "they are not torn down, rings and all. They are here—I am here—the shadows of the things that would have been, may be dispelled. They will be. I know they will."

111

His hands were busy with his garments all this time; turning them inside out, putting them on upside down, tearing them, mislaying them, making them parties to every kind of extravagance.

"I don't know what to do." cried Scrooge, laughing and crying in the same breath; and making a perfect cocoon of himself with his stockings. "I am as light as a feather, I am as happy as an angel, I am as merry as a schoolboy. I am as giddy as a drunken man. A merry Christmas to everybody! A happy New Year to all the world! Hallo here! Whoop! Hallo!"

He had frisked into the sitting-room, and was now standing there: perfectly winded.

"There's the saucepan that the gruel was in," cried Scrooge, starting off again, and going round the fire-place. "There's the door, by which the Ghost of Jacob Marley entered. There's the corner where the Ghost of Christmas Present sat. There's the window where I saw the wandering Spirits. It's all right, it's all true, it all happened. Ha, ha, ha!"

Really, for a man who had been out of practice for so many years, it was a splendid laugh, a most illustrious laugh. The father of a long, long line of brilliant laughs.

"I don't know what day of the month it is," said Scrooge. "I don't know how long I've been among the Spirits. I don't know anything. I'm quite a baby. Never mind. I don't care. I'd rather be a baby. Hallo! Whoop! Hallo there!"

He was checked in his transports by the churches ringing out the lustiest peals he had ever heard. Clash, clang, hammer; ding, dong, bell. Bell, dong, ding; hammer, clang, clash. Oh, glorious, glorious.

Running to the window, he opened it, and put out his head. No fog, no mist; clear, bright, jovial, stirring, cold; cold, piping for the blood to dance to; Golden sunlight; Heavenly sky; sweet fresh air; merry bells. Oh, glorious. Glorious.

"What's to-day?" cried Scrooge, calling downward to a boy in Sunday clothes, who perhaps had loitered in to look about him.

"Eh?" returned the boy, with all his might of wonder.

"What's to-day, my fine fellow?" said Scrooge.

"To-day?" replied the boy. "Why, Christmas Day."

"It's Christmas Day," said Scrooge to himself. "I haven't missed it. The Spirits have done it all in one night. They can do anything they like. Of course they can. Of course they can. Hallo, my fine fellow."

"Hallo," returned the boy.

"Do you know the Poulterer's, in the next street but one, at the corner?" Scrooge inquired.

"I should hope I did," replied the lad.

"An intelligent boy," said Scrooge. "A remarkable boy. Do you know whether they've sold the prize Turkey that was hanging up there—Not the little prize Turkey: the big one?"

"What, the one as big as me?" returned the boy.

"What a delightful boy," said Scrooge. "It's a pleasure to talk to him. Yes, my buck."

"It's hanging there now," replied the boy.

"Is it," said Scrooge. "Go and buy it."

"Walk-ER!" exclaimed the boy.

"No, no," said Scrooge, "I am in earnest. Go and buy it, and tell them to bring it here, that I may give them the direction where to take it. Come back with the man, and I'll give you a shilling. Come back with him in less than five minutes and I'll give you half-a-crown."

The boy was off like a shot. He must have had a steady hand at a trigger who could have got a shot off half so fast.

"I'll send it to Bob Cratchit's," whispered Scrooge, rubbing his hands, and splitting with a laugh. "He shan't know who sends it. It's twice the size of Tiny Tim. Joe Miller never made such a joke as sending it to Bob's will be."

The hand in which he wrote the address was not a steady one, but write it he did, somehow, and went down-stairs to open the street door, ready for the coming of the poulterer's man. As he stood there, waiting his arrival, the knocker caught his eye.

"I shall love it, as long as I live," cried Scrooge, patting it with his hand. "I scarcely ever looked at it before. What an honest expression it has in its face. It's a wonderful knocker!—Here's the Turkey! Hallo! Whoop! How are you! Merry Christmas!"

It was a Turkey. He never could have stood upon his legs, that bird. He would have snapped them short off in a minute, like sticks of sealing-wax.

"Why, it's impossible to carry that to Camden Town," said Scrooge. "You must have a cab."

The chuckle with which he said this, and the chuckle with which he paid for the Turkey, and the chuckle with which he paid for the cab, and the chuckle with which he recompensed the boy, were only to be exceeded by the chuckle with which he sat down breathless in his chair again, and chuckled till he cried.

Shaving was not an easy task, for his hand continued to shake very much; and shaving requires attention, even when you don't dance while you are at it. But if he had cut the end of his nose off, he would have put a piece of sticking-plaister over it, and been quite satisfied.

He dressed himself all in his best, and at last got out into the streets. The people were by this time pouring forth, as he had seen them with the Ghost of Christmas Present; and walking with his hands behind him, Scrooge regarded every one with a delighted smile. He looked so irresistibly pleasant, in a word, that three or four good-humoured fellows said, "Good morning, sir. A merry Christmas to you." And Scrooge said often afterwards, that of all the blithe sounds he had ever heard, those were the blithest in his ears.

He had not gone far, when coming on towards him he beheld the portly gentleman, who had walked into

his counting-house the day before, and said, "Scrooge
and Marley's, I believe." It sent a pang across his heart
to think how this old gentleman would look upon him
when they met; but he knew what path lay straight
before him, and he took it.

"My dear sir," said Scrooge, quickening his pace, and
taking the old gentleman by both his hands. "How do
you do. I hope you succeeded yesterday. It was very kind
of you. A merry Christmas to you, sir."

"Mr. Scrooge."

"Yes," said Scrooge. "That is my name, and I fear it
may not be pleasant to you. Allow me to ask your par-
don. And will you have the goodness"—here Scrooge
whispered in his ear.

"Lord bless me," cried the gentleman, as if his breath
were taken away. "My dear Mr. Scrooge, are you serious?"

"If you please," said Scrooge. "Not a farthing less. A
great many back-payments are included in it, I assure
you. Will you do me that favour."

"My dear sir," said the other, shaking hands with
him. "I don't know what to say to such munificence."

"Don't say anything please," retorted Scrooge.
"Come and see me. Will you come and see me?"

"I will," cried the old gentleman. And it was clear he
meant to do it.

"Thank you," said Scrooge. "I am much obliged to
you. I thank you fifty times. Bless you."

He went to church, and walked about the streets,
and watched the people hurrying to and fro, and patted

children on the head, and questioned beggars, and looked down into the kitchens of houses, and up to the windows, and found that everything could yield him pleasure. He had never dreamed that any walk—that anything—could give him so much happiness. In the afternoon he turned his steps towards his nephew's house.

He passed the door a dozen times, before he had the courage to go up and knock. But he made a dash, and did it:

"Is your master at home, my dear?" said Scrooge to the girl. Nice girl. Very.

"Yes, sir."

"Where is he, my love?" said Scrooge.

"He's in the dining-room, sir, along with mistress. I'll show you up-stairs, if you please."

"Thank you. He knows me," said Scrooge, with his hand already on the dining-room lock. "I'll go in here, my dear."

He turned it gently, and sidled his face in, round the door. They were looking at the table (which was spread out in great array); for these young housekeepers are always nervous on such points, and like to see that everything is right.

"Fred," said Scrooge.

Dear heart alive, how his niece by marriage started. Scrooge had forgotten, for the moment, about her sitting in the corner with the footstool, or he wouldn't have done it, on any account.

"Why bless my soul," cried Fred, "who's that?"

"It's I. Your uncle Scrooge. I have come to dinner. Will you let me in, Fred?"

Let him in. It is a mercy he didn't shake his arm off. He was at home in five minutes. Nothing could be heartier. His niece looked just the same. So did Topper when he came. So did the plump sister when she came. So did every one when they came. Wonderful party, wonderful games, wonderful unanimity, wonderful happiness.

But he was early at the office next morning. Oh, he was early there. If he could only be there first, and catch Bob Cratchit coming late. That was the thing he had set his heart upon.

And he did it; yes, he did. The clock struck nine. No Bob. A quarter past. No Bob. He was full eighteen minutes and a half behind his time. Scrooge sat with his door wide open, that he might see him come into the Tank.

His hat was off, before he opened the door; his comforter, too. He was on his stool in a jiffy; driving away with his pen, as if he were trying to overtake nine o'clock.

"Hallo," growled Scrooge, in his accustomed voice, as near as he could feign it. "What do you mean by coming here at this time of day?"

"I am very sorry, sir," said Bob. "I am behind my time."

"You are," repeated Scrooge. "Yes. I think you are. Step this way, sir, if you please."

"It's only once a year, sir," pleaded Bob, appearing from the Tank. "It shall not be repeated. I was making rather merry yesterday, sir."

"Now, I'll tell you what, my friend," said Scrooge, "I am not going to stand this sort of thing any longer. And therefore," he continued, leaping from his stool, and giving Bob such a dig in the waistcoat that he staggered

back into the Tank again; "and therefore I am about to raise your salary."

Bob trembled, and got a little nearer to the ruler. He had a momentary idea of knocking Scrooge down with it, holding him, and calling to the people in the court for help and a strait-waistcoat.

"A merry Christmas, Bob," said Scrooge, with an earnestness that could not be mistaken, as he clapped him on the back. "A merrier Christmas, Bob, my good fellow, than I have given you for many a year. I'll raise your salary, and endeavour to assist your struggling family, and we will discuss your affairs this very afternoon, over a Christmas bowl of smoking bishop, Bob. Make up the fires, and buy another coal-scuttle before you dot another 'i', Bob Cratchit."

Scrooge was better than his word. He did it all, and infinitely more; and to Tiny Tim, who did not die, he was a second father. He became as good a friend, as good a master, and as good a man, as the good old city knew, or any other good old city, town, or borough, in the good old world. Some people laughed to see the alteration in him, but he let them laugh, and little heeded them; for he was wise enough to know that nothing ever happened on this globe, for good, at which some people did not have their fill of laughter in the outset; and knowing that such as these would be blind anyway, he thought it quite as well that they should wrinkle up their eyes in grins, as have the malady in less attractive forms. His own heart laughed: and that was quite enough for him.

He had no further intercourse with Spirits, but lived upon the Total Abstinence Principle, ever afterwards; and it was always said of him, that he knew how to keep Christmas well, if any man alive possessed the knowledge. May that be truly said of us, and all of us! And so, as Tiny Tim observed, God bless Us, Every One!

# Bibliography & Suggested Reading List

Adler, Jerry. "Kids Growing up Scared." *Newsweek*, January 10, 1994, 43-49.

Blair, Walter, ed. 1962. *Selected Shorter Writings of Mark Twain.* Boston: Houghton Mifflin.

Bleck, Robert. 1993. *Give Back the Pain.* Bedford: Mills and Sanderson.

Bradshaw, John. 1988. *Bradshaw on: The Family.* Pompano Beach: Health Communications, Inc.

Bradshaw, John. 1992. *Creating Love.* New York: Bantam Books.

Campbell, Joseph. 1986. *The Inner Reaches of Outer Space.* New York: Harper and Row.

————. 1968. *The Hero with a Thousand Faces.* Princeton: Princeton University Press.

Davis, Paul. 1990. *The Lives and Times of Ebenezer Scrooge.* New Haven: Yale University Press.

deMello, Anthony. 1990. *Awareness.* New York: Doubleday.

*Diagnostic and Statistical Manual of Mental Disorders* (4th Edition). 1994. Washington, D.C.: American Psychiatric Association.

Dickens, Charles. *A Christmas Carol.*

Flowers, Betty Sue, ed. 1988. *Joseph Campbell & The Power of Myth with Bill Moyers*. New York: Doubleday.

*Forrest Gump*. Paramount Pictures, Robert Zemeckis. 1994.

Foundation for Inner Peace. 1992. *A Course in Miracles*. Glen Ellen, CA.

Fox, Emmet. 1990. *Power Through Constructive Thinking*. New York: Harper Paperbacks, 1990.

Glass, Ira. "Chicago Gangs Influenced by Religion." *Weekend Edition*. National Public Radio. February 1994.

Goldsmith, Joel. 1986. *A Parenthisis in Eternity*. New York: HarperCollins.

———. 1993. *The Thunder of Silence*. New York: HarperCollins.

Gravitz, Herbert and Julie Bowden. 1985. *Recovery: A Guide for Adult Children of Alcoholics*. New York: Simon and Schuster.

Hearn, Michael Patrick. 1976. *The Annotated Christmas Carol*. New York: Clarkson N. Potter, Inc.

Hewlett, Sylvia Ann. 1991. *When the Bough Breaks*. New York: Harper Perennial.

Kort, Michael. 1985. *The Soviet Colossus*. New York: Charles Scribner's Sons.

Kubler-Ross, Elisabeth. 1969. *On Death and Dying*. New York: MacMillan Publishing Co.

Masland, Tom. "Will It be Peace or Punishment?" *Newsweek*, August 1, 1994, 37.

Matousek, Mark. "Boy wonder." *Common Boundary*, Volume 12, Issue 2, March/April 1994, 63-64.

Meyer, Marvin, trans. 1984. *The Secret Teachings of Jesus*. New York: Vintage Books.

Miller, Alice. 1990. *Banished Knowledge*. New York: Doubleday.

———. 1990. *For Your Own Good*. New York: The Noonday Press.

———. 1990. *The Untouched Key*. New York: Doubleday.

———. 1986. *Thou Shalt not Be Aware*. New York: Meridian.

Mitchell, Stephen. 1991. *The Gospel According to Jesus*. New York: Harper Collins.

Miller, James E., Roseann Dueñas Gonzalez, and Nancy C. Millet, eds. *Question and Form in Literature (Our Town*, by Thornton Wilder, pp. 184-217). Glenview, Illinois, Scott, Foresman and Co., 1982.

Moody, Raymond. 1978. *Reflections on Life After Life*. New York:  Bantam Books.

Peck, M. Scott. 1978. *The Road Less Traveled*. New York: Simon and Schuster.

Ring, Kenneth. 1985. *Heading Toward Omega*. New York: Quill/William Morrow.

————. 1992. *The Omega Project*. New York: William Morrow and Co.

Sagan, Carl. 1995. *The Demon-Haunted World*. New York: Random House.

St. Louis Post-Dispatch. "Board hears ideas to end child abuse." August, 1994.

Selby, John. 1992. *Kundalini Awakening*. New York: Bantam Books.

Shengold, Leonard. 1989. *Soul Murder*. New York: Fawcett Columbine.

Simpkinson, Charles. (Interview with M. Scott Peck) "The Importance of Being Civil," *Common Boundary*, Volume 11, Issue 2, March/April, 1993, 22-29.

"Spiritus contra Spiritum: The Bill Wilson/C. J. Jung Letters." *Parabola*, Volume XII, Number 2, May 1987, 68-71.

Stettbacher, J. Konrad. 1991. *Making Sense of Suffering*. New York: Dutton.

Whitfield, Charles L., M. D. 1987. *Healing the Child Within*. Pompano Beach: Health Communications, Inc.

Williamson, Marianne. 1992. *A Return to Love*. Boston: Harper Collins, 1992.

Wilson, Edmund. 1941. *The Wound and the Bow*. Cambridge: Cambridge University Press.

# Index

# STAY IN TOUCH. . .

**Llewellyn publishes hundreds of books on your favorite subjects!**
On the following pages you will find listed some books now available on related subjects. Your local bookstore stocks most of these and will stock new Llewellyn titles as they become available. We urge your patronage.

## Order by Phone

Call toll-free within the U.S. and Canada, **1–800–THE MOON**. In Minnesota call **(612) 291–1970**. We accept Visa, MasterCard, and American Express.

## Order by Mail

Send the full price of your order (MN residents add 7% sales tax) in U.S. funds to:
Llewellyn Worldwide
P.O. Box 64383, Dept. K198-8
St. Paul, MN 55164–0383, U.S.A.

## Postage and Handling

- ◆ $4.00 for orders $15.00 and under
- ◆ $5.00 for orders over $15.00
- ◆ No charge for orders over $100.00

We ship UPS in the continental United States. We cannot ship to P.O. boxes. Orders shipped to Alaska, Hawaii, Canada, Mexico, and Puerto Rico will be sent first-class mail.

International orders: Airmail—add freight equal to price of each book to the total price of order, plus $5.00 for each non-book item (audiotapes, etc.). Surface mail—Add $1.00 per item.

Allow 4–6 weeks delivery on all orders. Postage and handling rates subject to change.

## Group Discounts

We offer a 20% quantity discount to group leaders or agents. You must order a minimum of 5 copies of the same book to get our special quantity price.

## Free Catalog

Get a free copy of our color catalog, *New Worlds of Mind and Spirit.* Subscribe for just $10.00 in the United States and Canada ($20.00 overseas, first class mail). Many bookstores carry *New Worlds*— ask for it!

## WHEN SANTA WAS A SHAMAN
### ANCIENT ORIGINS OF SANTA CLAUS AND THE CHRISTMAS TREE
**Tony van Renterghem**

This is an ancestral detective story, leading back to prehistoric times and man's first concepts of religion. The American Santa Claus (a revamping of the Dutch Saint Nicholas by an artist for the Coca-Cola company!) represents only the tip of a very ancient iceberg. Beneath it lies Western man's oldest stories: (1) the myth of the Tree of Fire, the last vestige of which is our Christmas Tree, and (2) the persistent, vague memory of the shaman, in harmony with Gaia, now transformed into a jolly old man with flying reindeer.

Learn how these stories were remembered around the world, camouflaged for safety and interwoven with other myths. Always resurfacing—in Holland and Belgium as Saint Nicholas (or more accurately Black Pete, the Dark Helper) and in Britain, Germany, France, Russia, Scandinavia, Spain, Italy, North Africa—these myths eventually crossed the Atlantic to America, where they were sanitized, commercialized and exported back into the world from which they came.

1-56718-765-X, 224 pp., 7 x 10, color illus., softcover     $16.95

## THE POWER OF DREAMING
### MESSAGES FROM YOUR INNER SELF
D. Jason Cooper

Unlock the secret of your dreams and open the door to your inner self! Our dreams hold a wisdom which can guide us, protect us and better our lives, if we listen to it. *The Power of Dreaming* presents a new, reliable and effective "technology" for interpreting your dreams, as it is the first book to separate dream symbols from their context to better interpret each element: the nature of the dream and your role within it; its events, people and objects; archetypes in the dream; and the dream's class (whether it's a problem-solving dream, a house-cleaning dream, a psychological dream or an occult dream). Once you string meanings of all these elements together, you'll arrive at a complete, accurate and insightful interpretation of your dreams. This brand-new technique illustrates how events, rather than objects, are the key to unlocking your dreams' meanings. Includes three different dream dictionaries: one to interpret the meaning of events, one for objects and one for archetypes.

*The Power of Dreaming* gives you all the information you need to follow a program of self-knowledge and understanding through your dreams. Take this fascinating road to self-discovery every night!

**1-56718-175-9, 224 pp., 6 x 9, softcover**                    **$12.00**

**To order, call 1-800-THE MOON**
All prices subject to change without notice

## THE ULTIMATE CURE
### THE HEALING ENERGY WITHIN YOU
**Dr. Jim Dreaver**

*The Ultimate Cure* will open a door into consciousness and literally bring you into a direct, first-hand experience of illumination—an experience that will stimulate your mind, warm your heart and feed your soul.

Dr. Jim Dreaver provides a first-hand account of the spiritual journey and outlines the steps needed to live in the world with an authentic sense of wisdom, love and power. He addresses the issues of meditation, work as a spiritual exercise, harnessing the power of the mind, conscious breathing, and healing the wounds of the past. Dr. Dreaver's main theme is that spiritual presence, which is the source of all healing, is an actual, palpable reality that can be felt and tapped into.

To realize enlightenment, you must have a tremendous hunger for it. This delightfully honest and wonderfully human book will stimulate your appetite and, by the time you turn to the last page, will leave you feeling totally satisfied.

**1-56718-244-5, 288 pp., 6 x 9, softcover**               **$14.95**

## New Chakra Healing
### The Revolutionary 32-Center Energy System
**Cyndi Dale**

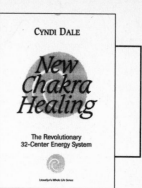

Break through the barriers that keep you from your true purpose with *New Chakra Healing*. This manual presents never-before-published information that makes a quantum leap in the current knowledge of the human energy centers, fields, and principles that govern the connection between the physical and spiritual realms.

By working with your full energy body, you can heal all resistance to living a successful life. The traditional seven-chakra system was just the beginning of our understanding of the holistic human. Now Cyndi Dale's research uncovers a total of 32 energy centers: 12 physically oriented chakras, and 20 energy points that exist in the spiritual plane. She also discusses auras, rays, kundalini, mana energy, karma, dharma, and cords (energetic connections between people that serve as relationship contracts). In addition, she extends chakra work to include the back of the body as well as the front, with detailed explanations on how these energy systems tie into the spine. Each chapter takes the reader on a journey through the various systems, incorporating personal experiences, practical exercises and guided meditation.

1-56718-200-3, 288 pp., 7 x 10, color illus., softcover     **$17.95**

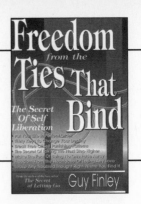